Film and the Imagined Image

# Film and the Imagined Image

Sarah Cooper

EDINBURGH
University Press

Edinburgh University Press is one of the leading university presses in the UK. We publish academic books and journals in our selected subject areas across the humanities and social sciences, combining cutting-edge scholarship with high editorial and production values to produce academic works of lasting importance. For more information visit our website: edinburghuniversitypress.com

© Sarah Cooper, 2019, 2021

Edinburgh University Press Ltd
The Tun – Holyrood Road
12(2f) Jackson's Entry
Edinburgh EH8 8PJ

First published in hardback by Edinburgh University Press 2019

Typeset in 11/13 Monotype Ehrhardt by
IDSUK (DataConnection) Ltd

A CIP record for this book is available from the British Library

ISBN 978 1 4744 5278 6 (hardback)
ISBN 978 1 4744 5279 3 (paperback)
ISBN 978 1 4744 5280 9 (webready PDF)
ISBN 978 1 4744 5281 6 (epub)

The right of Sarah Cooper to be identified as the author of this work has been asserted in accordance with the Copyright, Designs and Patents Act 1988, and the Copyright and Related Rights Regulations 2003 (SI No. 2498).

# Contents

*List of Figures*     vi
*Acknowledgements*     vii

**Part I Dual Vision**
1. Seeing Pictures     3
2. Feeling Pictures     22

**Part II Making Mental Motion Pictures**
3. Layering     39
4. Volumising     66
5. Supplementing     89
6. Reshaping     113
7. Erasing     134
Conclusion: Broadening Out     156
Postscript     168

*Notes*     169
*Filmography*     177
*Bibliography*     179
*Index*     191

# Figures

| | | |
|---|---|---|
| 3.1 | *Black Sun* (Gary Tarn, 2005) | 40 |
| 3.2 | *Heart of a Dog* (Laurie Anderson, 2015) | 48 |
| 3.3 | *Heart of a Dog* (Laurie Anderson, 2015) | 51 |
| 3.4 | *London* (Patrick Keiller, 1994) | 58 |
| 3.5 | *Jane B. by Agnès V.* (Agnès Varda, 1988) | 63 |
| 5.1 | *Shirin* (Abbas Kiarostami, 2008) | 94 |
| 5.2 | *Shirin* (Abbas Kiarostami, 2008) | 96 |
| 5.3 | *The Fall of the House of Usher* (Jan Švankmajer, 1980) | 104 |
| 5.4 | *The Fall of the House of Usher* (Jan Švankmajer, 1980) | 104 |
| 5.5 | *The Pendulum, the Pit and Hope* (Jan Švankmajer, 1983) | 110 |
| 6.1 | *London* (Patrick Keiller, 1994) | 115 |
| 6.2 | *London* (Patrick Keiller, 1994) | 116 |
| 6.3 | *Cézanne* (Jean-Marie Straub and Danièle Huillet, 1989) | 124 |
| 6.4 | *A Visit to the Louvre* (Jean-Marie Straub and Danièle Huillet, 2003) | 128 |
| 6.5 | *Effi Briest* (Rainer Werner Fassbinder, 1974) | 133 |
| 7.1 | *Le Camion* (Marguerite Duras, 1977) | 142 |
| 7.2 | *Le Camion* (Marguerite Duras, 1977) | 143 |
| 7.3 | *Les Mains négatives* (Marguerite Duras, 1979) | 149 |
| 7.4 | *Césarée* (Marguerite Duras, 1979) | 151 |
| 7.5 | *Césarée* (Marguerite Duras, 1979) | 152 |

# Acknowledgements

In her rules for writers, Hilary Mantel stresses how important it is for a writer to write a book that they themselves would like to read. I have done that here, but it would not have been possible without the generosity and encouragement of many people.

First and foremost, Gillian Leslie, Richard Strachan, and the editorial team at Edinburgh University Press have been simply brilliant to work with from start to finish. I thank also the organisers and attendees of events where I presented aspects of my work in progress: ARTHEMIS, Concordia University, March 2015; Film and French Studies Research Seminar, Edinburgh University, April 2015; University of Oxford French Research Seminar, May 2016; Studies in French Cinema Annual Conference, London, June 2016; *DOKUARTS* Essaydox Symposium, Berlin, October 2016; Visualising Theory Research Seminar, University College Cork, February 2017; CRASSH, Cambridge, Images of Care and Dying Research Seminar Series, March 2017; SCMS, Chicago, March 2017; and Society for French Studies Annual Conference, Durham, July 2017. Some of that initial research appears in *Screen* 59:4 (Winter 2018); *Understanding Merleau-Ponty, Understanding Modernism*, ed. Ariane Mildenberg (Bloomsbury, 2018); and *Women and the City in French Literature and Culture*, ed. Siobhán McIlvanney and Gillian Ni Cheallaigh (University of Wales Press, 2019): I acknowledge the editors for their permission to feature parts of that material here in modified form. My day-to-day work environment has played a vital role in sustaining my research and I am grateful to my colleagues in the Department of Film Studies and beyond at King's College London who make it such a special place to be. I am also indebted to my students at all levels who are such great interlocutors and from whom I continue to learn so much. Colin Davis, Sam Girgus, Judith Mayne, David Rodowick, Emma Wilson, and Mike Witt offered me welcome support at a pivotal moment in the progress of the manuscript. The first time that I made public the planned shape of the book in its final format was when I sent the proposal and sample materials to Edinburgh University Press for consideration and review. I extend heartfelt thanks to the anonymous readers for their feedback, which spurred me on to complete the project.

When I began working on film and imagination during a period of sabbatical leave after a lengthy and intense stint of senior administrative duties, I joined a gym, took up a range of activities, and met some wonderful people as a result, including Bogusha Demucha, Saori Funawatari, Sharon Saker, and Julie Wilkins. More particularly, I have spent many an evening with Alex Duran, Helen Livermore, Marilena Nicolaou, Paul Smith, and Tara Stimpson, along with others from Fitnationuk, following up workouts with some very fine wines. Laure Platford introduced me to a circle of artists whose creativity has been awe-inspiring. I wrote most of this book in London but I also got away from my desk frequently in order to advance further with it – another of Mantel's rules, which I took to geographical extremes. I was inspired to write and rewrite parts of it in various places, from Westcliff-on-Sea to Paris, Palermo through Massa Lubrense to Alghero, all of which trips involved spending precious vacation time with my parents. I finished a first draft of the manuscript in Bodø while staying with my sister, brother-in-law, and three gorgeous nieces who reminded Auntie Sarah on a daily basis of the vivacity of their own imagination. It is to Ella, Ava, and Onna, along with my beautiful Clare and Bjørn, and my amazing mum and dad that I dedicate this work, with all my love.

# PART I
# DUAL VISION

CHAPTER 1

# Seeing Pictures

'Startin' to see pictures, ain't ya?' To be asked this question over halfway through a film by someone speaking directly to camera is to invite an affirmative if incredulous response. Of course we are – we have been for around eighty-five minutes: we are watching a narrative film and 'seeing pictures' is a fundamental part of this experience. The question is not addressed primarily to spectators, though, whose vision has just been aligned momentarily with that of a specific character. The words are spoken by Major Marquis Warren (Samuel L. Jackson) during a scene in Quentin Tarantino's *The Hateful Eight* (2015) after he has described in graphic detail to General Sanford Smithers (Bruce Dern) what he did to Smithers's son prior to killing him some time after the American Civil War. Warren, a former Union soldier turned bounty hunter, describes visiting upon the son a slow and torturous death after finding out that his father was the racist white Confederate general who executed a command of black soldiers who were in his charge at the Battle of Baton Rouge. Warren's actions are a combination of revenge and self-preservation. The film cuts between flashbacks to what Warren claims he did to Smithers's son and the present, focusing at one point on Smithers's forehead and eyes, as images of his son overlay his face before replacing it, showing viewers what Smithers may be picturing as he listens. Tarantino's multi-layered and self-reflexive mode of storytelling thus points briefly here to how narration can prompt the formation of pictures in the mind. To locate picture-seeing at the heart of storytelling is not to give a rather obvious and basic account of what is visible on screen, then, but to suggest that this is a mental activity and to link it to imagining. Through the camera alignment and Warren's question to Smithers, spectators are also being asked whether pictures are seen in the mind and not – or not only – on the screen.

I first saw this particular film shortly after its release in a London cinema belonging to the Odeon chain. One of the instructions given in voice-over and written on screen prior to the start of every programme at that time, after audience members were told to finish conversations and switch off mobile phones, was to 'free your imagination'.[1] This positioning of imagination at the centre of the film experience contrasts with the way in which film is sometimes understood to do the work of imagining for spectators and is thereby deemed less powerful than the novelistic or poetic text. After all, the images that General Smithers might be supposed to be picturing are visible on screen, and this leaves little, if anything, to the spectator's imagination in this film when this process is understood in terms of its image-making capacity. Seeing mental pictures is not therefore an obvious part of the definition of what it means to imagine at the movies, and a wealth of film scholarship supports this view. Much has been written on imagination being neither inferior nor incidental to audio-vision: it has been the subject of many studies that think it central to film spectatorship.[2] Cognitive film theorists who led an earlier wave of work on imagination touched on its image-making capacity but distanced it largely from cinema. Gregory Currie is emblematic in advancing an understanding of imagination as stripped of its close association with 'the faculty of image-making or visualization' (Currie 1991: 131).[3] This film theoretical research ran parallel in the 1990s to the more widespread and contrasting rise of interest in image-making or visualisation in literary studies.[4] That the verbal arts can prompt the image-making capacity of the imagination is something that literary writers have long known and relied upon, even in the twentieth century when imagination, the 'sovereign ghost', as literary critic Denis Donoghue terms it, was no longer an essential power, and literary criticism and theory made the object of praise language rather than the individual writer as creator (Donoghue 1976). Adept at probing mental images in their own minds and conveying them in writing, poets and novelists encourage the creation of mental images on the part of their readers too. The experience of image formation is the subject of Elaine Scarry's *Dreaming by the Book* ([1999] 2001), in which she explores in exquisite detail the ways that writers stimulate readers to make and move mental pictures that play across the backlit tissue of the human brain as they read. My contention in this book is that these labile images of the mind can be created and experienced when viewing film too.

While visualisation and mental image formation have been recognised in more recent writings on spectatorship, the emphasis to date has been on pointing to the activity and the filmic conditions for their emergence.[5] What is missing from current scholarship is an account of the felt experience of image-making: a step-by-step exploration of the processes that combine to form, transform, deform, and dismantle mental images while watching film. Although rarely the sole goal of any film experience, since spectators are immersed in so many other ways while attending to both onscreen and off-screen space, the appearance of imagined images, however quick at times, can be strikingly vivid and palpable. The vivacity and substantiality of the image-making that Scarry outlines in her literary study therefore has relevance to film spectatorship, as do the ensuing processes that set those images in motion, even though reading must be distinguished from film viewing.[6] Merely to acknowledge without fully activating the possibility of spectators seeing mental pictures, as Tarantino does in my opening example, is therefore just a gateway to a vast and endlessly shifting mental landscape that some films invite spectators to create more readily than others. To explore aspects of this potentially infinite terrain my study will move into a realm of essay films and documentaries, art house cinema, and experimental blank screen works in which words and sound still feature prominently. Such films as will be discussed in the successive chapters of this book create more ample space for spectators to imagine in images, and yet my study will still have something to say in conclusion about the sporadic manner in which more mainstream cinema can activate imagining in the ways it outlines too. It is important to recognise from the outset, however, that the existence of this mental arena in which pictures are seen is not beyond dispute, as cognitive film theory's predominant focus on mental activities of imagining aside from that of image-making already suggests. In this respect, and in addition to taking us from screen to mind, Major Marquis Warren's question leads us to the nub of a lively, ongoing imagery debate.

Not everyone reports seeing pictures in their mind when they imagine.[7] Nor can such mental activity be induced artificially if there is not already a propensity to visualise, as Aldous Huxley found out to his chagrin when he entered a mescaline-fuelled state, hoping to access the kind of intensely visual inner world that William Blake bears witness to in his work (Huxley 1954). The debate as to the form that mental images take, if they appear at all, is longstanding and spans the history of philosophy, in addition to psychology and cognitive science, reaching its heyday in the 1970s and 1980s.[8] Psychologist Zenon Pylyshyn, a foremost advocate of what has been termed the propositional or descriptive account, argues that mental imagery is not represented in pictures at all but in descriptions that depend upon the same symbolic codes used in language (Pylyshyn 1973).[9] Indeed, the very fact of calling mental images pictures raises an important question for what has been termed pictorialist or depictive theory. If mental images were kept as pictures to be brought back for inspection in front of the mind's eye, our brains would never be large enough to accommodate them. Additionally, we would only ever be able to imagine something that we had already perceived, and imagining would just be a matter of recalling or combining stored images, which is clearly not, or not always, the case. The literal figuration not only of inner pictures but also of an internal figure that observes them – the famed homunculus in our heads – has been subject to widespread criticism in twentieth-century philosophy in particular, with Daniel Dennett referring to pictorialist theory as the Cartesian theatre view of the mind (Dennett 1991: ch. 5). For Dennett, challenging the notion of mental visual images is the necessary starting point for questioning other kinds of mental representation, as he states wittily: 'We are less inclined to strike up the little band in the brain for auditory perception than we are to set up the movie screen, so if images can be eliminated, mental noises, smells, feels, and tastes will go quietly' (Dennett 1981: 51–2). Understanding imagination as the faculty for forming and seeing mental pictures is still somewhat against the intellectual mainstream, as cultural scholar Eva Brann noted in an earlier landmark study (Brann 1991: 18), but this notion of forming imagery is key to the way in which pictorialist theory has countered some of the charges levelled against it.

From his perspective as a leading late-twentieth-century proponent of pictorialist theory, Stephen Michael Kosslyn, in his work on creating and using images in the brain, agrees with the problems that are raised above regarding the characterisation of mental images as pictures. As he notes, there is a two-dimensionality to standard understandings of a picture but this does not quite tally with the experience of those who visualise and who are able to examine mental images through practices such as mental rotation, as well as place themselves within them, rather than just observing flatly from the outside (Kosslyn 1983: 2). In his conceptualisation, there is no inner screen watched by miniscule inner eyes, and rather than describing mental images as pictures to be retrieved, they are generated when needed. Moreover, he argues that something does not have to be a picture to function as one: in the brain 'nerve cells can *function* as if they composed something like a television screen without actually *being* one' (ibid.: 25). He describes the mind's eye as consisting of the various tests that evaluate and interpret the information in a matrix as in a computer: 'The pictorialness of images lies in the way they are interpreted within the mind' (ibid.: 27). As Kosslyn and his collaborators confirm in later experiments: 'there need be no actual picture in the brain to have a depiction: all that is needed is a "functional space" in which distance can be defined vis-à-vis how information is processed' (Kosslyn et al. 2006:

14–15).[10] Essentially, then, although images are configured as pictorial in this understanding, they are not literal pictures. Since not everyone claims to see visual mental images, the depictive emerges as just one format, and Kosslyn presents a useful sliding scale on which people are 'mainly visual' or 'mainly verbal', suggesting that most people have the capacity to shift their thinking in the other direction when it is helpful to do so (Kosslyn 1983: 59). The fact that my own study concentrates exclusively on the visual mental image and continues to talk of pictures interchangeably with images does not deny that there are other ways of thinking about mental representations or imagining: its focus does aim quite deliberately, however, to shine a light on an area that has received little attention in film studies to date.

To return to Major Warren's question about seeing pictures, we can add more nuances to the definition of mental pictures on the basis of this now classic work in cognitive science. These images are not always and only two-dimensional and, when generated, they come into being through interpretation, allowing those who experience them to perform mental activities that already imply the three-dimensionality that more recent cognitive research has focused upon in the inter-disciplinary fields of psychocinematics or neurocinematics. Differentiating his terms but nonetheless implicitly in keeping with Kosslyn's multi-faceted understanding of what it means mentally to picture something, Jeffrey M. Zacks speaks indeed of event models, explaining: 'Event models are not just *pictures* in the head. Pictures do not have components, but models do' (Zacks 2015: 32). Zacks notes how components are crucial for running simulations and understands such activity to be at work when processing events of a story, whether seen on a screen or read on a page (ibid.: 35).[11] Talk of running simulations echoes implicitly Kosslyn's computer model of the mind, but in the intervening years the rise of functional magnetic resonance imaging (fMRI) that has provided increasingly more detailed images of brain activity brings with it the mechanics of the scanner too. The computer in particular has served as a metaphor for the brain, but I do not seek to cement that metaphor in the context of film spectatorship. Philosopher Catherine Malabou warns against mechanical analogues for brain functioning, which in her view suggest a form of flexibility and pliancy to the brain complicit with neoliberal control (Malabou [2004] 2008).[12] My study is attuned to the brain's plastic and formative capacities, and I return to Malabou explicitly in a later chapter. Suffice it to acknowledge here that mental 'pictures' are more complex than the term makes them appear – open as they are to mobility and three-dimensionality – and so too is the act of 'seeing'.

Seeing with one's eyes relies on at least two kinds of vision. The dual visual systems (DVS) model put forward by scientists David Milner and Melvyn Goodale in the mid-1990s shows how vision depends on ventral and dorsal streams. The former, bearing a strong connection not only to immediate visual experience but to its storage for future reference, is called upon in the more active analysis of abstract dynamics of the visual field, and the latter is associated with the coordination of our own sensorimotor system or registering that of others in real time (Milner and Goodale 1995). The ways in which these streams of vision-for-perception and vision-for-action interact has been acknowledged as potentially important for sustaining mental images, bridging the action of mirror neurons, visual memories, and image schemas.[13] More specifically rooted in film studies research and focusing on what is seen on screen, psychocinematics in recent years has taken up eye-tracking technology and has sought to provide empirical perspectives on ways of looking that screen theory has theorised using different frameworks drawn from psychoanalysis, reception studies, and phenomenology over the decades. As William Brown cautions astutely, though, to fixate on seeing rather than not seeing becomes problematic since it ignores the need for temporary sightlessness that the sighted are fully aware of in the regular involuntary action of blinking (Brown 2018). Brown's sense that in order to see, we must look away is not only true for seeing but also for my understanding of imagining in this book. The relation between imagining and looking away assumes several different forms when watching film, as will become clear in my unfolding discussion; the first of these stems from a scientific study of blinking.

In research carried out by a neuroscientific team led by Tamami Nakano, participants were monitored while watching videos of the British television comedy antics of Mr Bean, with fMRI scanning of the parts of the brain that are active or inactive while viewing. The findings showed that the aspects of the brain that are activated when participants in the experiment attend to something are deactivated when they blink; cortical activity momentarily decreases in the dorsal attention network and the default mode or task negative network implicated in internal processing becomes more active as a result (Nakano et al. 2013). This default mode network has been understood as synonymous with introspection and self-referential activity (ibid.; Davey et al. 2016). More specifically, it has been associated with mind wandering, along with daydreaming, as explored in research led by cognitive scientist Alexander Schlegel.[14] These insights, especially when they broach the question of visual mental representation, complement research into activity of the visual cortex when sight is absent, supporting the view that we see with our brains.[15] Such findings indicate some of the neural correlates for imaginative activity that variously connect it to and disconnect it from seeing with one's eyes. What philosopher Colin McGinn terms mindsight may not always need eyesight to function (McGinn 2004), but it is the relationship between the two that informs my own study of imagining in images.[16]

Attending to the conscious act of seeing pictures in the mind *as well as* those on screen when viewing film will be a major aspect of this book and forms the focus of Part II in which analysis of a range of films will enable such mental images to be brought into view. The experience of the mental image as well as an onscreen image prompts a kind of dual vision between mind and screen that is split in a manner not dissimilar to a divided daydreaming consciousness but whose imagined images become stronger than reverie without blocking out the film being viewed. It is guided imagining that will inform the possibility of seeing vivid mental pictures in this book, with the processes of mental image formation being derived from an engagement with the films under discussion. Before we reach the chapter-by-chapter exploration of the processes integral to the formation and experience of such imagery, my initial cognitivist and neuroscientifically informed discussion of imagery needs to be opened out in order to help flesh out the key characteristics of the mental pictures stimulated by film. The blink of an eye that momentarily suspends what can be seen – the look away – and which reveals a connection to brain activity associated with the unguided imagining of mind wandering is the conscious and frequent, if transitory, mechanism of the more sustained act of closing our eyes. We do this, of course, in order to dream, and there is an ongoing dialogue on dreams between neuroscience and psychoanalysis, which considers how the default mode network might operate during sleep (see Zellner 2013; Domhoff and Fox 2015). The dream images that we experience differ from consciously created imagined images: they have their own logic and even though we generate them, we undergo rather than direct them in all their strangeness. They do, however, provide evidence of mental images that many people will attest to far more readily in experiential terms without the kinds of distractions that can beset a focus on imagining by day. Scarry pre-empts this in her figuration of imagining when reading as *dreaming*-by-the-book; a more film-specific lineage will reveal an important connection between dreams and the first of the two main aspects of the consciously formed mental images that will concern me too in this study: vivacity. In order to see such images more clearly, we need to journey counter-intuitively into darkness and to slip momentarily from the conscious into the unconscious realm.

## Closing the Eyes, Vivifying Mental Pictures

On the way to the kind of dreaming that is not daydreaming, you have to shut your eyes. 'You must . . . close your eyes,' declares the eponymous Alice during the opening credits of Surrealist Jan Švankmajer's first feature-length film (1988), 'otherwise . . . you won't see anything'. Whether or not Alice is talking to me, to us, whoever we are, this seems a peculiar thing to be told to do when watching a film, and it seems better to disobey. I rarely close my eyes in the cinema if I am gripped by action, moved by sentiment, or altogether engrossed intellectually. I do, however, close them momentarily if scared witless, repulsed, or just wanting to blot out what is on screen because it disturbs me (although sound can perturb even more chillingly). More positively, I shut my eyes sometimes to concentrate when listening intently, but I also do so very occasionally when tired or bored, removing myself subtly from an experience that I might simply stop with the remote control at home. What Alice knows, though, ever wiser than her years, is that the paradoxical vision she is talking about is commonplace, as any dreamer who experiences the richness of mental imagery while sleeping will concur. It is actually rather useful, then, to obey Alice's command and orient ourselves first towards the inner vision of dreaming, the better ultimately to return to the conscious realm of image formation and to see what else there is to see when watching film.

To begin: an archaic dream of dreams that has inspired writers and artists for centuries, its vivacity that of a vision that provides a dual sense of direction for my own visit to a world usually only accessed when asleep. As recounted in Genesis 28: 10–22, the biblical Jacob dreams of a ladder connecting earth to heaven before hearing God's prophecy telling him that his offspring will be many and blessing all the peoples of the earth. As Jacob closes his eyes and falls asleep so the stairway climbs, which angels ascend and descend. As the scales fall from his eyes and he sees more clearly as a result of his dream, vision is purified, cleaned out, descaled upon waking up – the upwards motion akin to a return to consciousness. The falling and rising of Jacob's dreaming connect the dream world of the depths to the waking state of the surface; these are the depths to which author Hélène Cixous refers when commenting on the importance of dreams to writerly creativity (Cixous 1993). But these motions, insofar as they are underpinned by the scaling of a ladder, are not quite mine. For me, and when not waking up with a jolt, the return to consciousness needs to be figured through water rather than air, visually akin to the distortions of artist Alexander James's secular photographic-painterly world of submerged mortality, with awakening still being the possibility of rising upwards to the surface, but a liquid, resistant return through fathoms, not a clambering up rungs. Displacing Jacob's dream and ladder as imaged through millennia in the history of art, James's *Transparency of a Dream Illuminated* comes to my mind here: a series of cobalt blue butterflies photographed on a black background underwater and then reworked with oils, vibrantly beautiful even though dead, archaically resonant with the soul.[17] A butterfly for a ladder, I trade surreally in symbols and metaphors as I think and write but with a desire to hold on to the visual mental image brought to life and light in dreams.

Through a slippage of association on the wing of an insect I move from seeing to remembering, from brilliant blue butterflies to a death's head moth in black and white, a memory image courtesy of filmmaking duo Salvador Dalí and Luis Buñuel. To begin again, with film images this time: a thin, dark, horizontal cloud cuts across the moon, and with a sideways swipe of a razor blade, a man slits open an eye. So frequently a young woman suffers even if she does not appear to (Švankmajer's Alice visits a wonderland that is terrifying; James's Ophelias are as stunning yet as entombed as his watery butterflies but do not have the same historical connection to the alchemy of soul). The opening shots of Dalí and Buñuel's *Un Chien Andalou/An Andalusian Dog* (1929) are – more extreme and irreverent than the purifying, cleaning, and descaling of vision in Jacob's case – a direct assault on vision accessed through a woman's gaze to camera. The gelatinous fluid that spills so visibly from that infamous sliced eye suggests, more aggressively than Alice's instruction to close our eyes, the inaugural sightlessness of a different kind of vision, one which was valorised by Surrealists whose startling wake-up call to their spectators involved an obligatory encounter with irrationality on screen. The Surrealists lauded the illogic of the unconscious across the arts, yet in their films as well as film theory, dreams furnish the royal road to the mental image, as visualised at an earlier juncture, although not without difficulty, by Freud.

Freud actually confesses to struggling with conscious mental visualisation when citing from and commenting on a letter from his friend Wilhelm Fliess:

> 'I am very much occupied with your dream-book: *I see it lying finished before me and I see myself turning over its pages.*' How much I envied him his gift as a seer! If only *I* could have seen it lying finished before me! (Freud [1900] 1991: 257)

The workings of the unconscious in dreams, however, take a pictographic form that Freud describes in such fine detail using himself as a case study much of the time that his first-hand knowledge of the strong visual component of dreaming is never in doubt. For Freud, the eyes are the most important sensory channels and the action of closing them also signals a move to protect other senses from stimuli acting on them, even though this can never be fully achieved (ibid.: 83). Visual images are the main component of dreams – he speaks frequently, as does the literature he cites, of dream-images and dream-pictures – and with the exception of hearing, the participation of the other senses is deemed intermittent and less important (ibid.: 95). From early on, though, the dream-images and dream-pictures are connected to thought and language, and interpretation is a matter of translating and decoding. His famous definition of the dream as the (disguised) fulfilment of a (suppressed or repressed) wish (ibid.: 244), overturned some years later when he moved beyond the pleasure principle, depends on stripping away the disguise in order to recover the wish. It is not the pictorial value of the dream that is important to him – as it is for me – but the symbolic relation. Unlike Jacob's dream vision, taken at face value, Freud's always requires deciphering. For Cixous, *The Interpretation of Dreams*, while a marvellous book, is a dream-killer precisely because it interprets (Cixous 1993: 107). Surrealist film theorists also praise Freud's magnum opus, but they place far more emphasis on the visual aspect of mental imagery.

Prior to Freud's detailed mining of the unconscious, particularly through the portal of the dream, the flag of the imagination had been flying at half-mast, according to André Breton, and it is through the combination of dream and reality that Breton's oft-cited definition of Surrealism is established (Breton [1924] 1985: 24). The Surrealists arise singularly from what philosopher Richard Kearney otherwise terms the wake of imagination in the twentieth century (Kearney 1988).[18] When Surrealist film theorists take up reference to dreams they comment on the parity between the pictorial nature of cinema and mental images, straddling conscious and unconscious worlds, onscreen images and the mental images of spectators. Paul Ramain summarises this relationship when he explains that cinema and dream, as well as daydream, correspond with one another: 'The simultaneity of actions, soft-focus images, dissolves, superimpositions, distortions, the doubling of images, slow motion, movement in silence – are these not *the soul of dream and daydream*?' (Ramain [1925] 1988: 363). In contrast to Ramain's sense of synergy between dream and daydream, Jean Goudal distinguishes dream images from other mental images, defining film as a 'conscious hallucination' in the process (Goudal [1925] 1988: 355). For Goudal, film deludes us, and though I do not follow him that far, his observations on the relative strength of different mental images are notable for the varied qualities he lends them, as is his thinking on the mental processes that inform the creation of Surrealist poetry and its hypothetical transition into film.

Goudal comments that when we are awake, the images that enter the imagination 'have an anemic, pale color which by contrast makes the vigor and relief of real images stand out, the ones, that is to say, we get through our senses' (ibid.: 356). When our eyes close and we fall asleep, in contrast, and declaring more definitively than Freud did that our senses do not cross the threshold into consciousness, Goudal holds that the imaginary succession of images comes to the fore with nothing to contradict them, and this is how we believe in their actual existence (ibid.: 356).[19] Goudal is not ignoring a potential distinction between dream images and the aforementioned 'real images'; his point is that the conditions of sleep eliminate any comparison to the real, and the dream images assume their place, with a vivid quality akin to the perceived world. He carries this riveted concentration on the dream image over into the conditions of cinema. Although Goudal's spectator is more attentive to what is seen on screen, his assertion of the unchallenged strength and pictorial nature of the mental image in dreams bridges waking and sleeping worlds in a manner that connects later in his article with conscious mental image-making. The fusion of dream and consciousness that Breton says is key to accessing the future surreality is, for Goudal, more approachable in film than in literature. Goudal cites from the work of French poet Philippe Soupault in order to demonstrate this, using a poetic line also referred to by Breton in his first manifesto to illustrate the arbitrariness best suited to the Surrealist image: 'A church stood dazzling as a bell' (*Une église se dressait éclatante comme une cloche*) (ibid.: 357). For Goudal, the cinema better approximates the cerebral process that would have suggested the poetic image to the writer in the first place: to show a dazzling church, then a dazzling bell in quick succession gives the almost simultaneous sight of two things, which the mind combines without having the time to think about logical connections. This seeing of two things at almost the same time relies to an extent on the spectator's memory, rather than imagination, but it is the fact that the mental image is prioritised here that is important. Taken to be closer to mental processes due to its basis in and privileging of pictorial images, cinema is closer than verbal language to the Surrealist aim to defy logic and reason in order to imagine a new and different reality. Goudal's image-making example that draws from Soupault's words suggests that picturing two objects in quick succession is the imagined first stage in this endeavour.

It is impossible entirely to escape language. As Linda Williams argues, the Surrealists reveal 'the ways in which the image, too, is structured by processes similar to those at work in language' (Williams 1981: 41). Where the Surrealists declared their debt to Freud, aligning the filmic image with a fusion of dream and reality, or with the conditions for experiencing dream images, but privileging the image as doing something distinct from language with regard to logic and rationality, such subsequent scholarship reframes this through Lacan's reading of Freud's work in terms of structuralist linguistics, reintroducing language to the image. Goudal's play of simultaneity and succession through the example of the images of church and bell would thus become figurative and metaphorical, reliant on the very form of condensation (and displacement) that Freud was interested in within the dream work and that Lacan translated into linguistic tropes. It is enough for the purposes of my argument here, though, that Goudal, in addition to recognising the strength of visual mental images while sleeping, speaks of the creation of mental imagery on the basis of a line of poetry while awake, both of which he related to aspects of the film experience. My interests lie in mental images that do not pale anaemically in comparison to the evidence of the senses and in how they can be consciously created rather than dreamt. This latter activity will involve shifting Goudal's emphasis on the spectator's absorption in film as in a dream to the production of vivid mental images as they view. Later theorists who look in more detail at spectatorship than Goudal did test the relation to the dream state that so enthralled the Surrealists and take us smoothly from a dreaming to a waking state.

The closed eyes invoked by Švankmajer's Alice at the outset of this foray into the world of images of the mind and screen are aided or, more accurately at the cinema, replaced by a constitutive absence of light. As Breton exclaims: 'Cinema? Bravo for the dark rooms' (Breton [1924] 1985: 59). Darkness is crucial to the viewing experience in these early years, as it still is within auditoria today, with the main illumination emanating now from the screen. Apparatus film theorists influenced by Freudian and Lacanian psychoanalysis rather than Surrealism use the passive state of the spectator seated comfortably in the dark as the starting point for comparing the act of watching film to a position that first resembles falling asleep and that also reconnects with psychical structures of infancy. Moreover, the concept of the dream screen that Bertram Lewin hypothesised in the 1940s – that surface on which he argues a dream appears to be projected – and which Robert Eberwein develops with more extensive reference to film in the 1980s, forms part of Jean-Louis Baudry's exploration of the relationship between film and dream in the 1970s (Lewin

1946; Eberwein 1984; Baudry [1975] 1986).[20] Christian Metz also speaks at length about the relation between dream and cinema, distinguishing them when it comes to positioning the spectator:

> The filmic and dream states tend to converge when the spectator begins to doze off [*s'endormir*] (although ordinary language at this stage does not speak of 'sleep' [*sommeil*]), or when the dreamer begins to wake up. But the dominant situation is that in which film and dream are not confounded: this is because the film spectator is a man awake, whereas the dreamer is a man asleep. (Metz [1977] 1982: 108)[21]

Aside from his brief reference to those hypnagogic transitional states – the kind that so fascinated visionary Stan Brakhage – Metz keeps dreamer and spectator apart on the basis of the distinction between sleeping and waking. Metz makes a more direct link between film and daydream later on in his text, saying: 'the dream belongs to childhood and the night; the film and the daydream are more adult and belong to the day, but not midday – to the evening, rather' (ibid.: 137).[22] Yet the analogy between film and daydream does not lead any further than the exploration of dreams did when it comes to the mental activity of the spectator. Metz argues emphatically that the perception of film images involves the spectator's perception of real, as opposed to mental, images (ibid.: 109). Conscious mental image formation is not Metz's concern in the predominantly perceptual field, even though he is attentive to the spectator's wakened state.

Like Metz, I too distinguish between waking and sleeping states, positioning spectatorship in the former dimension; but the perception of film images will be bound up in my study with imagining mental images in a way that Metz could not entertain because of his segregation of the two. Bringing the interior production of images together with perceived onscreen images will rely on the strength of the mental images that can appear in dreams and that, like Goudal, I contrast with pallid daydreams. In such dual vision, it is the imagined image rather than just the onscreen image that partakes of this vivacity. The consciously generated imagined images of my book will appear neither as (religious) visions nor conscious hallucinations; nor will they belong to an illogical, irrational world that requires interpretation as Freud suggests. I borrow only the pictorial vitality of the dream world, not the state of passively experienced, unconscious complexity in need of decipherment or linguistic translation: neither film nor imagined images are dreams in my account. Alice's paradoxical instruction to close our eyes therefore leads more straightforwardly yet just as intriguingly to a kind of vision that accompanies the viewing of what is on screen: this inner vision that is indebted to how the dream image appears is a vivid seeing with the mind while awake. As we return now from the netherworld of dreams we still need to heed the instruction to shut our eyes, if only for a little while longer, since this is the way that some filmmakers have explored the conscious visualisation of mental images. These may yet lack the vigour of the imagery that will be explored in Part II of this book, but they provide an indispensable bridge between the pictures of sleeping and waking life, leading us gradually towards what it means for spectators consciously to imagine in images.

## Picturing with Closed and Open Eyes

The title of one of Alfred Hitchcock's early articles stresses the necessity of mental visualisation when starting work on a film. 'Close Your Eyes and Visualise!' is not an instruction to spectators but a reminder to himself and a plea to other directors.[23] He argues that the motion pictures are visual first and foremost and that pictorial action needs to be imagined initially in the mind, favouring this over forming a film script by dialogue alone. For Hitchcock, there is too much writing done in the studios. He understands writing as the enemy of this visual sense, as he declares: 'I try to do without paper when I begin a new film. I visualize my story in my mind as a series of smudges moving over a variety of backgrounds' (Hitchcock 1936: 12). While not a detailed description of depictive mental images, Hitchcock's smudges nevertheless bring out a salient element of the mental arena in which he sketches his films, already indicated in Kosslyn's aforementioned research. The fact that the smudges move across different backgrounds suggests a spatial configuration to the mind: the ground covered in Hitchcock's visualisations is revelatory of mental space.

Although Hitchcock is not the subject of scientific study undergoing extensive analysis with high-tech equipment of what is going on in his mind in the introspective planning of his films, he has evidently scrutinised his own conscious mental pictures painstakingly, and even the little he says about them here is corroborated by later research into visualisation. Images are representations that are similar to those that occur in perception, and neuroscientific research has demonstrated that the same regions that mediate representations in sensory perception are also involved in mental imagery (see Schlegel et al. 2013). There are differences between the two, however, and just as percepts – the mental impressions left as a result of perceiving things – are distinct from mental images of the kind we create, our way of viewing them is too. Hitchcock's smudges – admittedly of uncertain dimension and proportion – reveal something about the mind's eye as opposed to the actual eye. Being a structure in the brain, the mind's eye does not move over a scene as our eyes would; rather, the image moves across a centre of focus (Kosslyn 1983: 128). In Hitchcock's example, it is the smudges that move over a variety of backgrounds that come to his attention, and this is not as a result of a mind's eye scanning across them as the actual eyes would.

Hitchcock's visualisation techniques that are facilitated by closing his eyes while remaining awake, in order to activate the mind's eye and conjure mental images, position him within a historical lineage that precedes and exceeds him, not just in the philosophical and scientific study of imagery. The English Romantic poets were especially sensitive to this – Samuel Taylor Coleridge declares: '[m]y eyes make pictures, when they are shut' (Coleridge 1895: 193) – and so are other filmmakers. In the opening paragraph of Brakhage's seminal meditation on vision in *Metaphors on Vision* (1963a), for example, the instruction to imagine appears three times, lending it quasi-Romantic sovereignty as he writes of the innocence of an untutored eye that goes on an adventure of perception. The fall from this original state of grace in the journey from childhood to adulthood is one that can never be reversed, yet Brakhage seeks nonetheless to develop what he terms the optical mind, asserting: '[t]here is no need for the mind's eye to be deadened after infancy' (Brakhage 1963a: 29). In addition to open-eye vision, Brakhage is captivated by what he sees with his eyes closed, not only when dreaming but also while awake. Borrowing Michael McClure's term, he speaks of 'brain movies', which correspond to images that flash before the eyes, normally when closed (Brakhage 1963b: 23).[24] Filmmakers and poets who laud the mental pictures that appear when their waking eyes are closed join up momentarily with the more permanent state that the blind who visualise testify to across texts and films and that we will encounter in Part II.[25] Jean-Luc Godard recognises this in *JLG/JLG: autoportrait de décembre/ JLG/JLG: Self-Portrait of December* (1995), supporting the belief that seeing – and seeing film – can be understood as an affair of the brain. In this film, Godard tells the blind woman who comes to him for the job of assistant editor to visualise a cube and to divide it up by drawing straight lines from its centre to each of the corners, before asking her how she manages to see all of this. She replies: 'In my head, just like you.' She edits film through a combination of listening to Godard, running her hands along an imaginary filmstrip, and thereby seeing both the film and the act of editing in her head: she speaks the dialogue from the point at which she arrives by touch and cuts the film using her fingers as scissors. The mental pictures that result from her following his instructions to divide up the three-dimensional cube are part of a visualisation process that she shares with the sighted filmmaker and also proffers suggestively to sighted spectators. They also link to an activity that literary and critical theorists have addressed in other contexts, which harks back to William Brown's sense that in order to see, we need to look away.

Speaking about the reading of poetry, Gaston Bachelard describes how imagination begins at the point that readers suspend their reading: what the poet evokes causes readers to turn their heads away from the book, as the poet succeeds in opening the door to reveries (Bachelard [1957] 1994: 14).[26] Writing in a different field about the visual image of photography, Roland Barthes declares: 'Ultimately—or at the limit—in order to see a photograph well, it is best to look away or close your eyes' (Barthes [1980] 2000: 53). The turn or lifting of the head, or indeed the closing of the eyes, are the actions that correspond with what the aforementioned filmmakers and poets posit as fundamental to picturing, visualising, imagining, and exploring inner vision with the mind's eye. When writing about his appreciation of photography, Barthes notes a difference between the photograph and cinema, saying that he cannot treat cinematic images in the same way: 'I don't have time: in front of the screen, I am not free to shut my eyes; otherwise, opening them again, I would not discover the same image' (ibid.: 55). The moving image moves too quickly for Barthes.[27] Yet this act of looking away or closing one's eyes in the cinema is pertinent to an experience that Barthes posits cinematically in a different piece.

In some reflections upon leaving the cinema, Barthes confesses rather deliciously and furtively to flirting with two spectatorial bodies in the auditorium space: not only the narcissistic kind born of apparatus theory but a perverse kind, luxuriating in the darkness of the hall with other bodies, doubly fascinated by looking away from the screen as well as at it (Barthes 1975). This combination of attention and distraction, of looking at and looking away from the screen, has something of the spirit of closing one's eyes in order to see in the cinema, while recalling his thoughts on reading and looking at photographs too. The looking away that alludes to the closing of the eyes is not the sleeper's absorption in the dream world (how could it be, given his desiring relation to what surrounds him?), and as Metz reminded us when specifying the difference between viewing films and dreaming, the spectators' eyes remain open. Barthes's dual focus with his eyes open takes us closer to the perceptual conditions necessary for the open-eyed imagining that film prompts. Crucial to such prompting and the resultant vivacity of the images, as Scarry notes in her literary study, is an instruction given on what to imagine (Scarry [1999] 2001: 31–9). While we have encountered spectatorial instructions already, thanks initially to

Švankmajer's Alice, we can turn now to consider an example in which spectators are told once again to close their eyes in the first instance but additionally to think of something once the eyes are closed. The instructions given are precise yet broad, and they are delivered in the absence of any representational images on screen. But by participating in this brief and playful experiment, we nevertheless get a glimpse of an aspect of the action of imagining that will be important to imagining in images while watching film.

David Wharry's experimental short *Wishful Thinking* (1978) alternates between a blank black and blank white screen, directing instructions at the viewer through a voice-over.[28] Spectators are told to make a 'very special personal wish', then close their eyes and project this onto their eyelids, then open their eyes and project it onto the screen, and then close their eyes and project it through their eyelids onto the screen. Wishful thinking is normally consigned to the realm of hopes and fantasy, serving as an acknowledgement of something that one wants to happen but that probably will not occur. Here, although the activity is literalised and turned into a form of mental projection, it is also imbued with improbability and impossibility. The visualisation processes that cognitive scientists use in their experiments are tied to concrete objects: picturing a cube that will then be rotated, for example (Godard's choice of a cube for his aspiring editor to visualise is far from arbitrary). When the images to be pictured and manipulated are complex or even abstract, they can be shown first as drawings to those involved who then reconstruct them for manipulation and examination in their minds. In contrast, Wharry is asking people to think of any (very special personal) wish. If I wish I were on a beach, sipping coconut water while lounging on a straw mat under a palm tree, I could visualise that partially or as a pictured scene and project that; but if I wish for something more abstract, this is far harder to do. And in any case, my wish remains just a wish. Moreover, while Wharry's instructions may prompt the creation of mental images, the absence of any directive as to what to picture means that the mental event is as likely to involve the recall of images as it is the formation of new ones, hence the appropriateness of the title that refers to (wishful) thinking. There is, though, an element of transformation involved in engaging with this film – changing a blank screen to something with a projected wish on it, whatever form this might take – and therein lies the link to imagining.

Whereas vision occurs whether we like it or not whenever our eyes are open, mental images are not present all of the time, and while the percept is comparatively stable, the mental image is mutable: as Kosslyn notes, it is possible to add to and modify the latter in ways that transform the sense evidence of the eyes (Kosslyn 1983: 91). For Bachelard too, altering the images of perception is fundamental to imagining: '[w]e always think of the imagination as the faculty that *forms* images. On the contrary, it *deforms* what we perceive; it is, above all, the faculty that frees us from immediate images and *changes* them' (Bachelard [1943] 1988: 1). Without this deformation there would be no imaginative activity for Bachelard; there would just be perception or the memory of perception, of something familiar and habitual (ibid.: 1). Wharry's screen is the barest of surfaces proffered for transformation, and some of the films that inform my study work with such blankness at greater length and in more detail, but there is a constant in that what is perceived is different from what is imagined. Although the mental images that are stimulated by film are more noticeable against a blank screen, this does not mean that they do not operate in films rich in onscreen images. Directors interested in engaging the image-making capacity of the imagination create space for it within image-laden films, opening up the possibility for spectators to peruse the mental space in which images can be variously formed and transformed. Thus, the German director Alexander Kluge's belief that film comes about in the mind of spectators recognises how film engages the imagination, or what he terms 'Phantasie' (Kluge 1981). Writing at an earlier juncture about the relation between word, image, and film in 1965 with Edgar Reitz and Wilfried Reinke, Kluge and his colleagues explore and envisage formally innovative films that make the spectator active, and recognise how such films might call for spectators – in addition to exhibitors and distributors – 'with a high level of filmic imagination' (Reitz et al. [1965] 1988: 86).[29] However, in contrast to their belief that film, unlike literature, 'cannot convey any really precise mental images' (ibid.: 88), my own study explores the generation of such mental imagery on a par with the precision of the perceptual world. Perception and imagination have to work alongside one another for this to be possible, and imagining needs to be guided.

For perception and imagination to work simultaneously without interfering with one another there has to be a difference between them, as observed in the context of discussing Wharry's work above. Wittgenstein sums this up neatly when he describes the impossibility of looking at an object and imagining it simultaneously, while recognising that the 'tie-up' between imaging and seeing is close (Wittgenstein 1967: 109).[30] If spectators are so fully absorbed in seeing pictures on screen, if all of their senses are totally engaged in an embodied film experience, how is it also possible to notice the formation of images of the mind if and when they appear? Perception frequently overrides imagination in the conscious realm for this very reason, as Metz opined, and this also confirms Daniel Frampton's belief that '[t]he filmgoer's experience seems primarily perceptual rather than imaginative' (Frampton 2006: 154). At those moments when the onscreen images and aural dimension do not overwhelm the spectator's imagination, though, there is a potential opening to enjoy what Georgina Evans terms the 'unfettered private freedoms' of mental imagery (Evans 2008: 224). Yet the strongest images are those that are formed under guidance and that emerge more clearly as a result than Hitchcock's smudges and more precisely than if spectators are just told to close their eyes and think of something, as Wharry suggests, because viewers are instructed upon exactly what to picture. Godard recognises this through his instructions to his blind editor, but we now need to explore how this more detailed direction extends to the spectator. To point to the strength of belief in the vivacity of mental images and to cite testimony of those who see them, while waking rather than just sleeping, in life and in film, as I have done so far is an important initial step in accounting for the existence of the imagined image; to explain how such imagery can be formed is quite another. In order to reach this elaboration that will unfurl in Part II of this book, the next step is to probe more deeply the relationship between perceiving and imagining.

CHAPTER 2

# Feeling Pictures

Imagine that you are seated in the darkened space of a cinema auditorium. Now you are going to imagine the sudden arrival of light. You are in a screening and it is well over halfway through the film. This light is not the sudden unwelcome intrusion of the houselights, nor is it a blinding brightness that appears on screen. Images that were interspersed with black leader in the film that you have been watching have now gone and the screen is totally black. The arrival of light occurs only in your head on the basis of subtle directions from a woman's voice after a silence. She says, simply: 'And then the sun rose.'[1]

With these words, French writer-director Marguerite Duras partakes of the radiant ignition that Elaine Scarry elaborates upon as one of the ways in which literary writers initiate the creation of moving pictures in their readers' minds.[2] The significant difference in this context is that Duras is speaking the words in voice-over to be listened to against the predominantly black screen of the latter part of *L'Homme Atlantique/The Atlantic Man* (1981). The light of sunrise is the precondition for seeing what there is to follow in the dawning of this day, all of which must be imagined. There is a house, a terrace, a bird, and a single rose. The bird crosses the terrace, coming so close to the house that it grazes the rose, as Duras explains: 'I heard the bird's brushing of the rose in its velvet flight. And I looked at the rose. It moved first as if animated with life and then little by little it became an ordinary rose once again.' The illumination of the sun inaugurates the imagining of the bird and the movement of the flower, which is enlivened momentarily before resuming its usual state, all of which is heard and seen by the speaking I. Birds and flowers hold a special place in Scarry's discussion of imaginability, with flowers in particular lending themselves to vivid imagining due to their size, shape, and localisation, along with the rarity of their petals (Scarry [1999] 2001: 40–71). A fuller understanding of precisely how Duras's description of the bird and flower prompts the making and moving of imagined images will emerge from the fruits of subsequent chapters that will work through the principal processes of mental image formation in a filmic context. For now, let us stay with the dawning pretext for these mental motion pictures and focus first on what it might mean to feel the initial stirrings of their unfolding.

The movement encapsulated in this scene is described in the lead-up to this moment as brutal (it is no coincidence that the bird is masculine, the rose feminine in French). The rush of the sea is heard faintly all the while as this is recounted, suggesting that the suffering caused by her lover's departure that imbues the entire film is present in the air, on the wind, imprinted in the sounds and movements of nature, through what is ethereal and invisible and yet still experienced, enduringly and painfully, when she chooses not to shut it out. Regardless of whether spectators remain looking at the screen throughout this film – looking as if with eyes closed in the later stages, thanks to the abiding darkness of the screen – it was made to be looked at and listened to, a stripped back appeal to the senses, rather than an audio reading encounter with the author merely vocalising a text. The emergent conditions for making and moving mental images that are conjured by Duras's voice and prompted by the sunrise involve a velour feathery wing of a bird touching a rose on the mental retina in the presence of a black screen. The film encounter that Duras reduces to an absolute minimum thus fascinates, not just because it focuses attention on what is to be imagined but on what is – and is not – there to be perceived.

Similar to the distinction that Scarry makes between the guided image-making of dreaming-by-the-book and the images of reverie, there is a difference between the formation of mental images under direction in film, as in this example, and those that emerge for other reasons. These latter may take myriad forms and will come and go so rapidly in some films that they are easy to miss: they could be part of a projective thought process of what is going to happen next, which may involve visualising actions in advance of them actually happening and creating mini pre-emptive scenarios that may or may not ever occur; they may be more reflective and indebted to memory, the film stimulating recall of images that appeared earlier, or the memory of images from other films, or still more diffuse memory images drawn from other life experiences. I will return later in this chapter to the question of memory images and their relation to the imagined images that concern me. For the time being, it is sufficient to observe that these mental images, if and when they occur, will mostly have a faintness to them, since they serve the purposes of processing what is occurring on screen and are not the point in and of themselves. Like the images of daydreams or reverie mentioned in the previous chapter, with the pallor of which Jean Goudal spoke when talking of imagining by day, the mental images in these examples are for the most part wraith-like in comparison to the images that are on screen. In this, one of their characteristics might be understood as faded in relation to the evidence of perception, thereby positioning them within a long tradition of description that the British empiricist Thomas Hobbes epitomised as 'decaying sense' and which can be traced back to Aristotle (Hobbes [1651] 2008: 11). Yet they also correspond in a different way to Jean-Paul Sartre's notable twentieth-century philosophical critique of classical conceptions of imagination, in which the translucence of imagined images contrasts markedly with the vivacity and solidity of the world of perception. I have already begun tacitly to delineate my own difference from Sartre's understanding of imagining, inspired by Scarry but also indebted to film and film theory, drawing an allegiance between vividness and the imagined images that will be central to my study with recourse to the realm of dreams and to what it is possible to focus on in conscious visualisation not only with closed but also with open eyes. It is that more substantial quality too now that will slowly come to the fore as spectators are directed to bring mental images into being in a film context; it is necessary first to pass through Sartre to a revision of his thinking by one of his contemporaries in order to begin to feel their texture.

Rather than view imagination in terms of images in the mind, Sartre thinks of it as revelatory of some of the workings of consciousness, and his theory depends on transparency. Aided by Husserlian phenomenology, Sartre posits the image as an intentional structure. He writes:

> The image of my friend Pierre [. . .] is one of the possible ways of aiming at the real being, Pierre. Thus, in the act of imagination, consciousness relates directly to Pierre and not by the intermediary of a simulacrum, which would be *in* it. (Sartre [1936] 2012: 132–3)

The image is defined as an act rather than a thing within, as consciousness *of* something; in his subsequent work, Sartre talks indeed of the 'imaging consciousness' (Sartre [1940] 2010: 7). As a result, imagination, as Sartre configures it, lacks the vitality of the perceived world, taking us instead to the 'irrealizing' function of consciousness (ibid.: 3). Two-dimensional and diaphanous, the world that emerges through the imaging consciousness is one with which we may be familiar in reverie, not to be taken or mistaken for the substantial world of perception, even though it can be absorbing. In the filmic context, the incidental mental images of which spectators may become aware while viewing film attest to this ultra sheerness, visible to the mind's eye but only just. The phenomenological ghostliness of the realm of imagination, the 'essential poverty' of the image (ibid.: 9), to coin Sartre's phrase, is, however, open to question in ways that expand upon the vitality of this realm that I have already pointed to thus far.

In everyday life, and distinct from delusions, the occasional, brief feeling that we did, said, or saw something that we only in fact imagined doing, saying, or seeing, or that we experienced something that we actually dreamt is quite common. This would not be possible if imagining and perceiving were not tied to one another in some way. Wittgenstein recognised this in different terms when he declared the impossibility of perceiving and imagining the same thing at once, and neuroscience researchers account for this in their studies of the mental mechanisms shared by perception and imagination. Maurice Merleau-Ponty sensed this too in his late work. While he carries forwards the Sartrean understanding of imagination in his magnum opus *Phenomenology of Perception*, as he positions perception in the full sense of the word as the antithesis of imagining (Merleau-Ponty [1945] 2002: 40), he adds qualifications and finally queries this belief as his work progresses. His interest in the increased substantial qualities of the imagined world comes neither from considering psychotic episodes nor hallucination but, rather, a more everyday, or every night, occurrence when we go to sleep. Again, then, we return to the realm of dreams, repeating the closure of the eyes so important to imagining too across the many works that I have referred to so far. When beginning to set out the intertwining of the body with visible things and admitting the double polarity of reflection through which, in Hegelian terms, retiring into oneself also involves leaving oneself, Merleau-Ponty writes in *The Visible and the Invisible* of the persistent issue of our access to the world:

> For there remains the problem of how we can be under the illusion of seeing what we do not see, how the rags of the dream can, before the dreamer, be worth the close-woven fabric of the true world, how the unconsciousness of not having observed can, in the fascinated man, take the place of the consciousness of having observed. (Merleau-Ponty [1964] 1968: 5–6)

Dreams may be tatters of fabric, continuing the broken-up quality of one part of the imagined world outlined in his earlier work, but here it is their being taken, and indeed mistaken, as the complete fabric of the world that dogs the philosopher, albeit while dreaming rather than awake. Merleau-Ponty invokes a tactile quality, which lends the dream the malleable firmness of cloth. In this posthumously published work, he continues to distinguish between perceiving and imagining, between the real and the imagined sphere, and the latter still remains weaker than the way in which its existence was outlined in my previous chapter. Yet there is a growing sense throughout this late work of a thicker texture being granted to the otherwise ethereal sphere and a stronger palpability accrues as a result to the act of imagining than was hitherto apparent. For, Merleau-Ponty also articulates the simultaneity of perception and imagination that occurs with the eyes open, while tapping into the textural quality accessed with the eyes closed.

To exchange Sartrean gossamer for a denser, more closely woven fabric is still not yet to explain how the bird in Duras's garden causes the rose to move in a way that is more substantial than a daydream. This remains the task of the following chapters. More immediately, it is the presence of the latent or the hidden that Merleau-Ponty is aiming to convey at this juncture of his late work, and he compares this with Bachelard's observation that each of the senses has its own imaginary field. He furthers this in a later entry in his notes: 'Being and the imaginary are for Sartre "objects", "entities" – For me they are "elements" (in Bachelard's sense), that is, not objects, but fields' (ibid.: 267). The element or field of the imaginary sphere is to be understood through the imaginary sphere of the body, and the main point is that, whether in dreaming or conscious imagining, this is always related back in some way to vision. Spectators are, after all, invited by Duras to see the effect of the bird's contact with the rose even though it is unavailable to visual perception on screen, and while this experience may be accompanied by affective responses, such vision is not dissipated into these alone. In 'Eye and Mind', Merleau-Ponty characterises the imaginary dimension as that which clothes vision within (*ce qui la tapisse intérieurement*) (Merleau-Ponty [1960] 1993b: 126). Towards the end of the text, he stresses the importance of vision to the imagination:

> even our power to imagine ourselves elsewhere – 'I am in Petersburg in my bed, in Paris, my eyes see the sun' [Robert Delaunay] – or freely to envision real beings, wherever they are, borrows from vision and employs means we owe to it. (Merleau-Ponty [1960] 1993b: 146)

Vision, then, for Merleau-Ponty, is the starting point for imagining, and the imaginary texture of the real is there wherever one looks, as the lining of sight. Rather than antithetical positions on parallel lines, perception and imagination are brought together here in their distinctness like the outer material of a garment in relation to its lining. They fit together, move with one another, and in such movement, imagination acquires substance.

Merleau-Ponty has been criticised for placing too much emphasis on vision in his phenomenology that sought to make perception an affair of the entire body.[3] It is indeed because of this latter element of his philosophy that film scholars have turned to his work in more recent years in order to challenge ocular-centrism and to speak of the film experience with reference to senses other than sight.[4] To reintroduce imagination through a connection to audio-vision is to bring out an inner vision frequently occluded when sight is decentred.[5] It is not unequivocally to reinsert sight at the top of the sensorial hierarchy, though. As Merleau-Ponty's reference to the world of dreams suggests, as the blackness of Duras's screen attests – and as the blankness of Wharry's screen showed, as Hitchcock's instruction to 'close your eyes' affirmed, as Godard instructs his blind editor, and as Švankmajer's Alice also declared – imaginative vision is just as entwined with what is *not* seen with the eyes.[6] It is fitting, then, that when Merleau-Ponty credits Marcel Proust with being the best at describing the lining or depth of the sensible world, he plunges us into darkness:

> the 'great unpenetrated and discouraging night of our soul' is not empty, is not 'nothingness'; but these entities, these domains, these worlds that line it, people it, and whose presence it feels like the presence of someone in the dark, have been acquired only through its commerce with the visible, to which they remain attached. (Merleau-Ponty [1964] 1968: 150)

This felt experience of the inhabited soul as the presence of someone in the dark, which is arrived at through commerce with the visible, sheds light on what thrives in the hinterland of visual perception. As my study advances, later chapters will explore such darkness in ways that shun the light otherwise so important to visibility in phenomenology, broaching post-phenomenological terrain and deconstructing the binary of presence and absence in the forging of imagined images. Furthermore, the light of the mind can be as destructive as it is formative of mental vision. For the time being, though, and these developments notwithstanding, Merleau-Ponty still has much to offer an understanding of the feel and texture of imagining, and his praise of Proust connects back to his more explicit remarks on imagining in 'Eye and Mind'.[7]

The bond between perception and imagination suggests that imagination is always there as the lining of sight. In filmic terms, this corroborates the sense that, moulding to perception of onscreen images, the imagination is always accessible even if only intermittently accessed. It can be understood to partake of a chiasmic structure that Merleau-Ponty outlines in his late work, not remaining always in the background of perception, but coiling round frequently to the foreground along the Möbius strip of the embodied mind's contortions. When imagining is brought to the fore, especially through the guidance that Duras gives us briefly yet evocatively of the encounter between the bird and the rose, it assumes the position that perception may otherwise have done, giving rise to a kind of mimesis of perception of which Scarry speaks and that successive chapters will give more shape to in filmic terms. It lends the mental pictures the degree of vivacity and substance usually only characteristic of the perceived world without replacing it. These imagined images are not incidental to the film that is unfolding and not merely a part of spectators processing the film: they feature at the forefront of the film experience for those who visualise. In a more extreme sense than Kluge envisaged when he spoke of film being created in the mind of the spectator, Duras nonetheless provides the most pared down conditions for this creative activity through which mental images emerge with precision. This stripped back point of departure for imagining in images while viewing film has a distinctive feel: that of the brush of a bird's wing against a rose, feather to petal in the dawning imagery of the mind, conjured by what is heard and seen, as well as what is not perceived, on screen.

The vivacity of which I spoke in the previous chapter joins, then, with the substantiality of a close-woven fabric by means of Merleau-Ponty's musings, which also stem from the dream world but extend to waking life. His awareness across his late work that sight has a lining, which connects with a sense of being in one place and simultaneously seeing something somewhere else, involves a layering of vision that is not disconnected from the other senses but which can still be focused on specifically. The first of the processes that inform the emergence of vivid and substantial mental images that are then set in motion while watching film will be explored in more detail in the next chapter, and the cumulative processes explored as my study advances will permit a return to the Durassian bird and rose in conclusion. Moreover, Duras's films will be discussed further in a later chapter, since her conflicted relation to cinema prompts spectators to dismantle the very images they may create in their minds, and of which the black screen is both harbinger and climax. For the moment, we are in a better position now to weave together the final threads of the modalities of the dual vision that has been referred to over these opening chapters. Imagining and perceiving work together but in different ways in this unique way of seeing, yet they dovetail regularly with other mental processes, which need to be acknowledged too and from which imagining in images can be distinguished.

## Directing Dual Vision

In day-to-day life, seeing one thing while imagining something else is not an unusual occurrence. Jean Goudal was alert to this when he first differentiated the anaemic pallor of the imagination from what he termed the 'real images' that come to us through our senses. As seasoned daydreamers will know, though, often it is the real world surroundings that blur or fade in comparison to the images of reverie even when these latter remain paler. The important thing is that two things are kept in mind at once. Eva Brann explains how perception and imagination relate to one another on a daily basis by making reference to the linguistic trope of metaphor by means of which two things are brought together in an interrelationship (Brann 1991: 776–7). Referring to how metaphors are processed when reading, Brann writes: 'a metaphor is realized when the reader recognizes the sameness of a conceptual element in a comparison, while visualizing, like a pictorial palimpsest, two disparate pictures simultaneously' (ibid.: 777). The simultaneity crucial to metaphor that Brann describes here in visual form as a pictorial palimpsest and elsewhere as a superposition supports her conclusion that '[a]ll imaginative play requires double vision' (ibid.: 779). This doubleness relates to what I have been terming dual vision in the filmic context – although such vision will substantialise in the following chapters in ways that Brann does not fully account for in her discussion of metaphor. Recognising such duality of vision was in fact fundamental to the work of two signal early filmmaker-theorists who show how a succession of mental images can be stimulated by images on screen. For both Maya Deren and Sergei Eisenstein, the images that form in the spectator's mind are as important as those on screen, and they broach both imagination and memory in their own writings on this topic.

Across her theoretical writings and with reference to her own experimental films, Deren invokes the spectator's everyday experiential knowledge when speaking of film viewing, suggesting that there is a constant and necessary comparison to be made between this and the film they are watching. While she and her then husband and co-director Alexander Hammid work carefully with the juxtaposition of shots in the groundbreaking *Meshes of the Afternoon* (1943), it is across sequences and indeed the entire film that this comparative activity takes place, in her view, as a seamless corollary to the act of visual perception. She reflects on this at a later date: 'As we watch a film, the continuous act of recognition in which we are involved is like a strip of memory unrolling beneath the images of the film itself, to form the invisible underlayer of an implicit double exposure' (Deren [1960] 2005: 116). Perception as recollection recalls the philosophy of Henri Bergson (whose work Deren knew of through T. E. Hulme), but this dual layer of the visible and invisible also pre-empts Merleau-Ponty's sense in 'Eye and Mind' that sight has a textural lining. Deren is explicit about the visibility of this lining even as she terms it an 'invisible underlayer', since spectators are creating a double exposure that is not visible on screen but figured as a palimpsest or superposition between mind and screen, and in this double exposure both images – the mental and the onscreen – are equal in importance. Implicitly in keeping with Brann's foregrounded figure of metaphor to explain her sense of imaginative double vision, Deren's privileging of verticality (the poetic axis linked to metaphor) over horizontality (the metonymy of prose) combines eye and inner eye simultaneously to generate the poetic visual experience of film.

Slow motion is the specific example Deren gives as existing in the embodied mind of spectators rather than on screen: knowing the rhythm and pulse of an action and experiencing what is occurring on screen in relation to this produces what she terms a 'double-exposure of time' (Deren [1960] 2005: 121). As the second Maya goes upstairs in *Meshes* her sandaled feet float and bounce gently, breaking continuity with known speeds of climbing stairs, as the camera angle changes and the top half of her body is also seen. The altered climb is shown across several shots, and it is knowledge of bodily motion in time in comparison with this other kind of motion that forms the imagistic double exposure between mind and screen to which Deren refers. This is in part enabled through the memory of the first time that the first Maya climbed the stairs at a more conventional pace, yet it also taps into that experiential knowledge that allows spectators to feel the relative pace of this different gait, the combined elements of which form an imagined image that may be drawn from memory but that does not have to be.

Deren's visual aptitude for a 'picture language', as Rudolf Arnheim terms it (Arnheim [1962] 2000: 86), is inimitable.[8] She is not, however, the first filmmaker-theorist to be concerned with images of the mind being stimulated by images on screen, and her most famous forebear in this regard is Eisenstein. For Eisenstein, montage prompts spectators to create imagined pictures, although he recognises that each person's images will be different (Eisenstein [1939] 1970: 33). Unlike Deren, who refers the spectator back to their everyday experience, Eisenstein invokes the vision the creator/s may have had in mind when conceiving the film. Eisenstein speaks of the necessity for the filmmaker of seizing the imagination of the spectator and locates this as essential to the power of montage (ibid.: 37). Whereas this may not involve the formation of complete mental pictures on the part of the spectator and can just generate details and fragments, the resultant visual images still correspond with those the director has in mind:

> In fact, every spectator, in correspondence with his individuality, and in his own way and out of his own experience – out of the womb of his fantasy, out of the warp and weft of his associations, all conditioned by the premises of his character, habits and social appurtenances, creates an image in accordance with the representational guidance suggested by the author, leading him to understanding and experience of the author's theme. (Eisenstein [1939] 1970: 33)

At the root of this possibility of communing with the images that someone else (the author/director) had in mind is a rational process that is carefully calculated to produce particular ideas and that stems from early on in Eisenstein's oeuvre. When, for example, images of the lion statues are edited together in the oft-cited sequence of *Battleship Potemkin* (1925), this is a means of symbolic, pictorial expression, figured across the image chain from the dormant to the upright animal. In the later essay, 'Word and Image' (Eisenstein [1939] 1970), and even though this piece sets up a freer sense of creativity in some respects, there is an intended visual image, rather than just an idea, that the director is aiming to get across. That mental image may not always pass successfully from director to spectator, but the suggestion of the generation of imagery on the basis of the succession of images on screen is what is pivotal here. As Martin Lefebvre notes, Eisenstein's doctrine of *imaginicity* (*obraznost*) involves the combined work of imagination and memory, evident in the above reference to the creation of an image through the 'warp and weft' of all manner of associations from the spectator's own experience (Lefebvre 1999: 482). As for Deren, albeit in different terms, imagined mental images for Eisenstein are not always entirely separable from memory images, yet importantly too imagination and memory are not the same. Indeed, there are felt differences in the experience of acts of remembering and imagining, and while these 'mates of the mind', as Edward Casey terms them, feed each other at times, they are also distinct (Casey 1976: 2–4).[9]

In the ensuing chapters of my own study, imagined images are created rather than recollected, and though they may draw from and bear a relation to what has been seen and felt, known and remembered within the film experience or beyond, they are not memory images based solely on recall. Moreover, the vivacity and palpability of the imagined images that I have pointed to across this and the previous chapter will arise from films that direct spectators more precisely with words and sounds to construct them, as in the case of my earlier example from Duras's corpus, thereby contrasting with the silent filmmaking and more exclusive focus on montage that first prompted Deren's and Eisenstein's pioneering reflections on the spectator's mental images. Inter-titles in films of the silent era, when they appear, present viewers with words that may indeed generate mental images in excess of those seen on screen, but it is the more persistent vocal or sonorous elements of later films that concern me in this study of the guided image-making of the imagination in the era of audio-vision.[10] Guidance serves image-making more gently than any authoritarian directedness, and there is freedom within instruction to shape and reshape mental images in ways that can never be fully controlled. This relative freedom harks back to Kluge's interest in the spectator's imagination, since unlike Eisenstein, he had no ideal meaning in mind when speaking of the role of the spectator in the production of meaning (Kluge 1981). Yet guidance is crucial to the formation of vivid mental images and is coupled with freedom within constraints. Quite apart from the fact that the exact forms that such images take can never be imposed on anyone, nobody can be forced to make them. Indeed, Part II of this book offers an explanation of how mental images form *if* they appear to spectators, and it explores some of the processes that give rise to them without ever implying that this is exactly how and what everyone should be seeing. As the range of films included in this study will demonstrate, mental image-making is not just stimulated by one particular kind of filmmaking, nor is it associated principally with the work of one director, and their international scope is also tied to this recognition. Furthermore, no single film prompts the process of mental composition for the entirety of its duration. Indeed, I spend considerable time in several chapters outlining how a particular sequence of a film prompts the generation of mental images, such that this experience, while recurrent in some films, is recognised as more transient in others. The fleetingness of the experience at times is, however, exactly what enables me in conclusion to broaden the relevance of this study still further.

Imagining in images operates in the film experience as spectators see and hear, feel and think, occasionally looming prominently and occasionally being eclipsed, but nonetheless as important as other perceptual and cognitive processes. A major strand of film philosophy has been devoted to thinking rather than imagining in images. For Gilles Deleuze, filmmakers think in movement- and time-images and they do so through cinema such that the thinking in images is externalised rather than being something that is traced in visual terms in relation to the filmmaker's mind (Deleuze [1983] 2005: xix). Hitchcock's visualised smudges understandably have no place in such an account. When indeed Deleuze discusses

Hitchcock's films at the end of *Cinema 1*, he addresses the question of the mental image in film as part of the crisis of the action-image beyond affection- and perception-images, using Charles Sanders Peirce's definition of thirdness. Deleuze notes:

> thirdness gives birth not to actions but to 'acts' which necessarily contain the symbolic element of a law (giving, exchanging); not to perceptions, but to interpretations which refer to the element of sense; not to affections, but to intellectual feelings of relations, such as the feelings which accompany the use of the logical conjunctions 'because', 'although', 'so that', 'therefore', 'now', etc. (Deleuze [1983] 2005: 201)

The mental becomes the proper object of this image but is defined in terms of relations, symbolic acts, and intellectual feelings. With reference to Hitchcock's films, Deleuze notes that action, perception, and affection are 'framed in a fabric of relations', stressing that '[i]t is this chain of relations which constitutes the mental image, in opposition to the thread of actions, perceptions and affections' (ibid.: 205). For Deleuze, naming a pleonastic 'imagination-image' in *Cinema 1* would not have made any sense, since the sensorimotor linkages that propel the classical cinema forwards feature the imaginary elements that he talks about in more detail in *Cinema 2* as part of them rather than constituting a principal defining feature of the essence of the cinematic image that he is searching for throughout. When he reaches his lengthier meditation on the mental terrain in *Cinema 2*, inaugurated with reference to Hitchcock at the end of the first text, the imaginary plays an important role in relation to the real, the virtual, and the actual in his description of images, although all of these categories in their indiscernibility are superseded by time in the passage from the crystal image to the chronosign, with thought as their goal. Referring to the spectator, he writes:

> It is true that bad cinema (and sometimes good) limits itself to a dream state induced in the viewer, or – as has been the subject of frequent analysis – to an imaginary participation. But the essence of cinema – which is not the majority of films – has thought as its higher purpose, nothing but thought and its functioning. (Deleuze [1985] 1994: 168)

As in the first cinema book, so in the second, thought surpasses imagination, from Deleuze's extensive discussion of film images to this passing reference to the state induced in the viewer.

My focus on imagining in images on the part of the viewer in this book turns attention to the images of the mind in a manner that does not seek to surpass thought. Yet my study recognises the image-making capacity of the imagination as distinctive, rather than only working in the service of thinking, without consigning it to a dream state. The consciousness of mental images as more than translucent, *pace* Sartre, may reintroduce what many twentieth-century philosophers were keen to banish from the mind, but the fact that there is still a debate about imagery points to the persistence of a felt experience of mental image formation that cannot be explained away. Daniel Dennett's humorously made observation about getting rid of visual mental images so that other kinds of mental impressions also disappear may have been adhered to in the sense that even ardent pictorialists do not envision a homunculus sitting down with popcorn and a beverage to watch an endless stream of movies in their heads. But there is still a widespread and popular analogy for visual mental images as a kind of inner cinema: that is to say, a continual succession of images, rather than the imagined presence of an apparatus, screen, and seating. We will encounter this belief most poignantly in the testimony of artist Hugues de Montalembert in the next chapter as we explore the first aspect of mental composition in the film context. Yet the imagined images of the kind that interest me more broadly in this book are generated in a more fragmented and discontinuous manner than the metaphor of a perpetual inner cinema of images suggests. While the vivid mental pictures that will take shape over the course of the ensuing chapters are in motion and frequently sustained, they still come and go, both inviting and interrupting the cinematic analogy. The images of the mind take on opacity and free themselves from intentionality, at times assuming a life of their own, as philosopher Gilbert Simondon suggests when he writes:

> images are not as limpid as concepts; they do not obey the activity of thinking with as much suppleness; they can only be governed indirectly; they conserve a certain opaqueness, like a foreign population at the heart of an organized state. Containing in some measure will, appetite and movement, they appear almost like secondary organisms at the heart of the thinking being: parasites or adjuvants, they are like secondary monads living at certain moments in the subject and leaving them at certain others. (Simondon [1965–6] 2014: 9)

The opaqueness of the mental image in Simondon's account contrasts explicitly with Sartrean translucence, associating it with visibility rather than invisibility. In the following chapters, and in keeping with such palpable comings and goings, imagined images are occasionally primary rather than secondary and are sometimes more powerful than what is on screen, yet inevitably they also disappear entirely; the overriding point here is to recognise them alongside the evidence of the senses and workings of the intellect that process what is heard and seen, all of which play a role in dual vision. Imagined images are not everything but nor are they nothing; to see and feel the formation of images in the mind is to witness how they inhabit, as Edward Casey suggests, a spatial-temporal limbo that seems neither internal nor external to the imaginer at times (Casey 1976: 14). Dual vision partakes of both internal and external worlds, and while indebted to the dual visual systems theory referred to in the previous chapter, it is not to be reduced to a function of this visual system alone, occurring as it does in excess of what and how the eyes see, as my discussion so far has sought to make clear.

The myriad screens on which films can be viewed in the twenty-first century necessarily widen out some of the conditions that have underpinned several of my examples in these opening chapters, from my own initial reference to where I first saw *The Hateful Eight*, through André Breton's praise of the darkness of auditoria (also the apparatus theorists' ideal forum), to the setting I evoked for the imagining of Duras's bird and flower. While I do not incorporate installation art in my study, not all of the other films that will be discussed are made for or viewed exclusively in cinemas. As a result, my charting of imagined images in the subsequent chapters weaves the auditorium space in and out where relevant, mindful of the specificity of its screen as one among others, especially today. The processes that I focus on just require a screen and a seated viewer for what is not always a solitary pursuit of unalloyed attentiveness but is one which takes place nonetheless between an embodied mind and screen, forming a dual vision unique to each individual who experiences it. When Maya Deren speaks of the 'invisible underlayer' of the implicit double exposure that she suggests spectators experience while viewing film, she points to a fundamental aspect of dual vision: layering. This is the first of five processes of mental composition that will now be explored in depth. The way in which films direct the layering of perception and imagination confers upon mental images the vibrancy and substance that this opening section has introduced, serving as the foundation of the dual vision of onscreen and imagined images in the next chapter and beyond.

# PART II
# MAKING MENTAL MOTION PICTURES

CHAPTER 3

# Layering

Midway through Gary Tarn's essay film *Black Sun* (2005), Hugues de Montalembert recalls in his voice-over narrative a particularly strong memory. French artist De Montalembert was blinded in a vicious bungled robbery when he was living in New York in 1978. He is the narrator of Tarn's film who is heard but never seen. The film focuses on the life-changing consequences of losing his sight, and the visual memory that he describes at this midpoint dates back to the time when he could still see. He tells of how one day in 1973, while working in Vietnam as a freelance reporter for Italian magazines, he saw a young girl of around twelve years old standing alone in the playground of an orphanage in Saigon. She was not playing with the other children because her arms had been blown off in a landmine explosion. In keeping with the non-illustrative image track that predominates in the film, the onscreen images do not seek to represent his verbal account and do not show the young Vietnamese girl in the playground. They focus instead and at length on filtered images of a young western girl (Figure 3.1), smiling as she plays on a rope-swing. De Montalembert's story is all the more jarring for being told over this onscreen image. It is the image that is not shown, though, that is more striking.

Whenever I think back to this film, I feel sure that I saw the tragic image of the young girl in Saigon standing to one side in the playground as the other children play on, even though this scene never materialises on screen.[1] In memory, of course, both this and the onscreen image of the girl on the swing are mental images, and one could respond by saying that this is why they feel equivalent. Yet, the division in perception between what is seen and heard gives rise to an imagined image that is different from what appears before the eyes and makes an equally powerful mental impression *at the time of viewing the film*. Believing that one has seen something that one has imagined is a reversal of a classic psychology experiment. The experiment carried out by Mary Cheves West Perky in

Figure 3.1 *Black Sun* (Gary Tarn, 2005).

1910 asked people to imagine a list of things by means of simple verbal instructions (Perky 1910). Unbeknown to them, very faint images of the things that they were being asked to imagine were projected on a screen in front of them: the visual stimulus was presented 'gradually and with increasing definiteness' (ibid.: 428). Perky's experiment takes the perceived image of an object back to the almost translucent state with which imagery is frequently associated and which is familiar from daydreams, increasing its intensity until it rejoins the consistency of the world of perception. As a result of the joining together of an instruction to imagine and a gradual perceptual experience, most people mistook perceptual for imaginative consciousness, and Perky thereby demonstrated that vision and imagery could be indistinguishable. An overlap between vision and imagery is clearly in play when I think I have seen the scene with the young Vietnamese girl, but the other girl who is there unequivocally to be seen on screen contrasts with the gradual appearance of the objects in the Perky experiment. The question, then, is how the mental feat of image-making is orchestrated here to produce an experience akin to that of perceiving a film image with one's eyes while one is looking at something else.

As with the Duras extract discussed in the previous chapter, the power of words to direct imagining resonates in this example; Tarn's film, like the other essay films and documentaries that will feature in this chapter, has a narrative voice-over that draws in this respect from the verbal arts. Speaking of his time as a reporter in Vietnam when the film first cuts to the filtered image of this sequence, De Montalembert's precise words are as follows:

> I was interested in the people who were innocent and still had to endure the consequences of such madness. I remember arriving in an orphanage in Saigon and there was something like one thousand children in a courtyard playing wild, and in the corner a little girl – a very, very beautiful little girl – around twelve years old, looking ashamed, not playing, because she had no arms any longer: they had been blown up by a mine. Those visions are still very vividly in my mind.

The present participles set the scene that he describes in motion and keep it moving in sync with the onscreen moving image – 'I remember *arriving* ... and ... children ... *playing* wild'. The space of imagining is defined – a courtyard – with the contrast between the vast numbers engaged in frenzied play and the little girl providing the coordinates of her isolation 'in the corner', which in turn focuses attention on the static, ashamed countenance of the beautiful twelve-year-old with no arms. Just enough information is given here to direct the mental composition of the scene: the exact shape of the courtyard, the time of day, what the little Vietnamese girl is wearing, and so on, are not recalled, leaving this open to be imagined, still on the basis of the linguistic constraints but with a degree of freedom. Just as important as the verbal direction for image-making to be prompted to come into being, though, is the relation to the onscreen visual image and to what is also heard alongside De Montalembert's narration.

The sound of voices shouting and crying out coincides with De Montalembert's declared interest in the innocents who had to endure the insanity of the Vietnam War. The sonic reverberation of suffering runs into the sound of children at play. These voices are faint and do not emanate from the diegetic space – all sound in this film is non-diegetic, accompanying the voice-over – but combine with Tarn's abstract musical composition that has entered a decidedly sombre key in this sequence. The voices gain somewhat in intensity and become more perceptible in the pauses between De Montalembert's words. Perky's experiment lives on in these gaps, translated into sonorous rather than visual terms, as the line between perceiving and imagining is blurred. Spectators are hearing about a scene imprinted in a mind that can never of course be entered in order to see precisely what he saw, and the film recognises this by not attempting to recreate his mental recollection on screen. But the words and the sound effects set up an oblique relation between De Montalembert's memory and a mental space that spectators can access – their own. The playground that is not seen has a perceptual point of contact with the faint sound of shrieking and shouting from which image-making can borrow. Yet even more important and persistent in this regard is the duration and content of the onscreen visual images in this sequence, which do not deviate from their focus on the young western girl.

This is not the first time in the film that filtered images are used. De Montalembert tells at an earlier juncture of how his brain was craving images to such an extent that he felt that returning to a place where he had had an intense visual experience would help the images to reach him through his blindness. As he describes a trip back to Bali, the film images take on bright colours reminiscent of Chris Marker's *Sans Soleil/Sunless* (1982) in which some of the images are solarised and enter the space that, in homage to Tarkovsky and Cocteau, is called the 'Zone'. For the most part, though, De Montalembert's voice-over accompanies a range of unfiltered visual images, blurred and clear, many of which were filmed on 16mm by Tarn on location in New York, Maine, Paris, London, India (Ladakh, Rishikesh, Rajasthan), and Iceland (see Bowen 2007). Just prior to the appearance of the filtered image of the young girl on the swing, there is an unfiltered shot of a staircase in New York that captures glimpses of people going up and down. The abrupt contrast of the smiling girl looms large and in close-up first of all, conveyed in white, green, brown, cream, and black blocks of colour as she moves away from the camera and then returns to it, giving disorientating views of her face, arms, and hands from different angles for the first few seconds. As the distance between subject and camera increases, she appears more clearly with long, wavy hair, holding on to a rope and swinging around, albeit still filtered. She swings about for around forty seconds prior to the transition in De Montalembert's narration from speaking about being in Vietnam to the particular story of the young girl at the orphanage. A young boy emerges briefly behind her at one point, suggesting that she is not entirely alone even though she is the main focal point throughout. I spoke in the first chapter of this study about directors leaving space for the viewer's imagination to go to work in the form of their films, and this may take the form of spaces within shots, or between them, of lacunae and ellipses that may or may not be signalled visibly with the kind of experimental use of black or clear leader that we have already considered in a couple of its manifestations, with reference to Wharry and then Duras. Here, there is no temporal or spatial ellipsis in narration. There is, however, time to build a mental image, not only the time that it takes for De Montalembert to describe the girl and the scene, but also the time that the girl playing on screen on the rope-swing has been present prior to his recall of his vision and the moments that she remains there after this. Time is the space needed for a mental image to be generated and held for long enough for it to appear as if it has been seen.

The visual shots, narration, and soundtrack that I have been describing in this sequence run for around one minute and forty-five seconds, and the mental image forms far more quickly, yet the duration of the perceived image helps the imagined image too to endure. Precisely how it acquires substance too, though, is what we now need to explore.

The perceived and imagined images are kept in view between eye and mind, and the relationship between perception and imagination harks back to Merleau-Ponty's sense of the connection between the two, as well as fleshing out Brann's notion of superposition that we also explored in the previous chapter. When Brann outlines how it is possible to keep two things in mind at the same time in everyday situations, she speaks of the 'transparencies' of the imagination overlaying the perceived world (Brann 1991: 776–7). The imagined image of the young girl in the playground is not, however, transparent: to reiterate my opening observations in this chapter, it is as if she has been seen rather than seen through. There is therefore more to the notion of dual vision in this filmic context than an imagined transparency being placed over a perceived image, as the mental collision between the bird and rose on Duras's terrace already intimated in the previous chapter. Scarry's discussion of translucence when outlining how writers of literary prose and poetry get readers to establish the foundations upon which to form images of the imagination is helpful in introducing why this is the case. Scarry refers to the famous passage towards the beginning of Proust's *In Search of Lost Time* in which the brightly coloured images of the magic lantern move around young Marcel's bedroom, with the figure of Golo surmounting all of the material obstacles in the room. As she reminds us, the room at Combray occasions Marcel's meditations on habit, but it is what is not remarked upon explicitly that is important in imaginative terms: 'the perceptual mimesis of the solidity of the room brought about by the "impalpable iridescence" of Golo fleeting across its surfaces' (Scarry [1999] 2001: 11). This overlaying of a visual transparency on the walls is key for Scarry in showing how Proust gets readers to bring a solid surface into being in their minds. Both Golo and the wall have to be imagined by the reader and it is the relation between the two, one sliding over the surface of the other, that not only builds but also firms up the walls of the room in the reader's mind. The result of this mental activity is that the room comes to life with the kind of solidity usually characteristic of the world of perception. While transparency plays a key role here, then, it is just an element of what is imagined rather than the sole quality of the mental image whose emergent substantiality it serves under the writer's expert instruction.

As Scarry elaborates on the ways in which transparent substances move across solid substances in a number of texts by different writers, lending the imagined world weight in the process, she also notes instances of this principle in the interior content of film, as well as pointing to this as film's most essential feature: the projection of an insubstantial moving image on a wall (ibid.: 17). The implication here is that film embodies the workings of the image-making that she has been arguing literature occasions in the mental arena. Writing at an earlier historical moment, but in keeping with Scarry's trajectory from the magic lantern, through the mental image, to film, Theodor Adorno likens the magic lantern slides of childhood to the movements of the inner images of dreams and daydreams, suggesting that it is in the objectification of the subjective experience of such mental images that film's potential as an art form lies: 'Such movement of interior images may be to film what the visible world is to painting or the acoustic world to music' (Adorno [1967] 1981: 201). Adorno is drawing upon the immaterial and insubstantial qualities of the mental image in order to make his argument and for Scarry too these remain undeniable properties of the imagination, even though the kind of instruction that writers give readers when they teach them how to dream-by-the-book in Scarry's account lends mental images more weight. For my purposes here, the imaginative process that film embodies for both writers is something that I am relocating to the subjective sphere of the spectator – without denying its presence in film and without fixing in mind a perpetual inner cinema – and in so doing the reader's mental manipulation of layers of translucence and solidity in Scarry's account also applies to the mental processes activated while listening and viewing. It is not therefore the case that the imagined image merely forms a translucent layer over the perceived image; rather, what is heard and seen generates a procedure of mental composition that borrows from the perceived world as it passes over it, acquiring more vivid qualities in the process. Nor is this to say that it blots out or replaces the perceived images of film, even though it may capture more attention at times; it is, however, to posit it in the first instance as a shifting surface as substantial as that of the perceived images of the film. The imagined image thus becomes something that viewers have the impression of seeing rather than seeing through but it never entirely blocks vision of the screen. It is worth pausing momentarily on this description of the imagined image because its architecture is foreshadowed in the form of some of the shots of *Black Sun*.

The film is fascinated with showing surfaces that are seen as well as seen through, thereby creating a broader field of vision within the space on screen. For example, a window of a diner early on in the film shows the people inside but also reflects the people, cars, and buildings behind the camera, outside. The transparency of glass is not entirely occluded, but what is visible in the reflection of the glass is as important as what is visible through it. This layering of the onscreen image combines with De Montalembert's words to suggest the perceptual and imaginative spaces of vision, as spectators are called upon to participate in creating what lies outside of ordinary sightlines but not out of mind. De Montalembert explains that when he first went blind his brain was producing images 'exactly like a film' all the time, as images of New York appear on screen, returning to aerial shots similar to those that feature at the outset. These 'brain movies', to recall Brakhage's term, also relate in part to what he has never seen with his eyes and thereby form the very creative vision he praises. De Montalembert speaks of vision indeed as a creation not perception, describing at a late point in the film how walking with a sighted painter friend of his is a treat akin to an adventure: his friend sees everything with an acute eye, elaborating on the environments that they pass through in a way that brings them to life for him. To see, for De Montalembert, borrowing the words of his painter friend, is always to 'see beyond', rather than just perceiving. Sight overspills its status as one of the five senses and becomes something that goes beyond them, bringing images to life vividly by means of the mind's eye.

To return to the young Vietnamese girl in the courtyard, whose image is created mentally rather than seen on screen, it is thanks to the brush with the perceived world of sound and vision in Tarn's film that the imagined image takes on substance that it lacks in Brann's discussion of transparencies overlaid on the world of perception and that it acquires in Merleau-Ponty's work in his brief foray into the world of dreams. The visible smile of the western girl and the strength in her arms needed to hold on to the rope are a cruel contrast with the shame and maimed body of the girl in Saigon whom De Montalembert describes. Yet the mimesis of perception aids the formation of the imagined image of the girl in the courtyard in spite of this glaring difference, as properties of the perceived image transfer to that which is imagined. There is a readiness to picture a girl because a girl of around the same age is already on screen, and while there is no literal mimetic transfer and the difference between the two is immense, imagining the young Vietnamese girl who cannot play borrows from perception of the girl on screen in terms of gender and age, lending her something of her substantiality too. The onscreen image has already been transformed to the extent that it is filtered rather than photo realistic and this too aids the transition from sight to mind. Indeed, the way in which imagining borrows from the comparative solidity and audibility of that which is perceived through audio-vision spans the scene more broadly. The girl on the swing moves about constantly in many different directions, combining with the motion of the imagined scene that is ignited by De Montalembert's description ('arriving' ... 'playing' ... 'wild') and fuelled by the sounds of child's play that are heard every now and again. Lingering with her moving image blends stasis and movement akin to that of the imagined image in which the young girl is standing still as her fellow orphans play.

The kind of dual vision called for here on the basis of borrowing from the perceived world in a filmic rather than solely literary sense will be encountered in different guises not only across other examples discussed in this chapter but also across later chapters in conjunction with further facets of the mental imaging process. For the time being, I want to bring in other examples that are based on the same principle but that contrast with this opening instance of layering, since it is not always a question of forming an image that diverges from what is shown on screen but of adding to the content of the onscreen images as the play of surfaces acquires further depth. This closer relationship between what is spoken about and what is imaged on screen is operative in Tarn's film too in sequences where there is a more direct link between the onscreen images and the story that De Montalembert is telling, but I want to consider a different film to show how this is not just a function of Tarn's particular aesthetic. Laurie Anderson's essay film *Heart of a Dog* (2015) directs imagining in this manner.

## Materialising and Filling In

Anderson's relationship to her beloved pet dog Lolabelle, a rat terrier, lies at the very heart of her meditative film, which runs from the dog's dream birth through her blindness to her death and beyond, as Anderson traces her journey through the bardo towards the new life thereafter. Anderson's reflections on the love and loss of Lolabelle broaden to include her relation to others who have passed away: from the personal – the passing of her mother, her friend Gordon Matta-Clark, and husband Lou Reed – to the political – victims of the 9/11 terror attacks in New York. Drawings, animation, and 8mm footage supply contrast throughout with other film images, which at times are slowed, rewound, tinted, and distressed. A number of the onscreen images in *Heart of a Dog* are seen through glass, which is rendered visible by what appears on it, most effectively by rain or snow that has fallen on it – on a car windscreen, for example. As in *Black Sun*, albeit as part of an aesthetic that does not also play with reflections, this normally translucent substance calls attention to itself by becoming visible. More broadly, the surface of the image is rarely smooth, uninterrupted, or unaltered: there is frequently something that gets in the way of clear-sighted vision, akin to Anderson's mention of the 'prisoner's cinema' of phosphenes that float on the surface of vision and behind the eyelids, which recall Brakhage's description of closed-eye vision, and which appear on screen too. It is this visual accretion that inclines towards images being seen both on screen and by means of the mind's eye, guided frequently by the soundtrack. Music and the words spoken in voice-over appeal to the ear, as the eye watches something similar to what is described or indeed different, affirming the importance of hearing in keeping with one of Anderson's constant points of reference, *The Tibetan Book of the Dead*. The film has the quality of a dream from the outset, and the haziness of many of the images – similar to clouds in the physical world that appear billowing out on screen at intervals, white against blue or in black and white – lends it properties that approach the condition of the imagination in gauzy daydreams. Citing David Foster Wallace, Anderson declares: 'Every love story is a ghost story', suggesting that her film too is a haunted tale of love. Ghosts are relatively easy to picture because they share the insubstantiality of those aforementioned clouds, yet Anderson gets spectators to flesh out what is imagined by filling in particular onscreen images.

Almost midway through the film, as she comments on her growing awareness at a younger age that some people live in different worlds, she speaks in voice-over of a man called Moses. She explains:

> I'd be walking to school and I'd look up and there was Moses, hanging by his tool belt. Every day, no matter what the weather, Moses would climb up the telephone poles, and attach his belt to them and open the phone boxes and move the lines around; sometimes he'd take out his tools and do some hammering. In the winter, you could see him really well, outlined against the bright sky, hammering, and spinning round and round up there. Now, Moses did not work for the phone company. He just lived in another world, a kind of dream world of trees and circuits and electronics. But everyone in town made a point of thanking him for fixing their phones. The men would be walking home from the train station in the evening and they'd yell: 'Hey Mo, good job on the phones. The reception on my line is really great now. Nice job. Clear. Thanks a lot.'

Anderson recounts this over black-and-white images of telegraph poles and wires, along with skeletal trees and their branches silhouetted against a wintry sky (Figure 3.2). A low-angle tracking shot follows the wires, telegraph poles, trees, and sky from the right to the left of the screen, pausing only briefly to pan more closely across a mass of branches above, before resuming its journey along the horizontal axis of the wires. Moses,

**Figure 3.2** *Heart of a Dog* (Laurie Anderson, 2015).

the focal point of her narrative, is entirely absent from the screen, but the camera angle that reinforces Anderson's declaration 'I'd look up', and the provision of a winter setting in which 'you could see him really well, outlined against the bright sky', predisposes viewers to see him too.

As with the onscreen images of the young girl on the rope-swing in Tarn's film, the duration of this sequence with its focus on one setting provides the space in temporal terms for imagining with the film, picturing images on the basis of Anderson's narrative, in excess of what the visual track shows. Here, though, the stage is set explicitly for the appearance of Moses on the telephone lines that he is said to have moved around come rain or shine. Viewers are given something to attach him to – telegraph poles pass by as the tracking shots run along the lines – so do not need to conjure the sturdiness of his support and can focus instead on bringing him into view. As Anderson announces Moses' presence 'every day, no matter what the weather', hammering can be heard as part of the musical soundtrack, prior to the declaration that this is one of his daily activities on the lines. The hammering recurs later in the sequence too, ensuring that he persists in a manner more akin to the world of perception than that of imagining. It is an outline of a man working against a bright sky that spectators are asked to picture, and given that the trees, wires, and telegraph poles are precisely outlines against a bright sky, Moses is the mental continuation of the perceptual experience, the ingredients of which serve to form a moving silhouette busying himself with his repairs. Imagining borrows from perception as it slides over the onscreen images, like the translucent mobility of Golo at Combray, gaining substance from them that it also draws from the soundscape, but this time it adds to what is there on the screen.

Anderson speaks about the Moses sequence in interview, likening it, along with the film as a whole, to a radio play on the basis of the words that encourage viewers to make their own pictures and to 'fill things in' (Anderson 2016). It is fitting that Tarn also makes reference to a radio play for the planning of *Black Sun*. While he specifies that he looked to François Girard's experimental biopic *Thirty Two Short Films about Glenn Gould* (1993) in order to work out how to structure his film, this was on the basis of his interest in Glenn Gould's radio play *The Idea of North* (1967), the combined effects of which gave Tarn a sense of how the film could flow with a musical rhythm (Bowen 2007). Although the audio tracks of these films differ markedly from one another and give rise to an audio-visual form distinct from the radio play, the voice and soundscape emerge necessarily from a zone that cannot be seen on screen. Rather than leave this zone to be consigned solely to the terms that conventionally designate the space beyond the screen and that are associated with sound – as non-diegetic, as hovering somewhere *over* the image (voice-over) or just *off* screen (*voix off*), or ghosting it acousmatically – it is the role it plays in the conversion into the images of the mind that has been crucial in the preceding examples. What Michel Chion terms the capacity to see with one's ears or hear with one's eyes is a form of sensory substitution associated with the correspondences and crossings of synaesthesia in audio-vision (Chion [1990] 1994). Combining that which is fundamental to listening to a radio play and its concomitant stimulation of the image-making capacity of the imagination with the presence of a rich succession of visual images on screen, these films also engage other sensorial connections but it is the way in which these too serve the generation of images of the imagination that is of interest to me.

The sequence in which Anderson remembers Moses is not the only instance in the film where the starting point for the layering of imagined images over those that are perceived is provided on screen. Exchanging the rarity of the air in which Moses is suspended for the slippery surface of ice, Anderson's final narrative of the film is the most affecting. She had confessed to her Buddhist teacher that she did not love her mother, and he suggests that she thinks of a moment when her mother loved her unconditionally. It is through a tale of walking her twin brothers across a frozen lake in a stroller that Anderson finds a way of reconnecting with her mother. The sequence that reveals her mother's love to her begins with Anderson's song 'The Lake' that opens with the words 'I walk accompanied by ghosts.' 8mm footage of Anderson appears with her skating around before the image broadens out to show others. This opening image had appeared towards the start of the film, after she had spoken of gathering with her siblings around her mother's deathbed and listening to her mother's confused last words. The skating tale takes her back to her mother in conclusion. The onscreen image is stretched frequently throughout this sequence, as the ice appears to split and the image itself is partially rent apart but repeatedly resealed. As she begins to speak, a clearer image of her appears skating around with a baby stroller: 'We lived by a lake and every winter it froze. We skated everywhere.' The image then cuts to close-up shots of the two baby boys, dressed in blue hats and anoraks, as she continues: 'One evening, I was coming home from the movies and I was pushing my little brothers, Craig and Phil, in a stroller.' It cuts back to the blurry image of the frozen lake with its stretched distortions and disturbances to the screen surface, as she explains: 'I had decided to take them over to the island to look at the moon that was just coming up.' As the onscreen image focuses on the border of the lake and the island, showing the stroller heading there, she declares: 'But as we got close to the island, the ice broke and the stroller sank into the dark water . . . .' Up until this point, the images on screen have kept pace with the narrative of events, but when she says that the ice broke and the stroller sank, this is not dramatised on screen. When she announces the breaking of the ice, a close-up of the white-textured, granular surface appears, followed by a faint superimposition of the face of one of her brothers (Figure 3.3). Anderson continues: 'My first thought was "mom's gonna kill me". And I remember the knitted balls on their hats as they disappeared under the black water.' She rescues her brothers and receives, wholly unexpectedly, high praise from her mother for her swimming and diving abilities. This provides her with the moment of unconditional love that she had been searching for all along. It is the knitted balls on her brothers' hats that I want to linger on here, though, and the slide of the stroller that continues as her narrative advances 'down the muddy bank, further down under the ice'. Viewers do not see any of this but the ease with which it can be imagined has as much to do with its play of surfaces as it does its vividly dramatic unfolding.

Crystalline and powdery white, blurred because it is filmed in close-up, with cracks in it that shift about as if an ice floe rather than being packed solid, the icy image that appears on screen as spectators are told that the knitted balls disappear under the black water is the treacherously unstable surface through which her brothers sank. Yet it is also the surface from which the imagination derives texture for the creation of its own

# LAYERING 51

**Figure 3.3** *Heart of a Dog* (Laurie Anderson, 2015).

images that slide over what is shown. The onscreen image appeals to haptic visuality in the sense that Laura U. Marks gives to this term, as viewers are brought into tactile proximity to the point that they lose sight of the broader picture of the optical visual mode. Haptic criticism, for Marks, is mimetic, pressing up to the surface of an object and taking its shape, getting close enough to the other thing in order to become it (Marks 2002: xiii). The surface-to-surface contact that I have been outlining in this chapter and that results in the formation of imagined images adds a further layer to the textural feel of such haptic vision. Rather than imaginatively completing the onscreen picture by seeing the close-up as a fragment of the whole lake, and positioning it in relation to the preceding images that viewers were presented with earlier of skaters on the frozen lake, the first generative point of contact between the perceived and the imagined image occasions a slippage from the coarse-grained surface of the ice that is seen on screen to the wool (of the knitted balls on her brothers' hats) that is not. Darkened water appears in the cracks of the surface as the knitted balls on the top of her brothers' hats are said to disappear under the black water. The second point of creative contact is to the sinking motion that exchanges the horizontal sliding that this sequence has been showing viewers on screen from the start for a vertical slide. We have already witnessed in previous examples in this chapter, drawing upon Scarry's observations, how surfaces moving against one another confer solidity to that which is imagined: here these sliding surfaces are shown first on screen – blades on ice, a stroller on ice – such that when it comes to imagine the stroller sliding down a muddy bank the motion of surface against surface, already established on screen, is taken up by the imagination just with a sinister change of direction. The moving cracked ice functions thus as a momentary blank screen that appears in order to permit the knitted balls disappearing into the black water to be imagined, its broken surface allowing the mental images to plunge into the depths with Anderson as she retrieves her brothers one by one before carrying them home.

From the emergence of Moses on the telephone wires to the witnessing of the knitted balls disappearing through the ice into the murky water, what appears on the mental retina draws upon what is seen and heard as both imagined and perceived images come into view. In this, Anderson prompts a similar process to that which we explored with reference to Tarn's film. Layering is an act of sliding mental images over those that are perceived but is an aesthetic principle of these films as well, such that viewers, sensitised by the films to looking at what is normally looked through, notice the imagined image too as more than just a transparency slipping across the field of vision in front of the screen. I want to further this exploration of this more opaque mental image now by granting more traction to this slippage, moving on from the ice of Anderson's frozen lake to the earth that is walked upon. Patrick Keiller's Robinson trilogy engages the strategies of layering outlined so far but also adds to them. The intricacy of the layering of perceiving and imagining that we have already seen in this chapter now requires the creation of fictive protagonists, unlike the stories that De Montalembert and Anderson recount in their own voices and that attach through their grain to their own lives.

## Grounding Fictive Protagonists

A white foxglove stands tall against a backdrop of lush woodland foliage in the English countryside; it sways gently with the wind in an atmosphere populated by the sound of birdsong. It is summertime. This flower appears within a film image towards the end of Patrick Keiller's *Robinson in Ruins* (2010), accompanied by voice-over commentary. The layers of drooping white bells are then captured in a close-up, dancing in and out of this shot that is held for nearly three minutes after a section of the commentary has ended. There are several such pauses on a long take in this film, where the need to listen intently to what is spoken in voice-over is momentarily relaxed. Just looking at the flower and listening to the sounds of nature, the mind is freed briefly to think of nothing, or, more accurately, not to think at all. Such is the precondition for unguided reverie: a space created for calmness and stillness through which the mind can wander unconstrained.

There is a fruitful tension that runs throughout Keiller's films between movement and such relatively brief moments of stasis, pacey voice-over commentary and short periods of almost silent repose. For the most part, though, and breaking any tendency towards prolonged, meditative contemplation, Keiller guides the wandering of his protagonists' feet while also shaping the image-making of the minds that accompany them.

The images of the trilogy are a documentary record of place, journeying from London throughout England more widely, as the voice-over narrative provides factual analysis and historical detail, interpreted from Keiller's political perspective, of the failures of capitalism and neoliberalism in the late twentieth and early twenty-first centuries and the effect these have had on the city and countryside. Robinson's heritage connects him to the nineteenth century and the figure of the *flâneur* of Poe and Baudelaire, through to Benjamin in the twentieth century. It also propels him forwards from the Surrealists to the Situationists and critical engagement with strategies of *dérive* (drifting) and the psychogeography that derives from this. Robinson and his companion move through lived space, and become 'livers' rather than 'spectators', as Guy Debord encourages when he chastens that the more spectators contemplate, the less they live (Debord [1967] 2004: 16). The *psycho*geographical element of their exploration of the ideological construction and sedimentation of late capitalism in the landscape takes place between perception and imagination. As the narrator declares at the beginning of *Robinson in Space* (1997), reading from Belgian Situationist Raoul Vaneigem's *The Revolution of Everyday Life*: 'a bridge between imagination and reality must be built'.

For Keiller, the combination of moving camera and interior monologue, as he characterises the image–word relationship in his films, is a comic attempt to represent consciousness: 'the inner experience of an alienated and rather unreliable artificial *flâneur*' (Keiller 2013: 79). This consciousness is split across two people, since it passes through a narrator distinct from Robinson the main protagonist, but who, like Robinson, is never seen. In the trilogy, and akin to Chris Marker's *Lettre de Sibérie/Letter from Siberia* (1957) and *Sunless* in this respect, only the narrator is audible (Paul Scofield in the first two films of the trilogy; Vanessa Redgrave in the third), but Keiller's narrator and protagonist have a more proximate relationship. The men, who maintain what the narrator describes in *London* (1994) as 'an uneasy bickering sexual relationship', are intermittently intimate across the first two films, but Redgrave's assertion of being the late narrator's wife in the third interrupts this. When talking about the first two films, Keiller aligns them with a shift in the history of the modernist avant-gardes, from the use of the poetic imagination to change appearances to the actual construction of new things, with modernity serving as a bridge between the two:

> Both films attempt to change reality with a heightened awareness in which 'I can always see how beautiful anything could be if only I could change it' – the words of the Situationist text quoted in the opening sequence of *Robinson in Space* – but in the second, the initial interest is in the production of (at least some of) this *anything*. (Keiller 2013: 36–7)

What is beautiful is what is not there but could be, and it is the role that imagination plays in bringing this potential into being that matters. Imagining, for both protagonists and spectators, is instrumental to the kinds of transformations Keiller is interested in.

One of the preconditions for imagining, as both Bachelard and Sartre remind us, is fundamental to Keiller's trilogy insofar as his protagonists are missing throughout from the onscreen images. When talking about images in the context of his literary and poetic analyses, Bachelard notes: 'If the image that is *present* does not make us think of one that is *absent*, if an image does not determine an abundance – an explosion – of unusual images, then there is no imagination' (Bachelard [1943] 1988: 1). Speaking more specifically about imagining a person, when Sartre conjures his friend Pierre in the opening lines of *The Imaginary* in the context of discussing everyday imagining, it is Pierre himself that he sets out to describe in so doing, but it is Pierre's absence that makes this possible for the philosopher (Sartre [1940] 2010: 4). If we follow Sartre's endeavour to conjure Pierre's face a little further on, he reports on an object that is 'very imperfectly attained: some details are lacking, others are suspect, the whole is rather blurred' (ibid.: 17). Pierre's face as imaged pales in comparison to that of the flesh-and-blood person who would be perceived when standing in front of him. When trying to picture Robinson, if viewers do so on the basis of the details provided by the narrator, it is guided picturing and therefore closer to the kind of direction that we have seen in the previous examples discussed thus far in this chapter in Tarn's and Anderson's work than to either the brief possibility of free-floating reverie glimpsed in pausing on the foxglove, or Sartre's imaginative labour. And yet the guidance on how to form any image of Robinson's face or body is initially scant, if relied upon alone, seemingly willing spectators to form only the kind of faint shades of people that Sartre was able to imagine when thinking of Pierre.

Neither Robinson's face nor body is ever fleshed out in description: apart from a problem with his liver that causes him to tire easily, Robinson is defined in terms of his low income and profession in the first film – he is a part-time lecturer in the School of Fine Art and Architecture at the fictitious University of Barking, living in Vauxhall. But he loses his job, plunging him into depression in the second film before he takes up a part-time job teaching English in a language school in Reading where he then lived. In the third film, and corresponding to the wraith-like mental impression furnished in fleeting descriptions in the previous two, he is said at the outset to have found 'a place to haunt' upon his release from the fictive Edgcott Open Prison, and is described as having 'increasing insubstantiality', eventually disappearing entirely such that the whole of the final film is a reconstruction of his last known whereabouts.[2] Daniel Defoe's *Robinson Crusoe* (1719) is referred to within the trilogy, and it is his *A Tour Through the Whole Island of Great Britain* (1724–6) that inspires the journey around England in the second of the three films, *Robinson in Space* (1997), providing one touchstone, as critic Robert Mayer notes (Mayer 2004). Yet Keiller's Robinson is not, or not only, that of Defoe. Keiller reports that he borrows the name from one of the itinerants in Kafka's *Amerika* in which the protagonist Karl Rossmann encounters two wanderers called Delamarche and Robinson. In surrounding writings on the film, Keiller also proffers a photographic image that Paul Scofield sent him in 1998 (August Sander's 'Itinerants' (1929)), suggesting that, in Scofield's absence, he had the idea that one of the figures slightly resembled Scofield, as well as Harun Farocki, albeit even more slightly, who plays Delamarche in Jean-Marie Straub and Danièle Huillet's version of the novel, *Klassenverhältnisse/Class Relations* (1984), while the other looked a little like Manfred Blank who plays Robinson (see Keiller 2012: 6; 2013: 7). He offers this only to withdraw it, though, saying that 'Straub and Huillet's Robinson [. . .] might also resemble my unseen protagonist. More recently, I have imagined he might look quite different' (Keiller 2012: 6). Indeed, in *Robinson in Ruins* Keiller destabilises even the name as something to cling to, as the man spectators are now told has been using Robinson as a pseudonym had apparently arrived in London in 1966 from Berlin and his history was uncertain prior to this moment. Yet Keiller had also located his birthplace in Shropshire in his earliest writings, making his origins mysterious to the point of coming from everywhere and nowhere (Keiller 2013: 7). Robinson can still be pictured, however, and more vividly than the faint transparencies placed under erasure that we seem to have encountered thus far.

Keiller's reference to Sander's photograph is pertinent in this respect. This is not at all because it furnishes a representational image that can be carried over to the film as a mental image: viewers may not read the accompanying writings and even if they did, that mental image would not be their initial creation but a memory of a photograph. Rather, in Sander's work, people are defined socio-culturally and by what they do and this is what Keiller's protagonists share with Sander's itinerants. In the Robinson trilogy, Robinson and the narrator are pictured through descriptions of their interactions with the aspects of the material world that do not appear on screen, rather than any isolated accounts of their physical features or states of mind. In other words, it is the contact between two imagined entities that produces the ground of the mental image here. This still happens over a series of onscreen images in keeping with the layering process that I have discussed thus far – Keiller's films are replete with onscreen visual imagery – but instead of happening all of a piece, as with Moses working with his tools silhouetted against the bright winter sky, the imagined entities are formed separately and brought together. If we consider, by way of example, the sequence of *Robinson in Ruins* in which Robinson is described as having 'increasing insubstantiality', we can look in more detail at one of the ways in which this process works.

At the start of the film, the house that Robinson found to haunt upon his release from prison is said to have once been a hotel – a place for transient visits that his own squatting presence continues in a different way. While he is as immaterial in this film as he and his narrator-lover are in the previous two, the explicitly referenced ghostliness of a male figure is relatively easy to imagine because it is so close to the consistency of daydreamed images. The derelict abode that he finds seems suited to his own disintegration: two shots reveal the dwelling, one that shows the boarded up exterior at the lower level, the second, filmed from the opposite side of the road, showing its scaffold-draped height behind the boarding. Ten minutes into the film, when Robinson's physical state of insubstantiality is referred to explicitly, as shots of the house appear again with more posters pasted now onto the exterior hoarding, the narrator reports:

> Despite his increasing insubstantiality, Robinson had returned from Lidl with two bottles of Putinoff vodka, a snow shovel, and several own-brand items in illustrated packaging that recalled the dwelling of Black Forest farmers which, for Heidegger, let earth and heaven, divinities and mortals enter in simple oneness into things. For which simple oneness Robinson began to search by visiting a well.

Imagining him returning from Lidl (the store is pictured in a previous shot with critical commentary pertaining to their mistreatment of their workers) to the place that is shown on screen, a squatter in this house that is being renovated, as Heidegger's 'Building Dwelling Thinking' is mentioned, creates a link to an outmoded vision of what it is to dwell from the perspective of Keiller's vision of modernity, which is summed up by the dilapidated dwelling. This is the intellectual point of the scene and the true direction of travel: for Keiller, the dominant narratives of modernity are about mobility and instant communication, work and travel, rather than home. But what has happened in the meantime without any attention being drawn to it, is that Robinson has gained imaginative substance through his trip to the supermarket and the objects that he has brought back with him: 'two bottles of Putinoff vodka, a snow shovel, and several own-brand items in illustrated packaging'. The weight of his purchases lends him weight too as he is imagined returning to his makeshift home shown on screen.

Even though the assorted objects are also imagined and therefore as flimsily ghostly in their insubstantiality as Robinson himself, it is difficult to imagine their heaviness being transported by a ghostly transparency; as a result, the weight of these items summons someone sturdier to carry them. Try picturing a ghost in your mind and then try making it walk along with Robinson's shopping: the vodka bottles, shovel, and other miscellaneous items with their 'illustrated packaging' will stand out comically against the faint figure and may seem as though they are floating along by themselves. In saying that the objects lend Robinson weight, though, this is not to imply that Robinson suddenly acquires bulging muscles at this juncture – bearing in mind his 'increasing insubstantiality' guards against such a distortion – but he is filled in, rather like the process that Anderson referred to in relation to the onscreen image of telephone wires, poles, and trees in *Heart of a Dog*. In *Robinson in Ruins*, it is through his contact with the imaginable materiality of bottles, a shovel, and other shopping that Robinson too comes to matter in the viewer's mind at this point in relation to the dilapidated dwelling on screen. All of this happens in just over thirty seconds – the length of time that it takes Redgrave to give the details of the shopping – before Robinson drifts off again, in the sense both that he resumes his journeying and that the mental image of him fades until he materialises again in the mental space at a gap in some blackthorn bushes on his way to the Physic Well which is shown on screen. The imagined protagonist ebbs and flows among the broader commentary of the trilogy that is punctured by such moments.

Continuing this focus on Robinson for the time being, it is a different encounter of imagined elements that confers materiality and contributes to Robinson's fleshed out existence in the first film of the trilogy, *London*. Viewers are asked in the following example to imagine Robinson dreaming rather than performing a physical act such as carrying his shopping back from the supermarket, and it is striking that this apparent regress works momentarily to erase the boundary of vivacity and solidity between the real

Figure 3.4 *London* (Patrick Keiller, 1994).

and the imagined world. Keiller achieves this not only through a combination of some of the previous processes that have been analysed in this chapter but by adding to them such that Robinson's dream emerges as vividly as his shopping did, even though it is a product of the fictive character's unconscious mind rather than something he is carrying in his hands.

Robinson's dream is recounted in *London* after viewers hear of his mistrust of the opinion polls in the run-up to the general election in 1992, reported by the narrator over images of one polling station. There is a brief cut to black before the image of a number 14 bus appears on screen, succeeded by that of The Green Man pub on Putney Heath (Figure 3.4). Robinson had apparently fallen asleep on the bus and woken up at the terminus opposite the pub, a place the narrator says he knew only through its description in *The War of the Worlds* by H. G. Wells. The music is dramatic throughout this sequence as the narrator continues:

> There were a number of men hanging about, mostly van drivers waiting for radio calls. As soon as he got off the bus, he was gripped by a ghastly premonition: in the bar, where he had tried to calm himself, a grinning stranger told him that in the eighteenth century The Green Man stood opposite a gibbet. He woke up trembling with fear and foreboding, and could not sleep for the rest of the night.

As the dream is narrated, the onscreen images cut between a view of the bus terminus from the pub and a view of the pub from the terminus, a kind of shot/reverse-shot in time with the incidental music that plays on the soundtrack from *The Lone Ranger*, credited to Alberto Colombo and Cy Feuer. Once the bus pulls forwards, it reveals the pub sign at a distance before a closer shot reveals more clearly a man with an axe on a gibbet-like structure as the narrator tells of how Robinson was unable to sleep for the rest of the night. The onscreen images furnish the material for the dream, rather than withholding it, but the scenes that are built around the bus and the pub are imagined. The means by which Robinson reached the pub – the number 14 bus – and the pub itself are shown. The man with the axe pictured on the sign and the gibbet-like structure from which his image hangs serve as the substantial basis on which to hang the nightmarish imagination of the history of this place.

The precision of the spoken word, coupled with perception of the elements of the architecture of the scene that viewers are to build and that are shown on screen, brings this example close to the layering and filling in that we explored through the work of Tarn and Anderson. The drama, heightened by the music, of waking at a bus terminus, being 'gripped by a ghastly premonition', and encountering a 'grinning stranger' unfolds between the bus and the pub that are shown. The door of the pub is open but it is not possible to see inside, inviting the mental positioning of Robinson and the stranger at the bar in the imagination, as the history of the place is revealed and the pub sign that is seen conjures the hangman's gibbet. Furthermore, the encounter between Robinson and the stranger lends weight to both through conversation, albeit without the physical contact that conferred the weight to Robinson through imagining him carrying his shopping in *Robinson in Ruins*. Even though Robinson and the stranger are no more existent than Robinson and his shopping were, the tale the stranger tells conveys solidity to them both: fleshed out beings converse in the pub, not transparencies or ghosts. And yet, the real trick of this scene – which is easy to forget – and the further layer that it adds to the formation of the imagined images explored so far is that none of this actually ever occurred in the physicality of the imagined world even though it appears and feels so similar.

Unlike the memories of experiences recalled by De Montalembert and Anderson, and in contrast to imagining the physical action of returning from the shops in the example from *Robinson in Ruins*, it is in Robinson's dream that he wakes up at the bus terminus, goes into the pub, and hears about the disturbing history. Viewers who visualise will have been imagining the images of a dream but these have achieved the same substantiality as those other images that were not positioned as the product of a fictive character's mind. The fact that spectators have imagined Robinson dreaming before imagining him waking up adds to the vivid and substantial image-making prompted by the grinning stranger's tale, with the images of Robinson's mind being recreated as if they had the materiality of his actual actions. Robinson's dreams are, to recall Merleau-Ponty's terms, worth the close-woven fabric of the true world, but this is not just apparent to the eyes of the dreamer in Robinson's case. It is the viewer's imagining that makes them so, conscious of the difference between the real and the dreamed worlds but imagining each as vividly as the other. When Robinson wakes up for real – that is to say, outside of his dream – he returns to the journeying across London that he has been engaged in with the narrator in his waking life, but he has now acquired an interiority as well as a physicality that is profoundly visual. It is thus not only through his erudition, evident in the commentaries of all of the films, that his subjectivity is registered but through his own dream life and imagination, which spectators too are invited to reconstitute and, in so doing, lay bare the processes of constructing their own imagined images.

We shall have reason to return to Robinson in a subsequent chapter, since the imaginative transformation of landscape that he and his narrator-companion engage in prompts the process of reshaping the perceived images on screen and we are not yet at this particular stage of mental composition. For the remainder of this chapter, I want to turn to one final example, from the work of Agnès Varda, who probes the imagined images of dreams on a vertical rather than horizontal axis, from flying to falling to the bottom of a well. The grounding of the mental image is still assured through the mimetic contact with the perceptual images, and it is from within this substantial world that Varda makes it possible to take flight.

## Taking Flight

When filming the English-born singer, model, and actress Jane Birkin in the multi-faceted portrait of *Jane B. par Agnès V./Jane B. by Agnès V.* (1988), Varda asks Birkin in one extended sequence how well she sleeps. They are sitting in a Parisian café, Varda audible but not visible, Birkin facing the camera, positioned with arms bent and hands behind her head, an upright version of her earlier reclining painterly pose in the film, in which she appears successively clothed and nude. She responds to Varda's questions about how she sleeps and about her dreams. The film cuts to a close-up of a dark green caryatid on the water fountain that is visible out of the window in the background of the initial shot of Birkin in the café.

Birkin's elaboration on her dreams shifts to a voice-over that continues over the next few shots. The film cuts to a close-up of her face, which is reclining at an angle and in a different space; her eyes are closed – like that of the caryatid – and then open. Birkin is then shown positioning a mirror in a shot taken in a wood – an image that recurs several times in this film about portraiture and that plays with reflections – before she runs towards the camera, with a floating cape of orange and silver foil, as she says in voice-over that the most magnificent dreams are those in which she flies. The image cuts back to Birkin's head reclining as she speaks now from within the diegetic space: 'I flew everywhere, over all the monuments of Paris. Once I even landed on the chimney of my own house. The most wonderful thing about those dreams is that when you descend gently, you're not even hurt.' As she reports on never being hurt, her eyes close again and the film cuts back to the close-up of the caryatid of the green water fountain, who also has her eyes closed. Birkin's presence on screen, adjacent to the caryatid through the cut of the film, aids rather than prevents imagined images taking flight.

Birkin is as substantial as the caryatid that she is pictured next to: visually, what matters about their juxtaposition is the fact that both the flesh-and-blood woman and the statuesque one have their eyes closed. They both shut out their field of vision at these moments, but the implication is that both are aligned in dreaming, and it is this inner journey that Birkin is externalising through her tale of flying, inviting spectators to make an inner journey of their own on the basis of her narrative. These juxtapositions resonate with Varda's earlier short, *Les Dites Cariatides/The So-Called Caryatids* (1984) in which she films a more diverse selection of these supporting statues of the female form across Paris as they appear on buildings. In the earlier film, Varda accompanies the onscreen images of these statues with a voice-over of poems from Baudelaire's *Les Fleurs du mal/Flowers of Evil*, the most significant of which is 'La Beauté/Beauty' in which the poetic voice speaks in the feminine: 'I am beautiful, o mortals! like a dream of stone.' Varda speaks of this earlier film as a collection of dreams of women of stone as muteness is given a voice, woman to woman. In *Jane B.* it is Birkin who speaks her own dreams, yet the imagination of matter is just as palpable here, and imagining borrows from the objective world, moving between flesh and stone to something more lightweight. It is Scarry who enables us to understand how these transitions assist the mental picturing of Birkin's dream flight.

For Scarry, the lightness of matter aids the formation of moving images when reading literary texts. She describes how one of the ways in which writers get their readers to set images in motion in their minds is through an association with rarity, already referenced briefly in the previous chapter with regard to the feathers and petals of Duras's bird and rose. When the mental image and the piece of the world being represented are aligned as almost identical because both are nearly weightless, it becomes easier to move something in the mind that is solid (Scarry [1999] 2001: 89–99). In this filmic example from *Jane B.*, as in those discussed previously in this chapter, the imagined image borrows from the substantiality of the perceived images – Birkin as she appears in the images, juxtaposed with the sculpted caryatids – but this cannot be all that it does here, since flesh and stone will only keep it grounded, weighing her down. When Birkin runs towards the camera prior to telling of her flying dreams she carries with her a material that billows out behind her as she runs, which is a light, shiny, thin foil membrane now stretched out and caught in air currents. Instead of telling viewers of an association between Birkin and rarity, Varda shows them this, lending them a sensorially present visual basis for a mental image in which solidity not only moves along the ground as in the images on screen but also takes off in the mind. When Birkin runs along with her cape behind her it is not the case that she is engaging on a runway that transfers her from ground to air as she disappears from the physical space to enter mental space: it is difficult, not to mention amusing, to think of making the grounded image of Birkin running along with her foil cape take off as an imagined continuation off-screen of what began in the onscreen image. But the subsequent mental images of her in flight that may form as spectators listen to her words after seeing her running along with the cape owe everything to this onscreen association of solidity with rarity. The process of visualisation occurs first on screen and then transfers to the mind: she takes a run towards the camera with her floating cape and takes off immediately afterwards in imagined images, light as air as she travels across Paris and settles on her roof, before drifting gently back down to earth. The flight of her dreams and that of the spectator's imagination commune in this sequence, and what is rehearsed on the screen is extended vertically through mental space. This space contracts momentarily as Varda invites Birkin to recall a recent dream before expanding once more, this time below the level of the ground, as Birkin recounts a nightmare.

Birkin is now outside, leaning against the water fountain, her head viewed in close-up, positioned just to the side of the caryatid seen earlier, and both have their eyes closed (Figure 3.5). Birkin recounts her nightmare from this position, partly from the diegetic space, partly in voice-over, but she completes the tale as the image returns to her seated

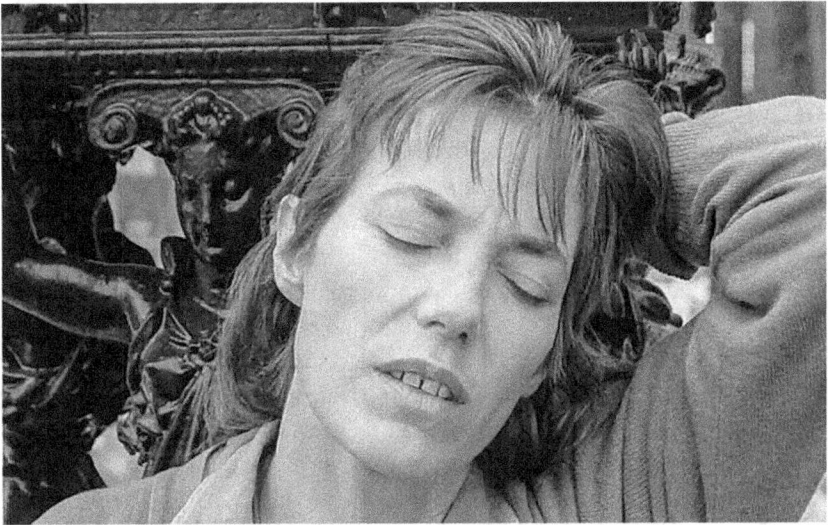

Figure 3.5 *Jane B. by Agnès V.* (Agnès Varda, 1988).

inside the café where this entire sequence on dreams began. She narrates her nightmare as follows, first from within the diegetic space:

> Two policemen came to find me [Birkin's eyes open] because they had found the body of a woman that I had killed years ago. [Switch to voice-over] I killed her in a dreadful way. She tried to cling on to the top of a well and I crushed her fingers with my feet before throwing her in. [Switch back to diegetic speech] But before she died, she had the time to scratch my name in her blood on the side of the well. And of course the police were able to read my name. They knew it was me – she had given me away. And when I woke up, my fear wasn't my crime, which was horrid, [cut back to the café] but of everyone finding out the next day in the papers that I wasn't a nice person.

There are a number of elements to this described dream that facilitate the formation of mental images as we have observed them thus far. The narration is dramatic and the shot is held for long enough for there to be no distraction other than listening to Birkin's voice, making the layering of the mental image over the perceived image possible. Furthermore, Birkin leans against the caryatid (she holds on with one of her hands behind her head throughout the narration of her dream), which forms a basis on which to imagine, through the mimesis of perception (hands on matter), contact between the stone of the well and the woman's hands, from her attempt at holding on to the edge, to scratching Birkin's name in her blood. When the film cuts back to Birkin sitting in the café, this coincides with her speaking of the fear that gripped her when she woke up, breaking with the space in which the dream was recounted.

When Birkin finishes telling of her nightmare and the shot returns to the café, Varda asks her whether it matters to her what people write about her in the papers. Birkin laughs, saying that she is only asking her this because there is a newspaper kiosk just outside the café, as the camera pans to the left, moving out of the space occupied in this sequence on sleep and dreams, and back to her public life of attention. The physical space mapped in this sequence is triangular, from café seat, to water fountain, to newspaper stand. Yet this space extends beyond this geometrical formation not only through other images that are offered to accompany Birkin's narrative and Varda's questions, but also through the imagined images prompted by their dialogue. Thus, while spectators have been listening to Birkin recount her dreams, Varda's film has been traversing and expanding physical space, such that the verticality of the imagined images from Birkin's roof to the bottom of the well intersects with the lateral movements across different filmed spaces. Neither the flying dream that takes spectators through the sky over Paris, nor the nightmare that leads down to the depths of the earth are imaged on screen – such images are withheld – but the onscreen shots that open out the initial space, that deform the geometry of physical space, displace her frequently as her narrative moves seamlessly between waking and dreaming life, imaging shifts of the imagination without seeking to image the imagination itself. Varda does not create onscreen images of Birkin's dreams, nor does she link them to Birkin's intending consciousness, that imaging consciousness of which Sartre speaks. Varda declares earlier in the film to Birkin: 'I can inhabit you with my reveries', but she does not inhabit Birkin in a literal sense of getting inside her head to create a vision of what Birkin sees as she dreams. Rather, the dreams are detached from the consciousness of both Birkin and Varda through images that remain absent, making them the immeasurable stuff of an expanded, distorted triangle that spectators amplify as they listen and view. The mutability of imagined space will not respect measurable space, as Bachelard notes: 'Space that has been seized upon by the imagination cannot remain indifferent space subject to the measures and estimates of the surveyor. It has been lived in . . .' (Bachelard [1957] 1994: xxxvi). And it is the configuration of such mental space that will be developed further in the next chapter.

The filmic examples that have been considered from the works of Varda and Keiller join with those of Anderson and Tarn in allowing us to see how audio-vision occasions the layering of imagined images over those that are perceived. We have seen how mental images are formed and sustained through their relation to the duration of what is perceived. This relationship permits the imagined image to be vivified, filled in, and grounded so that other activities then become possible – from imagining fictive characters to imagining real people flying in their dreams. We now need to delve further into the dimensions of the imagined image and peruse the space therein. Following on from Tarn's and Anderson's declared debt to radio plays, the next chapter concentrates on films that show no onscreen images and that rely solely on sound, music, and voices. This shift necessarily challenges the close relation that the imagination has had up until this point with the visual perception of the onscreen image. It is to the heightened importance of the aural dimension that I now turn.

CHAPTER 4

# Volumising

The previous chapter established the grounds on which to build mental images in the film experience and demonstrated how the mental space is populated in a manner that stands apart from what is seen on screen but is nonetheless guided by the films. Akin to the spatial-temporal limbo to which Edward Casey refers when discussing the locus of what is imagined, the mental space of the images can feel as though it is located ahead of spectators rather than within when engaging in the layering of the imagined over the perceived images; as a result, the boundary between inner and outer worlds also expands and contracts to the point that it reveals itself to be porous. That this space also feels enveloping at times, rather than being observed solely from the outside, contributes a further dimension to it, as will become clear as this chapter progresses. Layering will be operative as part of the processes of mental image formation discussed here too, but rather than the relation to onscreen images witnessed so far, now there is nothing to see but blankness.

British filmmaker and curator Matt Hulse knows the imaginative power of denying an audience pictures on a screen where images usually play.[1] He first established 'The Audible Picture Show' in March 2003 at the LUX Open conference held at the Royal College of Art. The show has toured widely across the UK at film festivals since then and has also travelled to Rotterdam and the United States. As Hulse observes:

> The title establishes an expectation in the mind of the audience: picture, show, theatre, entertainment. When the lights go down and this expectation is met with quirky, non-narrative, abstracted, minimal and conceptual work, something interesting happens. It is in this interaction that the 'show' takes place, entirely in the imagination. (Hulse 2011)

Hulse's show, which he notes appeals to a more cinephile rather than audiophile audience, comprises an eclectic yet carefully ordered series of short sound works, deriving from the local artists whose material is premiered at the event and his growing archive. The pieces are presented one after another in the darkness of a cinema auditorium and in the absence of any images on screen. As the conference website where Hulse presented his project in Chicago in 2004 attests, it 'gives the mind's eye a welcome stretch'.[2] This stretch registers the elasticity of the mental arena that expands and contracts in spatial, as well as visual, terms.

In a particularly evocative piece by Tony Hill, titled *A Sense of Place* (2003), and which Hulse declares to be the signature work for the picture show because it functions so well in the darkened space that encourages people to focus, it is indeed not only a capacity to visualise mental pictures that is rendered possible (Hulse 2004). Hill records a friend of his, a young blind woman named Sally Goode, walking around a place she has never been to before, as she commentates and speculates on her understanding of where she is by means of senses other than eyesight. Reliant on her narration, based on what she hears and what her hands make contact with, along with sounds of her environment – birdsong, a dog barking, loud bangs, along with her footsteps on different terrain, her hands tapping different surfaces, and the echo of her voice – it is a sense of space that is created, as she feels her way through the darkness, trying to work out the particular place she is in. Listener-spectators are identified momentarily here with her blindness, guided by Sally through the space of their imagination. Hill, who trained as an architect, presents people thus with the possibility of navigating mental space through sound, lending volume to it in the process.

Understood in spatial terms, the constitutive virtual volume of the film image has been theorised by philosopher Elie During through recourse to the work of moving image artists who take spectators behind and around what are effectively flat images on screen. For During, artist-filmmaker Mark Lewis offers salient examples in which viewers encounter this virtual voluminosity. Distinct from discussions of depth in relation to the filmic image (for example, depth of field), the volume image permits movement around the images to their other side. During notes: 'the back . . . is neither the material reverse side of the screen . . . nor the off-screen', and argues further that it is 'less material than the actual setting of the screen and more literal than the imaginary field extending off-screen' (During 2016). The volume image that During introduces in visual and spatial terms is useful to me here because of the sound dimension that is implicit in the term, even though my contrasting exploration of the imagined image will rely on making a mental journey against the blankness of the screen into a field without visible onscreen contours. Turning volume up and down is what we do to regulate electronic sound in our everyday environment when it is possible to control it, but the broader sonorous environment around us, which we do not always see, suggests whether things are near or far, even if we cannot pinpoint them exactly, and this in itself creates a sense of space. In a filmic context, when any trace of visual or representational images is removed entirely from the screen, it is the richness of the soundscape that pervades, as blankness becomes the sole but necessary point of contact for the formation of mental images and the configuration of mental space. I turn in this chapter to a detailed consideration of two examples from different ends of the twentieth century in order to explore how mental spatial volume is created through sound volume: Walter Ruttmann's *Wochenende/Weekend* (1930) and Derek Jarman's *Blue* (1993). We will, however, see the strategies that each deploys for the formation and transformation of mental space and imagery through the use of sound recur in other examples in this book.[3]

## Visualising Sound, Configuring Space

Imagine being seated in the darkness once again as you were for that Duras screening mentioned at the beginning of the second chapter. Now, though, instead of hearing words that set mental images in motion thanks to the radiant ignition Scarry speaks of, you hear resonant crashing sounds that crescendo to give way to alternating sounds of sharp grating back and forth and of metallic banging, setting up contrasting rhythms and tones. The screen is completely black and you are just experiencing a kind of abstract machine music. Or are you? The sounds that I have just described feature in the first few seconds of Ruttmann's *Weekend* and are part of a soundscape that captures in condensed form a period that runs from the end of the working day on a Saturday afternoon to the return to work on Monday. *Weekend* lasts eleven minutes and ten seconds and has six sections according to the structure Ruttmann originally set out (Ruttmann 1930). It is one of the work's most comprehensive historians who terms the opening of *Weekend* 'machine music' (*Maschinemusik*) (Goergen 1994: 13). Jeanpaul Goergen's description is interesting because he raises an issue for the mimetic account of mental image formation that I have been indebted to so far in my study: not only are there are no onscreen perceived images here from which imagining can borrow to shape vivid, substantial mental images, but the perceived sounds are also linked in his account to abstraction. Goergen is not alone in pointing to the abstract qualities of sound when discussing Ruttmann's piece. For Sabine Hake, the tendency of sound towards abstraction makes *Weekend* successful where Ruttmann's earlier city symphony *Berlin: Die Sinfonie der Grosstadt/Berlin: Symphony of a Great City* (1927) failed because of the mimetic quality of its onscreen images (Hake 2008: 252). While *Weekend* is not anchored in visual, representational terms, as Goergen and Hake observe, this has not however stopped others who engage with it from identifying sounds, linking them to the objects that made them, and entering more broadly into a sustained, albeit fragmented, experience of visualisation. To say that I hear sawing and hammering among the opening sounds of *Weekend*, for example, rather than the more abstract grating back and forth and banging, is already to place sounds in relation to objects – a saw, a hammer – and my opening aim is to show how these can give rise to mental images that serve rather than betray Ruttmann's unique sound experiment. The historical emergence of this artwork and the technology that enabled it bear mentioning before we explore in more detail how its sounds not only generate imagined images but also create a sense of space in keeping with the volumising that is the overall focus of this chapter.

Captivated by the arrival of the sound film, Ruttmann had already written several articles in 1928 on the possibilities it afforded, and had made *Melodie der Welt/Melody of the World* (1929), along with the sound film experiment *Des Haares und der Liebe Wellen/Waves of Hair and Love* (1929).[4] In mid-February 1930, when he was living and working in Paris, responsible for the sound on Abel Gance's *La Fin du monde/The End of the World* (1931), he went back to Berlin for a few weeks to produce *Weekend* (Goergen 1994: 8). *Weekend* was commissioned by radio pioneer Hans Flesch, who was then artistic director of the Berliner Funk-Stunde Station (Berlin Radio-Hour), and its hybrid status as a radio work that was broadcast as well as screened has caused debate around its categorisation since its original release. The leading question Murray Smith posed more recently – 'Is *Weekend* a Film?' (Smith 2015) – was very much in some reviewers' minds at the time of its initial broadcast and screening.[5] In the context of its initial reception and in keeping with the original commission, *Weekend* is referred to most frequently as radio drama or a radio play, a 'Hörspiel' that offers an appropriate counterpoint to Ruttmann's earlier animated 'Lichtspiele' (films – literally, 'light plays'), *Opus I–IV* (1921–5). More recently, as Dieter Daniels notes, it has been understood as a precursor to both the *musique concrète* of the likes of Pierre Schaeffer of the 1950s and the sampling techniques of modern techno music (Daniels 2004). In terms of its credentials as radio drama, as Daniels argues, it broke new ground. It was the first not to be performed by actors – the voice recordings were of non-professionals – and it was not dependent on a script. It was created solely from the natural sound material recorded in and around Berlin and was thereby freed from the linear progression and locality of live broadcast that had been predominant at the time, making it possible as a result to combine different times and spaces in one sound montage (Daniels 2017: 35). It is through its innovative sound montage, though, that it is indebted to the medium of film in spite of the fact that it is devoid of images.

Goergen notes how Ruttmann spoke variously about *Weekend* as 'Hörspiel' (radio play), as 'Tonmontagestudie' (study in sound editing), and as 'blinder Film' (blind film), with this unusual artwork being positioned thus by its maker between the established forms of film, radio play, music, and noise or sound art (Goergen 1994: 17).[6] Part of the reason for these different categorisations that span not only the aural but also the visual dimensions stems from the fact that the material used to make *Weekend* was film stock. It was recorded on optical film, since Tri-Ergon optical sound recording could bypass the technical limitations of the 78rpm record, permitting a style of filmic montage of the sounds recorded. Ruttmann produced *Weekend* in a workshop at Tri-Ergon Musik AG in the Berlin suburb of Marienfelde on the basis of the actual rather than manufactured sounds that he had captured in and around Berlin (Goergen 1994: 13). It was a kind of camera-less use of film that experimental filmmakers have had recourse to within the history of avant-garde filmmaking, but which in this instance, when run through the projector, generates nothing but blankness for the eye. The different categorisations of *Weekend*, from radio drama to imageless film, converge, as blankness connects with blindness, raising the question of the prompting of mental imagery in different media and of how such images arise from sounds.

To return specifically to the saw and the hammer that I generated from the opening sounds in *Weekend*, it is not entirely surprising that these emerge clearly to me, in contrast to the automated machinery that begins to make noise a few seconds later and that, in my experience, remains more inchoate. This has something tangentially to do with the 'hands on' approach to mental imaging that Scarry discusses in the literary dimension, even though Ruttmann's opening sounds are devoid of verbal instruction. Drawing upon work in cognitive science that shows that the part of the brain operative when one thinks of a handmade object (for example, the saw, the hammer) is not the same as that used when thinking about a non-handmade object (for example, a bird, a flower), she suggests that this is one explanation for how hands-on instruction assists readers not only in making pictures but in making them move (Scarry [1999] 2001: 146). This distinction between the parts of the brain that operate when one thinks of different objects is coupled with the fruits of cognitive research revealing that the part of the brain used in thinking about handmade objects is the area engaged in thinking about motion (ibid.: 146). Furthermore, research into sensory perception shows variations in size of the region of the brain devoted to sensations in different parts of the body and the relative size of the body parts as they exist in neural activity shows that the hand is by far the largest body part (ibid.: 147). The saw and the hammer are not only handmade but also, and in a crucial difference from the machinery of Ruttmann's work, hand-operated and manipulated.[7] These objects make contact with different materials and thus engage the surface contact that we explored in the previous chapter, albeit more vigorously in these examples of manual labouring. While not verbal, the impetus to imagine in the case of Ruttmann's artwork comes from the repetition of sounds that conjure the active motion of both tools hammering and sawing through their respective materials. Visualising sawing and hammering thereby draws upon the surface contact that confers solidity within the imagined realm, as these images layer over the black screen, forged in the workspace of the mind on the basis of sounds alone.

Several of the initial reviewers of Ruttmann's *Weekend* spoke of the rich mental images that they saw as they listened to this work. Writing in *La Revue du cinéma* in 1931, critic Janine Bouissounouse speaks of myriad pictures that emerge at various points throughout her experience of *Weekend* (Bouissounouse [1931] 1994: 46–7). Furthermore, Lea Schiavi, who interviewed Ruttmann in Italy in 1932, notes how he played *Weekend* to her on a record player. The effects, even without the blankness of a cinema screen and focus of the auditorium space, were pictorial: 'With eyes closed, sunk deep in my chair, I saw Ruttmann's record. Saw it: for the images that are preserved through their corresponding sounds come back together in the retina of our eyes with extreme vivid reality' (Schiavi [1932] 1994: 52). In articulating their experience of *Weekend*, Schiavi and Bouissounouse bring ear and eye far closer to one another than prominent contemporary theorists of radio did. Rather than visualisation, for example, Rudolf Arnheim speaks of acoustic bridges that arise between the different sounds that one listens to in this medium (Arnheim [1936] 1971: 194–5). For Arnheim, the ear moves from sound to sound, not from sound to inner vision, to build up the complete aural work of art, bypassing any relation to the eye. Kurt Weill too had spoken of the 'cancellation of the eye's activity' (Weill [1925] 2016: 588) in this domain and the 'dilettantish' idea that a listener should think of something while listening (ibid.: 589). Schiavi's and Bouissounouse's responses to *Weekend* show, however, that vision and inner vision are still operative even when they are not appealed to directly. This indirect appeal to vision is not intended to reaffirm the dominance and prevalence of the visual in a medium that might explore purely aural possibilities, as Arnheim and Weill understood it, but to suggest more simply that just as the image track of silent film reached frequently for inaudible music and sound, so the blankness of *Weekend* connects with visual imagery, which is imagined rather than seen on the screen.

For *Weekend* to be perceived as a montage of purely abstract sounds, these would need to detach themselves entirely from the objects that generate them, and as the example of sawing and hammering suggests, this is not fully possible. From the outline of his project in which Ruttmann names many of the objects that make the sounds (among other things, he names 'Hämmern' and 'Sägen', hammering and sawing (Ruttmann 1930)), to their actualisation, the soundscape retains contact with the visible, material world that is brought to life in the mind. This becomes even more prominent after the first few seconds. A church bell rings, before there is a cut to the sound of factory machinery. The montage quickens to a succession of staccato beats from a machine, and then cuts swiftly between different machines, hammer, and saw. Marching band music is heard faintly before a motor vehicle engine is started up, followed by some violin notes and a musical scale leading to a chord is played on a piano, a greeting – 'Hallo Fräulein' (Hello Miss) – is spoken by a man, and the cost of an item is stated and then rung up on a cash register. A man asks for a phone number: 'zweiundvierzig vier null' (4240). The voice of a child cuts in briefly to say 'Erlkönig' (Erlking) and the sound of a motor engine passes by. Sounds of factories, workshops, offices, homes, and shops emerge in the montage of this opening minute. These sounds introduce the end of the working week, and the structuring principles of succession and superimposition of sounds that occur here are operative throughout. As Lotte H. Eisner points out, however, the most important thing for Ruttmann in *Weekend* is the configuration of space (*die Ausgestaltung des Raums*) (Eisner [1930] 1994: 34). It is the space of sound that he is photographing through optical recording, grasped beyond the sense of sight and shaping the imagination of a physical space through the forging of a mental space with three dimensions.

Throughout the different sections of *Weekend* there are shifts in the volume of particular sounds as they are made – from the city environment to the pastoral retreat – which do not only create sonic variations but which also mould a sense of space through the suggestion of changing distances. Bells, choirs, and farmyard birds or animals, as well as voices, machinery, vehicle engines and sirens, position listener-spectators closer to them or further away, depending on how loud or quiet the sounds are. Sometimes the creation of the sense of space through changes in volume is the effect of sounds made by a range of sources, such as bell sounds heard faintly in the distance and then closer. The implication is not that the bell towers or the listeners are moving but that the montage of sounds is combining different bell rings from different towers at different distances, far to near. The effect of rising and falling volume also sometimes involves a slight rise and fall in pitch, which is associated with a moving object making a sound. The Doppler effect which causes shifts in wavelengths in sound and light involves waves – in this case just sound waves – being closer together in front of a moving object that is emitting sound and further apart in its wake. Thus, when a moving object making a sound travels past us, the pitch will drop slightly the further it disappears into the distance. Moving at the same speed as the object making the sound does not produce this effect. Whenever this effect appears in *Weekend*, the sense is that the device that records what is heard is static as things pass by it: moving vehicles demonstrate this through the sound of their engines, but the most effective example is the sound of the marching band that emerges briefly in the opening minutes, plays for a long uninterrupted period in the pastoral section, and then returns in the final sequence.

The marching band is one of the things that the French film reviewer Janine Bouissounouse says she saw vividly in her mind when experiencing *Weekend*. The mental image generated when the band plays at some length in the pastoral section is not static but moving, and the motion is signalled through the variation in volume and pitch. Were the music to be played at a constant volume, the corresponding mental impression would be of a band positioned for the duration in front of the listener. Thanks to the sounds of the music, the players would still be visualised playing their instruments, rather than frozen as in a snapshot, but they would be standing still. Contrastingly – and this is what Ruttmann presents – changes in volume and pitch correspond to alterations in location, and the mental image is set in motion. First the band is heard in the distance and therefore quieter and slightly flatter, then louder and marginally sharper, before it becomes distant once again and the pitch dips again before fading out. These alterations that correspond with movement also create the sense of space: the band is moving past the listener-spectator. The sound extends well beyond its proximity to the listener-spectator and Ruttmann's choice to focus on the marching band alone at this point without cutting to or overlaying other sounds is instructive. It is not simply a marching band that is brought forth here but the creation of a space through which the band passes, approaching listener-spectators and then leaving them behind, generating a moving image that is solely a product of imagined space created by the sound of the music. A sense of topography arises through these changes in volume that signal variations in proximity. This is how the blankness of Ruttmann's 'film without images' is rendered three-dimensional as the ear permits the mind's eye to picture what is heard. In the vivid example of the marching band, its image moves through a space that has been constructed sonically.

At the end of the weekend, the faint sound of distant church bells gives way to an alarm clock, a whistle, and a siren that go off one after another for work the next morning, as if the quiet bell came from a space as distant as sleep, and the alarm clock close by is a sudden wrenching out of this muffled soporific state. Yawning and reluctant sighs characterise the first greetings of the new day but these are soon followed by the mechanics of work again, returning to what Ruttmann terms its jazz, with a recapitulation of the succession and combination of sounds of typing, vehicles, music, voices, and machinery audible at the outset. However, there is a reminder of the pastoral sounds of Sunday through a brief return of the sound of the marching band, quieter now as if an aural memory, this time in sync with industrial rhythms and overlaid by different voices associated with the return to work. When Merleau-Ponty cited Robert Delaunay in 'Eye and Mind' to show how imagination owes a great deal to vision – 'I am in Petersburg in my bed, in Paris, my eyes see the sun' (Merleau-Ponty [1960] 1993b: 146) – envisaging the possibility of being in one place, yet imagining being somewhere else, it was sight that served as a point of entry into the imagination of being elsewhere. In this final sequence of *Weekend*, Ruttmann presents sounds that are part of the return to work on a Monday morning, additionally overlaying and intercutting sounds of the weekend: the sounds are generated from work and yet also from elsewhere, in Berlin and yet also in the countryside. Although this experience is less individualised than Delaunay's imagining being in Paris while in Petersburg – the aural remainder and reminder of the weekend cuts across different sounds of different work places – the sounds offer an aural equivalent here of that visual possibility of being in two places at once thanks to the imagination, hearing both simultaneously and yet registering their distinction. The sound of the band provides a memory of the weekend that was heard in the earlier sequence and yet now that it is replayed and remembered it forms part of an imaginative layering with the sounds of work, connecting not only different sounds but also different times and spaces.

By producing a sound piece which when presented in an auditorium has no accompanying image track, Ruttmann in one respect achieves the most extreme counterpoint of non-synchronisation that he and other contemporary directors had advocated in their writings on the potential of film sound. Ruttmann, like the Soviet directors of his time, had published a statement on sound in relation to image in their optical work. In August 1928, Eisenstein, Pudovkin, and Alexandrov stressed that sound should be used in counterpoint to onscreen images in order to enhance the hitherto silent medium without denigrating its future potential (Eisenstein et al. [1928] 1985: 84). A month later, Ruttmann too in his own first piece on sound calls for optical-acoustic counterpoint to be the basis of all sound design in film (Ruttmann [1928] 2016: 556). As Michael Cowan notes, though, the Soviet directors were interested in the dialectical conflict produced through their own advocacy of counterpoint, whereas Ruttmann was more interested in analogical relationships in his optical sound films (Cowan 2014: 87). In *Weekend* this analogical relationship can still be discerned, it is just displaced: it is formed between sound and mental image instead of visible onscreen optical-acoustic relations. Not all of the sounds of *Weekend* will generate vivid mental images, as my discussion of the opening few seconds suggested, but the work does prompt intermittent visualisations and, through the changing volume of its myriad sounds, also creates a sense of space. It is in this way that Ruttmann's unique sound work, which tends just as readily to mimesis as it does to abstraction, brings to life sound fragments as imagined images, between ear and mind.

Ruttmann can be understood therefore as a precursor to the kinds of experiments that the artists that form part of Matt Hulse's 'Audible Picture Show' are engaged in today, many of which use sound only and have no recourse to the verbalisation that we encountered in Sally Goode's descriptions in *A Sense of Place*. The limitless potential of blankness for the creation of pictures and scoping out of mental space need not always be signalled by a black screen, however: the topography can be set against a different colour, thematised and recognised as such, rather than as part of the surrounding darkness, signifying something rather than nothing and then being a constant perceptual presence along with the imaginative mental palimpsests created in response to the sounds. At greater length than any of the blank screen films mentioned so far, Derek Jarman's final work does just this, exploring a soundscape devoid of onscreen images and in which the blankness of the screen is blue. *Blue* has been positioned by scholars within many different aesthetic and media histories, from painting – prompted as much by Jarman's own career as painter as by the explicit homage it pays to Yves Klein – to the treatment of the monochrome in avant-garde film, and from the radio play to video poetry, both of which attend in varying degrees to the heightened importance of listening.[8] *Blue* has also travelled through different media and exhibition spaces, from radio and television to the gallery, as well as being programmed in cinemas.[9] As was the case for Ruttmann's work, I consider *Blue* here in its filmic incarnation. Changes in volume and pitch as explored in Ruttmann's work, which prompt the imagination of distance, acquire more layers and detail now as literal and figurative uses of language, along with sound and music, combine to create mental images that come and go in the expansion and contraction of mental space. Hulse's show was advertised as 'giv[ing] the mind's eye a welcome stretch'; it is Jarman who shows in more prolonged detail how the experience of such mental elasticity comes into being.

## Expanding, Contracting, Deepening

Written and directed against the pandemonium of images, *Blue* presents a serene field of colour on screen, at first glance easy on the eyes, especially those like mine that have had a lifelong love affair with blue.[10] The poignant and densely textured sound design by Simon Fisher Turner fleshes out gradually the daily personal battle with AIDS-related illnesses that Jarman fought throughout the time of its making, and which many of his friends had already lost. The growing knowledge of Jarman's descent into sightlessness, with which he is trying to come to terms, imbues my vision of the blue screen with melancholy and disturbs its apparent initial calm. Yet the colour is steadfast, accompanying the fragmented diary entries, poetry, citations, and music, along with the sounds of different environments, both real and imaginary. With words read by John Quentin, Nigel Terry, and Tilda Swinton, in addition to Jarman, *Blue* expands beyond Jarman's subjectivity, while still remaining intensely autobiographical, with many of the narratives stemming from his own experience. Dedicated to 'HB and All True Lovers', *Blue* testifies to a love stronger than death, as infinite as the sea and the sky. It also probes what there is to see beyond sight, as Jarman remains intensely visual in the face of impending blindness.

Jarman was writing *Chroma: A Book of Colour – June '93* and keeping his diaries while working on his film projects and paintings in his final years. The main part of the script for *Blue* is to be found in 'Into the Blue', one of the later chapters in *Chroma*. He declares earlier in the text: 'I've placed no colour photos in this book, as that would be a futile attempt to imprison them. [. . .] I prefer that the colours should float and take flight in your minds' (Jarman [1994] (1995): 42–3). In contrast, the initial plans for the film of *Blue* featured onscreen images and it was to be dedicated to Yves Klein.[11] But as the project evolved, the images dissolved. Jarman notes in his volume of posthumously published diaries: 'I decided to make *Blue* without images – they hinder the imagination and beg a narrative and suffocate with arbitrary charm, the admirable austerity of the void' (Jarman [2000] (2001): 198). The debt to Klein was preserved through the void of the blank blue screen. Jarman may replace the abundance of the onscreen images of his previous films with the vast expanse of blue alone, but this has the effect of channelling any further vision to the mind's eye. He asks in his diaries: 'If you woke on a dark day, had only the mind's eye with which to see your way, would you turn back?' (Jarman 1991: 307). He responds by carrying on into the darkness to produce his extraordinary final work. In so doing, he prompts an equally extraordinary journey through mental space on the part of the listener-spectator.

Jarman's ultimate decision not to make a film with a wealth of visual images gives *Blue* the power to speak out about the devastation that AIDS inflicted on countless lives for whom there is no representational image that could do them justice. Furthermore, the invisibility of the sufferers requires, as stated in the film, that the doors of perception be cleansed for things to be seen as they are, and imagination assumes an important role here as a result. When in the previous chapter Hugues de Montalembert described the images of his mind just after he went blind, he said that his brain was creating images 'exactly like a film'. At a late point in *Blue*, the narration asserts 'films chase through my mind' before talking of occasional dreams as magnificent as the Taj Mahal. Correspondingly, Jarman sets a rich and diverse series of images in motion by means of the mind's eye of the listener-spectator, and his skill as a writer means that he uses some of the techniques that Scarry speaks of in a literary context. Indeed, scholars have considered visualisation on the basis of the narration of *Blue* (Schwenger 1996; Higginson 2008: 79). While the mental image born of the spoken word plays a key role in forming the mental landscape of Jarman's film, other sounds and music are just as important, as is occasional silence. The light of the mind that Jarman directs listener-spectators to see on the basis of the broader soundscape in which words are embedded burns brightly in spite of his own physical decline and is evident from the outset of *Blue*.

To recall Scarry, the sudden illumination or flash of light that she terms 'radiant ignition' will set off the motion pictures of the imagination: when writers attach light to something more solid, this helps their readers to make the mental image move (Scarry [1999] 2001: 77–88). The opening invocation of *Blue* suggests the necessity of light to set things in motion in the mind, and is a modified passage drawn from the Leyden Papyrus, which reads as follows:

> You say to the boy 'Open your eyes'; when he opens his eyes and sees the light, you make him cry out, saying 'Grow (bis), O light, come forth (bis), O light, rise (bis), O light, ascend (bis), O light, thou who art without, come in'. (Griffith and Thompson [1904] 2007: 25)

In Jarman's revision of what is said to the boy, Blue replaces this light in the darkness: 'O Blue come forth, O Blue arise, O Blue ascend, O Blue come in'. He does, however, still open his eyes and see the light, prompting movement (comes forth, arises, and ascends) and creating an expansive mental space in which to operate. In Jarman's imagistic writing, in his poetry and prose, an influx of light prompts the creation of mental images that have elasticity: the boy Blue is in perpetual motion through these opening lines, against the blue of the screen. Yet there is darkness on the horizon from the very beginning, and I shall return to how this serves occasionally to cancel the light, thereby also affecting the visibility of moving images in mental space at times. For the time being, let us consider a sequence of imagined images that fly in from the dark and take flight in the mind early on in *Blue*, since they suggest a connection to processes of configuring space that we looked at in Ruttmann's *Weekend* and attach to Jarman's experience.

'Look where the fuck you're going!' Extracted from its context, this abrupt warning does not direct the formation of any precise mental pictures. Couple it with the whoosh of a bike and the sound of its bell, however, attribute it to a male cyclist passing by at some speed and wrap around it two brief sentences from a narrator's voice, and the ingredients are there for making mental images move through space. This is precisely what Jarman provides. The voice-over narration envelops the sound effects: 'I step off the kerb and a cyclist nearly knocks me down. [Sound of cyclist's bell, shouting, whirling of wheels.] Flying in from the dark he nearly parted my hair.' The cyclist's curt words, along with the sounds of the bike, emerge and are gone in a flash, and the changing volume of the shouted warning helps to create the mental space in which the scene takes place, far more quickly than the marching band sequence in *Weekend* and yet constitutive of an effective sound in motion all the same. Quieter, then louder, then quieter, as the cyclist approaches, is parallel, and then more distant, the bike apparently passes through a physical space that these slight volume changes recreate in mental space in an accordion-like effect of expansion and contraction of sound.

The cyclist is described as 'flying in from the dark'. As in the opening example in the previous chapter on layering in which De Montalembert remembers 'arriving' at the courtyard and seeing children 'playing', the present participle makes sure that the action is kept in motion even after the sound of the cyclist has been and gone. The verbal relation to airborne speed and movement conjured by a winged word ('flying') combines with the broader soundscape to create and sustain mental imagery in motion. The near miss is conveyed through the words that surround the sound effects, as a more suppositional mode of imagining is engaged faintly to intimate what could have happened: the cyclist '*nearly* knocks me down' and '*nearly* parted my hair'.[12] Imagining within an imagined image that this has happened to Jarman recalls the dreams that take place within the imagined images discussed in the previous chapter (those of the fictive Robinson and the real Jane Birkin), but here such suppositional imagining is much fainter, since listener-spectators are not instructed to imagine it directly, in contrast to the passage of the cyclist on the bike, only to imagine what might have occurred but did not. The fainter possible images that are so because the verbal instruction is more conditional serve to bolster the cyclist's proximity to Jarman as he steps off the kerb. But their suggestion of further motion within the motion that is already at work here (knocking him down, parting his hair) produces a second order of image-making within image-making that is not as vivid as the dreams recounted in the previous chapter because it did not happen and was not experienced. Jarman is left upright, his hair intact, but has taken a dangerous step downwards in literal and metaphorical terms.

Prior to this step off the kerb, he had been sitting in a café with friends, surrounded by sounds of background chatter and clatter, being served by Bosnian refugees and reading about the war in Sarajevo.[13] After stepping off the kerb to the abusive warning the narration declares: 'I step into a blue funk.' The actual, physical experiences of his day, which can be pictured, now shade into a figurative verbal image of melancholy, of feeling blue. The sound effect following this declaration is explosive – evoking the bombed echo of the talk of the war in Sarajevo, but more immediately it is as though he drops heavily into water, a depression given the mental shape of a depth charge, falling, going under and creating a massive splash. The mental imagery sinks into a mood that joins with the perceived colour of the screen and that also connects Jarman to others beyond himself, both the dead and the suffering. The move that Jarman's prose makes between literal and more figurative images is crucial to the expression of his experience of both an immediate environment and his pain, as his sight dwindles and the external light fades. He simply did not see the cyclist. His fading sight – the cause of the near collision and this blue funk – brings with it a shadow, and the tracking of this shadow later on in *Blue* shows how this initial example of the increase and decrease in the volume of sound is not the only way of configuring the mental space of moving images.

As Jarman's illness progresses, he has to go into hospital twice a day to be hooked up to the DHPG drip, which is said on one visit to trill like a canary. The narration describes how his companion and lover HB disappears into a shadow on one side of him, since he has lost the sight on the periphery of his right eye. It further outlines how he holds up his own hands in front of him and slowly parts them to observe how they disappear too. In her exploration of how readers can stretch mental images in their own minds, Scarry draws comparison between the mental image and a piece of cloth with a picture imprinted on it, that can be elongated or widened by manipulating it with one's hands (Scarry [1999] 2001: 111–12). Readers clearly do not reach into their heads to perform the action literally on mental pictures (but could visualise manipulating cloth if called upon to do so), yet Scarry's point that hands are involved in this expanding stretch of the mental image is pertinent here to Jarman's own exploration of vision. As with the visualisation of the handheld tools in *Weekend*, the more hands-on verbal instruction is operative here, yet it enables the picturing of something far more challenging: Jarman's diminishing sight.

If I place my hands in front of me and slowly part them, they remain in my field of vision. In visualising Jarman's actions, hands that part to leave a space between them create a mental space, stretched out on the mental retina, while also introducing a blank area into which HB has already disappeared, followed by one of Jarman's hands. The mental picture of sight loss and vision born from the description of HB and Jarman's own hands is accompanied by the regular squeaky electronic tweet of the canary-like drip until its initial regularity goes out of control, as the soundscape leaves its regular rhythm to be more in keeping with the crazed and erratic progression of the illness, harsh on the ears to drum home the harshness on the eyes. The sound of the equipment is represented first through comparison to the chirp of the little yellow bird before any such representational move is cancelled out. The mental image of a drip summoned by the tweet on the sound track is scrubbed out by its increasing unruliness, as the sound ends up being the only accompaniment to this description of how Jarman's sight is disappearing, closing in, conjured through the widening of his hands. The volumising of the mental image is created by hand here, accompanied by a brief burst of unbearable sound, all of which forms the space in which to see the onset of sight loss.

The shadow that Jarman explores with his hands and whose motion spectators can recreate in their minds has a visual corollary that he describes at a late point in the film on a visit to St Mary's hospital. The white flashes caused by Jarman's damaged retina unleash black floaters, as illumination and darkness are coupled ominously in the gradual formation of a subsequent mental image summoned by the encroachment of blindness. The narration likens these floaters to a flock of starlings in twilight as a faint sound of birds is heard in the background. Sound and mental image converge on the basis of the simile for the damaged retina, as birds swirl and trill scream-like in the fading light of the evening sky, from Jarman's eye to the listener-spectator's mind by way of the ear. The floaters are something he actually sees rather than imagines, darting across his visual field. Yet in comparing these to the black flock of birds and accompanying the description with their sounds in flight, what is described here makes the journey into imaginative space, and the starlings in their acrobatic murmurations flit past and around in the mind, akin to the course of the floaters across the surface of Jarman's remaining eyesight. The floaters that overlay or underpin whatever else he sees suggest a layering of vision, with birds silhouetted against a twilit sky, coming and going, moving around unbidden as he looks at something else, like the mental images set in motion for the listener-spectators throughout *Blue* against the blue screen. Those listener-spectators who have floaters in their own eyes may well witness the layering effect of seeing these in addition to imagining the starlings as a result of eye movements across or away from the screen while viewing *Blue*, the activity of the eye in this instance prompting an experience that chimes with the imagined movements of the black starlings in the mind. The multiple layering of perception and imagination – from Jarman seeing floaters in an eye examination to the floaters becoming starlings, and listener-spectators moving their eyes over the blue screen, not only perceiving the field of colour but aware of their own vision while imagining Jarman's literal situation and its figurative recreation – creates a sense of depth, not only between the screen and the imagined images but also within the imagined images themselves. While viewers may, for example, be picturing the black starlings against a blue sky in a way that equates to projecting a mental image of them onto the blue screen, the suggestion of depth here creates a space that is hollowed out rather than flat, which listener-spectators are within rather than viewing from outside as on a screen. Jarman's work thus prompts the creation not only of mental moving pictures but also of a mental space with dimensions.

## Enveloping

We have witnessed the creation of a space with dimensions from the outset of this chapter, from Sally Goode's narration in *A Sense of Place* through Ruttmann's marching band to the volumising effects of other sounds. I also mentioned at the start of this exploration of aural-spatial volume that it can feel as though mental space is enveloping at times, rather than being the forum for the formation and movement of mental images that are just observed from an external position and at a distance. This sense of being within space and moving through it in the mind is particularly palpable within dreams, but it is possible to have the feeling of inhabiting places that are visualised: for example, if asked to close one's eyes, picture one's living room, and then walk around it in the mind. It is pertinent to the development of my study of the imagined images of film that the foundations of the mental image in such instances serve a building process that connects with long-established ways of talking about mental space but that also breaches the boundaries of such accounts. Consciousness of a mental space that is three-dimensional furnishes both precisely delimited as well as potentially infinite expanses as loci for imagining.

Writing on the structure of the imagination, Marina Warner notes that from the publication of Conrad Gesner's *De Anima* (1586) through to more contemporary examples, most notably Freud and Dennett, the mind has been configured as a house, even though the map of the mind has been redrawn considerably over the centuries to give rise to different architectural configurations (Warner 2000: 163). For Bachelard indeed, the house is one of his primary instruments of analysis and constitutes the space in which all aspects of the inner life are lodged: 'our soul is an abode' (Bachelard [1957] 1994: xxxvii). In even grander terms in the past, the art of memory was associated with the building of memory palaces in the mind: orators would construct these elaborate structures and place things in different rooms in order to remember them and then walk through the palatial abode mentally as they did their talk (Yates 1966). Although the latter served memory rather than imagination and in its grandeur is probably very different from the aforementioned experiment of walking mentally around one's own living room, the palace had to be created in the mind and this means that it relied on the image-making powers of imagining in the first instance. Extendable built structures – which need not be literal palaces or even more modest houses – have thus been indispensable for categorising and activating broader aspects of the life of the mind as well as for showcasing mental image construction itself. Jarman prompts the building and inhabiting of such spaces but also expands and explodes enclosed structures to become an astronaut of the void, as Tilda Swinton's spoken words encourage midway through *Blue*. In the examples I have considered thus far – the cyclist, the parting of Jarman's hands, the starlings – *Blue* stimulates the visualisation of images from grounded positions, but the space through which the images move, whether along a street, in the airspace in front of a body, or in the sky, has been just as important. In the examples I go on to consider now, the experience of blindness intrudes into the mental space of image formation itself, instilling an intermittence of sight and its removal from the inside out but also creating a sense of space that is more expansive and fathomless.

The luminous condition for the appearance and disappearance of mental images presents itself as a transient flame within a fragment of poetry, read out in the film and accompanied by ethereal music: 'Your kiss flares / A match struck in the night / Flares and dies'. The metaphorical power of language that conveys the fire of passion through the effect of a kiss also brings the illumination necessary for the creation of a single mental picture of a match, struck in the darkness, which lights up suddenly and brightly before going out. The sound effect of a struck match precedes this entry into poetry, and both words and sound invoke a movement that is self-illuminating. As the words get listener-spectators to strike a match on the mental retina – an action of the hand – the lit movement of the flame through the dark night dies out, but it also reveals a cavernous space. To recall the neuroscientific research referred to in the first chapter of my study: for mental depictions to emerge, 'all that is needed', Kosslyn and his collaborators report, 'is a "functional space" in which distance can be defined vis-à-vis how information is processed' (Kosslyn et al. 2006: 14–15). From the relatively constrained space that exists around a struck match in the dark comes an expansive stretch within a far broader setting thanks to its 'flare'. This poem begins with the line 'The darkness comes in with the tide', and follows the more prosaic listing of the numerous, awful side effects of the DHPG drug Jarman is on, as it is explained that he has to sign a consent form to show awareness that he can contract any of the illnesses, and then declares that he cannot see what he is to do other than sign it. The flare of the kiss also links associatively to a flare sent up when lost, then, lost at sea, in the darkness of the incoming tide and night. The poem repeats several times the insatiable desire for more kisses, echoing the need to stoke the fire again and again, endlessly, to recreate the motion of striking up light in the dark, from intimate to infinite space, from a lit match in a room to a flare ascending in the sky, accompanied by the music, before closing with three lines: 'Greedy lips / Speedwell eyes / Blue skies'. The lips, ever hungry for more kisses in the night, lead on to mention of speedwell: in folklore, if you pick one of these delicate little blue flowers, birds come and peck your eyes out. 'Speedwell Eyes' was one of the early titles for this film (Jarman [2000] (2001): 247), and Jarman, losing his sight, eyes pecked out by his debilitating illnesses, lives in the perpetual incoming tidal darkness of the night, craving the moments of illuminated motion that the film also sparks off in the mental space, counteracting the blue flower of blindness – blue, as narrated elsewhere, brings black with it. Between the horizontal axis of the ebb and flow of the tide (heard occasionally on the soundtrack at different moments in the film), and the vertical axis of the night sky – the poles that Steve Dillon focuses on so aptly in his reading of Jarman's films, locating therein the debt to Cocteau who is also mentioned in *Blue* – this poem moves from the incoming tide at night to a vision of blue skies that joins with the perceived blueness of the screen, punctuated by kisses that light up and fade in the shadow of Jarman's own disappearing sight. To picture the self-illuminating motion of the mental image of the struck match, then, is also to witness it go out as listener-spectators continue to perceive the blue screen, the creation and extinction of light thereby entwined in the mind wherein even in the darkness there is a sense of infinite space.

Furthering this combination of illumination and darkness in the dimensions of imagined space, the inner eye is actually blinded in an earlier imaginative sequence devoted to Marco Polo and his travels. The sound of the wind whistles as the voyager is said to stumble across the Blue Mountain before taking a seat on a lapis throne. Listener-spectators are told that the caravan approaches, 'blue canvasses fluttering in the wind'. The fluttering of the canvasses introduces an association with the rarity that Scarry notes is one of the ways in which images are set in motion in the mind by writers: we encountered this in Birkin's account of her dream of flying in the previous chapter. Here the more substantial caravan is coupled with the lightness that characterises the flight of a butterfly or the wings of a bird. Listener-spectators are told: 'Blue people from over the seas – ultramarine – have come to collect the lapis with its flecks of gold.' Gold in the lapis brings with it radiant ignition, adding luminosity to the rarity of the caravan that is in motion as music plays that is made of interwoven yet distant voices. But the road to the city of Aqua Vitae is described as 'protected by a labyrinth built from crystals and mirrors which in the sunlight cause terrible blindness'. Multiple reflections of the sun in a glassy mirrored maze prompt formation of a crystalline image that is obscured immediately through an unbearable glare, ensuring that the city's secrets remain eternally safe from prying eyes but extinguishing radiant ignition. This is an instance of a process of erasure that will be explored more fully and with reference to different directors in a later chapter. Once the blinding image occurs here, though, a different relation to space arises.

As sight is blinded and the mental images are obscured by glare, the personified boy Blue is said to walk into the labyrinth in the silence of poetic excavation into the archaeology of sound. From within the depths of this labyrinth it is said that 'Blue watched as a word or phrase materialised in scintillating sparks, a poetry of fire which cast everything into darkness with the brightness of its reflections.' Listener-spectators may be watching Blue watching the materialisation of words or phrases, but they are also invited to experience what he experiences in the labyrinth of their own mental space, which seems to have become hollowed out, a space that it is possible to move through, a three-dimensional maze, rather than a flat image viewed from afar like a two-dimensional film. One of the haunting melodies from Rimsky-Korsakov's 'Scheherazade' is heard briefly and faintly in the background after the sound of a gong, a musical reminder of tales that were told by a woman to save her life across a thousand and one nights – music that conveys a nightly threat, but that also signifies an undoing of the work of death through the power of storytelling. The sparks of the words that are forged in the labyrinth reintroduce light to this dark space after the 'terrible blindness' of the glare of sunlight against crystals and mirrors. The mental image of the blinding gives way once again to the brightness of the light of the mind, thanks to the words, sound, and music that emerge from Jarman's own poetry of fire.

## Palimpsests

If the layering of images over a blank screen may initially have seemed simpler than negotiating the layering of images over onscreen images that we encountered in the previous chapter, I hope that by now the complexity of imagining in the audio-visual context of an imageless screen has become apparent. Ruttmann knew of this intricacy, as do the participants in Matt Hulse's 'Audible Picture Show', but it is on Jarman's work that I dwell now before I draw this chapter to a close.

Let us listen first to the footsteps that walk along a shingle shoreline towards the end of *Blue*. These feet have walked this way before but this will be the last time. They can be attached to Jarman, and yet are unattributed, reaching beyond this lone figure, as the film itself reaches beyond Jarman, to all those suffering and dying from AIDS, to tell their tale in the hope for change, if not for his generation then in the future. As the footsteps progress and get louder along the shoreline, the narration declares: 'I caught myself looking at shoes in a shop window. I thought of going in and buying a pair, but stopped myself. The shoes I am wearing at the moment should be sufficient to walk me out of life.' The footsteps then fade gradually out of earshot before disappearing forever. The aural-verbal and corresponding mental-visual palimpsest of Jarman looking in a shop window at shoes and a walk along the shoreline is formed through contact between the words and the sound of footsteps on shingle. The footsteps mark the passing time, the walk out of life, but are literalised in the sound effects that forge one image of footsteps walking along the beach and another of him looking at shoes in a shop window, the shoes pictured on the basis of their association with the footsteps and the space created by the changing volume of what is heard. But this is not where I want to leave Jarman, walking interminably along this desolate shore in my mind.

My own abiding mental impression of *Blue* whenever I think back to it, is of hazy summer days – a willed suspension rather than a denial on my part of the further AIDS-inflicted horrors that were to come for Jarman and that, as he repeats throughout, had already taken so many of his friends. The summery blues of his garden float unbidden from an early visit to the hospital for a check-up over light string music: 'blue bottle buzzing, lazy day, sky blue butterfly sways on a cornflower, lost in the warmth of the blue heat haze'. The rarity of the butterfly against the cornflower, light as air, causes it to sway in my mind, as the buzz of a blue bottle materialises and echoes through the word itself, and the lazy hot day takes shape in the fragment of the garden that I picture mentally in a haze of blue, a blue which lifts off gently yet vibrantly from the insects and flowers to imbue the entire scene. The blue takes flight in the mind, as was his desire for the colours of *Chroma*. It is impossible, though, to suspend the inevitable forever. The final poem of the film, also accompanied by string music and sounds of the wind and the tide crashing on the shoreline evokes what Kate Higginson terms 'an eternal queer sanctuary on the seabed' (Higginson 2008: 79). It tells of all these lives that will pass like the traces of a cloud, their names and work forgotten. But in the here and now there is no longer reference to suffering and pain, just to the lost boys who sleep forever in a deep embrace. The hell of waiting rooms, the skeletal bodies of those crushed by the disease are no longer present. The love that will drift on the tide forever is that of the man he wants to kiss him, on the lips and on the eyes. Blue is buried and respects are paid through the placing of a blue flower, a *pothos*, on a tomb: 'I place a delphinium, Blue, upon your grave.'[14] Clarity of sight may have gone forever but mental images remain as a single blue flower blooms luminously after the quickening of lives that 'will run like / Sparks through the stubble'. The mental laying down by hand of a delphinium on a grave over the blue screen is the final palimpsest of *Blue*, a movement of grace and humility, blue against blue, invisible yet imagined and observed fleetingly in the space viewed by the mind's eye before it too closes.

## Coda

The blank screen of the films discussed in this chapter constitutes fertile terrain and an ideal foundation for stimulating the imagination when accompanied by sound or music and a voice-over. We will encounter this blankness again, albeit in more sporadic fashion, when we chart the process of erasure in a later chapter. The process explored in the examples of this chapter that range from Jarman's *Blue* to Hulse's curatorial work in more recent years and stretch back to Ruttmann in early cinema also permits a connection to be made to other films. In this respect, it is worth emphasising that the examples discussed in most detail in my study are not the only ones to which these processes apply. The volumising that has been outlined at length with reference to the omnipresent blankness of these more experimental works is also occasionally in evidence in more narrative film. A salient example appears in the work of Spike Jonze in a scene in *Her* (2013), which appeals to the imagination and prompts both layering and volumising. Midway through a sequence focused on Theodore (Joaquin Phoenix) talking to Samantha (Scarlett Johansson), who is an advanced operating system who is present only ever as a voice, the film cuts to a close-up of Theodore's face as he lies in bed with his head on a pillow in the darkened environment of his bedroom. The close-up eventually gives way to a blank, black screen as he talks with Samantha in the darkness. He begins to tell her what he would do with her if she were in the room with him right now, detailing how he would put his arms around her and touch her. While he is still visible, Theodore's position on the bed and the framing of his face by the camera permits the mental positioning of Samantha over him, as he talks to her as if she were present in the off-screen space in front of his face. This exchange is suppositional at first, since her first question is voiced in the conditional tense: 'How would you touch me?' A profile shot of his face then serves as a brief reminder that there is no cheek against his cheek but the next shot, more fully over his face, returns to the closer vantage point. He has been closing his eyes periodically throughout this sequence so far and he does so one final time before the screen fades to black. At this point, their spoken sexual encounter deepens through his words first and then her reactions to what he says.

Theodore describes touching Samantha, running his fingers down her neck to her chest, and kissing her breasts, as she says that she can feel her skin: the mental image forms through the surface contact of flesh against flesh layered over the black screen in tandem with volumising that occurs courtesy of the music and their entwined voices. The music that has been a very gentle and quiet part of this sequence becomes gradually louder as Theodore describes entering her and she responds to this more and more vocally. The sounds of pleasure, occasional words, and the rising music contribute to the mental images in motion of lovers moving together and against one another in the darkness, as the increase in volume enables the creation of both mental space and pictures. The imagined physical encounter is engendered by the very real power of talking in the darkness, voice to voice. Duras will eventually return us in a later chapter to the voices of lovers in the dark as part of her very different aesthetic. For the time being, the play of absence and presence fundamental to imagining in images is what now needs to be interrogated as we move on to consider the process of supplementing.

CHAPTER 5

# Supplementing

When thinking of films that are particularly good at prompting spectators to imagine in images, whether sporadically or in a more continuous fashion, almost all of them appear to do so through some kind of omission. We have, for example, already encountered the memories of De Montalembert and Anderson, along with the recalled dreams of Robinson and Birkin, as missing images to be generated; we have also viewed blank screens that deploy sound, voice, and music only. Advancing further now in order to build upon the superposition of layering along with the expansions and contractions of volumising, I want to focus more specifically here on what I term the activity of supplementing what is on screen. In everyday parlance, something that is supplementary is something that is added to what is there. However, even this usage of the term may carry with it a sense of making up for something that is not there. It thus brings up the dual meaning that Jacques Derrida traces painstakingly through his readings of texts in his magnum opus *Of Grammatology* (Derrida [1967] 1997). The supplement as explored by Derrida derives from two different meanings of the verb *suppléer*: to add on to, and to substitute. Derrida shows how the supplement can add to something already complete in itself as well as adding on something to complete a thing. The term might point to a lack (something that needs to be completed) and aims as a result to put something in place of what is missing, but there is a paradox in that the very thing that supplements the lack in the original thing contains the condition of possibility for both. The supplement is one of the undecidable terms that characterise Derrida's deconstructive writing style, since it hovers incessantly between meanings without settling. Correspondingly, the logic of the supplement forms an important part of a deconstructive practice that disrupts the metaphysics of presence that holds systems of hierarchical binary oppositions in place. If we place such thinking on the supplement in relation to the absence that both Bachelard and Sartre point to as being necessary for imagination to be stimulated, for example, this prompts a rethinking of the notion of omission with which this chapter opened, since that which is imagined on the basis of being withheld becomes the condition of possibility for perception itself. Supplementing, as we will explore it throughout this chapter, is a matter of entering into an encounter with onscreen images that inscribe in varying ways the imprint of what is to be imagined within them. Neither wholly inside nor outside the onscreen image as a result, the imagined image is not only shaped by what is heard and seen but actually makes possible what is heard and seen in the first place. Indeed, the film experience in all its richness engages with the logic of the supplement here, deconstructing the binary of presence and absence on which definitions of imagining frequently depend.

### Supplementing Invisibility, Imagining Film

It is worth reiterating at this juncture that the imagined images that I have been scoping out from the beginning of this book are not created exclusively from the experience of viewing films within an auditorium space. This is not just because they are a function of the imagination rather than of a particular kind of external realm. As was noted in the previous chapter, even works that were made for the auditorium space travel far beyond that through various media and exhibition spaces, and wherever films are available for the home entertainment market today, the compositional workings of imagining can be experienced in less capacious surroundings, frequently through a one-to-one relationship between viewer and screen. Retaining this open viewing context, I want for the moment, though, to focus on the particular space of the cinema auditorium and its occupants by looking at films that take this arena as their own representational focal point. The reason for this is that the main such film discussed in this opening section is exemplary in prompting the activity of imagining in the supplementary sense that I have just outlined.

Imagine first of all that you are watching a film, either in an art house cinema or on DVD at home – the conditions will of course differ but what matters is that you are engrossed. You hear dramatic music accompanying the sound of a horse neighing then galloping, its hooves racing over the different textures of the ground it traverses, and then neighing again before it pulls up sharply and its rider dismounts. The visualised movement of the horse through the space configured by its sounds corresponds with the volumising of the imagined image that we considered in the previous chapter. As was the case for Ruttmann's marching band and Jarman's cyclist, the pitch and volume of the horse's sounds rise and fall; however, unlike these earlier examples, these sounds do not conjure up one continuous motion past one static point but several: the horse approaches, passes by, approaches again and only then comes to a halt. The dramatic music ensures continuity across the repeated sounds of the horse galloping past again and again, and the effect is to prompt the experience of a mental montage of images. In contrast to imagining a marching band or a cyclist passing by, you are in fact imagining a film sequence of a galloping horse, and the added complication in this instance is that whereas the horse is not shown, there is still a lot to be seen on screen. Instead of having a blank screen ahead of you, you are looking at a close-up of a woman in a cinema as you first hear the horse; she wears a veil that frames her brightly lit face and has a look of rapt attention that corresponds to what she appears to be seeing on a screen ahead of her. Her head is tilted to one side, rises, then tilts to the other, before the shot cuts to another shot of a woman who is more blankly absorbed, her face just as brightly illuminated, also framed by a hijab. These women fill the screen but you do not see the screen that you imagine them to be seeing. The formation of the imagined image of the galloping horse whose rider eventually dismounts must therefore also contend with the onscreen image of the women's faces, with knowledge of the fact that they are watching and reacting to a film.

The scene that I have been asking you to imagine is from Abbas Kiarostami's *Shirin* (2008), a film that begins with an ornate credit sequence in which viewers are shown a series of pages from an ancient text, yet which is formed thereafter of shots of women's faces in an auditorium space.[1] Their faces come to life in the darkness: ripples of light and shadow on their skin combine with emotions that cause their expressions to alter in many different ways as they also occasionally fidget or are momentarily distracted but otherwise appear concentrated throughout. The imagined film that plays invisibly across their changing faces and which *Shirin*'s spectators hear without seeing on screen is an adaptation of the tragic love story of *Khosrow and Shirin* based on a short story by Farideh Golbou and inspired by the work of the twelfth-century Persian poet Hakim Nezami Ganjavi (1141–1209), with a screenplay by M. Rahmanian. Kiarostami's film is based on the epic romance between a Persian king, Khosrow Parviz, and Shirin, an Armenian princess, and the tale is one of star-crossed lovers. Khosrow loves Shirin but marries Maryam, the daughter of a Roman emperor, for political purposes. Shirin too takes another lover, Farhad, a stone carver. Farhad loses the will to live when he is told falsely that Shirin is dead; she is in fact alive and is eventually united with Khosrow after Maryam has died, but Khosrow is killed in turn, viciously slaughtered. Shirin tells her tale of woe to her sisterhood, gathered around her and also grieving, before killing herself ultimately with a dagger. The rider of the horse in the sequence outlined above is Shirin, the main female protagonist whose name is the only one that features in the title of Kiarostami's retelling of the epic story. Commenting on the oscillation of freedom and constraint on the spectator's imagination when viewing this film, Kiarostami suggests that viewers should actually let go of the story and just keep their eyes on the screen and that in doing so they will see 'the Cinema itself' (Kiarostami cited in Khodaei 2009). Cinema as seen across the faces of its spectators without getting into their heads is what is perceived on screen, but this combines with what is heard of the story – words, music, and sound – to shape what is seen by the mind's eye. The hand-drawn illustrated images in the ancient text shown during the credit sequence set the scene of the era and attire. Imagined images derive not only from this initial anchor point and the ensuing story that is told, though: they also borrow from the mute imprint of emotion in the onscreen image and mimetic contact with sound as they come and go across the surface of *Shirin* between darkness and light. It is here that the dual vision of imagination and perception that has characterised the formation of the layers and volumising of the previous chapters acquires its further nuance. What is missing – onscreen images from a film-within-the-film – is that without which there would be no facial movements or emotions for viewers of *Shirin* to respond to on screen. The supplement of images from the film-within-the-film is lacking and yet fundamental, and the supplementary activities of imagining generate that without which there would be nothing to be perceived.

The onscreen focus on audience reactions to a film that is not shown is not unique to Kiarostami's *Shirin*. To name but a few brief examples, several of the contributions to the compilation film *Chacun son cinéma/To Each His Own Cinema* (Gilles Jacob, 2007), commissioned to commemorate the sixtieth anniversary of the Cannes Film Festival, do this too and also include a short film by Kiarostami. Among the shorts by different directors, various filmmakers turn their camera on the audience. In *Anna* by Alejandro González Iñárritu, this privileged relation to hearing and potentially forming mental images of the film-within-the-film rather than seeing it extends to its protagonist Anna (Luisa Williams), who is blind and is seen at a screening of Godard's *Le Mépris/Contempt* (1963). Anna's hands and then her expression are the spectator's primary focus. Viewers hear an exchange between Godard's Paul (Michel Piccoli) and Camille (Brigitte Bardot) and the sweeping soundtrack, as tears roll down Anna's face until the atmosphere reaches a point that she can bear no longer and she leaves the theatre. In another film, *Dans l'obscurité/Darkness* by the Dardenne brothers, it is hands again that spectators see first. This time, though, they do not belong to an onscreen spectator but are moving across the floor in the darkness as sounds from the final scene of Robert Bresson's *Au Hasard Balthazar* (1966) are also heard: sounds of gunshots, the bells of sheep, the barking of a dog. The hands belong to a thief (Jérémie Ségard) who enters a row and dips into a woman's open handbag. The woman (Émilie Dequenne) grabs his hand and pulls it to her tear-drenched face as Bresson's film and that of the Dardennes draw to a close with Schubert's haunting piano sonata no. 20. Kiarostami's contribution to the compilation – *Where Is My Romeo?* – concentrates solely on the images of a succession of several women's faces, streaked with tears, with no distractions from surrounding spectators or others in the darkness; the women are apparently watching the ending of Franco Zeffirelli's *Romeo and Juliet* (1968).[2] In Kiarostami's film, as well as those of the Dardennes and Iñárritu, something is left to the imagination because of what is not shown. Yet in all three of these shorts, while heightened emotion is visible on the faces of the women in response to films that viewers do not see, these films will be known to a cinephile audience. Mental images that arise to those who are familiar with the films that are heard will be those conjured from a memory of these films. Viewers unfamiliar with the original films may well imagine their own distinctive images, but the crucial difference from *Shirin* is that the missing images have an existence somewhere else: there is an actual film from which the sounds derive and it is not a matter of creating imagined images. *Shirin*'s uniqueness lies, then, in prompting mental images that have no basis in a pre-existing film.

The film-within-the-film of *Shirin* exists only in the imagination. Yet the radiance that we have seen ignite and set in motion certain of the mental images in previous chapters, following Scarry, mainly through words used in voice-over, shifts throughout *Shirin* to the onscreen image, and it is the women's faces that now illuminate a reaction to what *Shirin*'s spectators are prompted simultaneously to imagine. This light is not that of the metaphysics of presence since the imagined image is formed deconstructively between what is present and absent, onscreen and off, and even the images that *Shirin*'s spectators see on screen are a combination of light and shadow – illuminated women in the foreground, with other spectators, men and women, just about visible behind them. Mental images are prompted to come and go throughout, as words, music, and sound combine or succeed one another sometimes to generate vivid sequences, and at other times to leave the mind to wander back to the faces on screen. The latter moments occur particularly when guidance through the verbal narrative or sound is sparse and the faces are inscrutable. The contrasting vivacity of other sequences owes much to the verbal art of storytelling that, in spite of Kiarostami's instruction in the aforementioned interview, is difficult to relinquish entirely. Shirin's voice frames the film-within-the-film. The mode of address that calls her sisters to listen to her at the beginning of the film speaks directly from the outset both to those seated, silent women seen on screen and to those who are part of the imagined space generated by what is heard. The sound of sporadic dripping throughout Shirin's opening appeal to her sisters in grief creates a sense of cavernous yet contained space with unclear dimensions that gradually transforms into a brighter, more distinct meadow scene.

Even without the visual aid of an onscreen image from the film-within-the-film, the break between the call to her sisters to listen to her story and some lighter laughter that ensues thereafter is palpable as that of a slow transition through the orchestral score back in time (there will be many flashbacks in this audible film-within-the-film from Shirin's narration in the present). As birds sing and young women laugh and call to one another, this transition is imprinted in the facial reactions of the women on screen as the subtle lift of lips, gentle arising of emotion, and fleeting serenity (Figure 5.1). The sound of women's laughter in the film-within-the-film that opens this sequence is somewhat muted at first but rises in volume, as does the birdsong that accompanies it. This rise in volume of the women's laughter suggests their movement, as in the volumising chapter, and thereby the creation of space through which the laughing women move, yet what *Shirin*'s spectators have been witnessing here in the mental space is the gradual emergence of

**Figure 5.1** *Shirin* (Abbas Kiarostami, 2008).

a film image, a visual dissolve brought to mind through sound. The context of the auditorium setting in the film coupled with the expressions on the faces of the women shape the form of this emergence of mental images in filmic terms, as does the ensuing verbal exchange. Shirin, the narrator of the previous sequence, is now part of the group of young women (she will interject periodically as the film unfolds, sometimes suggesting her presence in voice-over alone as other images play on the imagined screen, rather than a perpetual return to the opening setting from where she is actually telling her tale). The other women call out to her and she asks where they are: they are playing a game in which she is blindfolded, walking around, and their voices explain her surroundings to her. The young women tell her that she is surrounded by flowers, and to choose one and enjoy its nectar. As the range of laughter and instructions floats across different voices, the mental image is configured spatially of a meadow filled with birdsong and bedecked in flowers. Women run through it, guiding one who, like Shirin's spectators, cannot see the surroundings, but the young women describe them for her – and the film's viewers – to picture.

The words that guide the formation of mental images in this sequence are those that direct Shirin, braided with flowers, birdsong, and laughter. At times, the use of language by Shirin and other characters is figurative rather than literal, lending itself less readily to picturing images on the mental screen of the film-within-the-film. At others, what she sees in her own mind is described for the film's audience to imagine without intimating that this is imaged on the screen of the film-within-the-film. This happens most notably when she recounts a haunting vision of a knight with a branch for a head where a dove has made its nest thus to be pictured as part of a dream or nightmare she is just recalling verbally. But sequences that dispense with verbal instruction altogether are just as effective at times in prompting the imagination in *Shirin*, aided by animated expressions on the women spectators' faces. Midway through the film, there is a ferocious battle, which erupts suddenly. The abrupt cut to this scene is signalled by the sound of a sword being drawn and swung through the air, followed by a groan and a bloodcurdling shout. The sound of the drawing of the weapon – a grating of material surfaces – causes the onscreen woman seen at the time of listening to this to jump forwards, startled; it also generates a mental image through the sound of surface contact. The ensuing scene is a din of clashing metal, cries, and flesh being plunged into and sliced open. The pace of the montage of onscreen women's faces in the audience speeds up at this point as the skirmish continues, and as one bites her nails and the next two look gripped, the next looks down and averts her eyes, the next looks to her side, the next closes her eyes before looking down and then to the side, and the next clasps her hands behind her head. This chain reaction is one that oscillates between absorption and aversion yet helps to shape and sustain the mental images that form in this sequence. Were the sounds to be heard alone against a blank screen, it would still be clear that this was a messy, bloody fight from the clashing of weaponry to the groans and cries of men accompanied by horses neighing with alarm. I spoke in earlier chapters of a mimetic relation between sound and the picturing of some of the objects that make it – especially the handheld, handmade kind – and this sequence is no different when imagining clanking, hand-wielded weapons such as swords being mobilised in battle. The surface contact – of sword and cover, weapon and flesh, clashing metal – substantiates the formation of the mental images of this battle. However, what intensifies the mental images here, making them even gorier, is the fact that some of the women are affected to the point that they have to block out what they see (Figure 5.2). It is thus not just that the sound of two metallic objects clashing and grating against one another forms an image of a fight, or that the sound of a sword slicing through skin brings with it images of a viscous blend of flesh opening up and sinew pouring forth: the women who watch this and show that they do not want to see it – bloodshed, aggression, fighting – heighten the vivacity of the battle that *Shirin*'s spectators picture and lend it further substance, conditioning and fuelling the way that this is seen in the film of the imagination.

From the levity of laughter when the young women play through to the horror of bloodshed in battle, the light and shade of what is imagined

**Figure 5.2** *Shirin* (Abbas Kiarostami, 2008).

runs across the onscreen women's faces and through spectators' minds, prompted by what is seen and heard. The emotions seen upon the faces of the women in the audience within these two contrasting sequences of the meadow and the bloody skirmish in *Shirin* form the perceptual surface with which imagined images make repeated contact, the former vivifying and helping to shape but also deriving from the latter. To imagine in relation to *Shirin* is indeed, then, to supplement the onscreen image in the sense that it is also to conjure an image without which the onscreen image would not assume the form and look the way that it does. Such is the power not only of cinema, as Kiarostami suggests when he encourages spectators to forget about the story and focus only on the screen, but of an invisible cinema with which his film is also in tune, dependent upon a dual viewing position that engages perception and imagination in equal measure. To return momentarily to Roland Barthes's reflections on his cinematic experience mentioned in an earlier chapter: to attend to an audience at the cinema, as he describes doing, is to behave perversely, since he is looking the wrong way, and this perverse body contrasts with a narcissistic engagement with the screen. Coupled with other references to closing one's eyes in order to see in the opening chapters of my study, Barthes's reflections initially provided a side-glance into the imagination that I aligned with the paradox of seeing and not seeing, of viewing film as if with one's eyes closed but keeping them open. When the camera rather than another spectator turns to the audience – as it has done variously in the work of Iñárritu, the Dardenne brothers, and especially Kiarostami in the examples discussed so far in this chapter – it also looks the wrong way, albeit from a different vantage point from Barthes's turn to other audience members. While there is still a very real possibility of fetishising what is shown on screen as a result – in Kiarostami's case, the faces of women – the imagination that is engaged in the process of perceiving disrupts the fetishism of the gaze, replacing such deceptive dual vision ('I know very well but all the same . . .') with the other kind that has been unfolding chapter by chapter in my study and which is less constraining and more emancipating for women in particular here. This is exemplified in an especially sensuous scene from *Shirin*.

Shirin arrives at a spring after a gruelling horse ride. She has been craving this moment of respite and explains so prior to finding this place of brief repose. Once she has descended from her horse – her feet are heard stepping down onto a gravelly surface – her breathing is heavy and her clothing is loosened before falling to the ground. After her immersion in the water, sounds of her splashing around in it reveal her enjoyment, her sighs ones of relief and release. She asks that the water embrace and caress her, holding her like a lover. All the while during this sequence, the faces of the women in the audience are relaxed and smile faintly; they seem to take gentle pleasure in her bathing. The sound of her horse neighing, followed by the contact of her feet on gravel, her breath, and then the muffled thud of material falling to the ground generates the surface contact necessary for the formation of mental images of this scene on a vertical axis – she climbs off the horse (feet/gravel), her clothing sinks to the ground (clothes/ground) – and her plunge into the water completes this journey of mental images of verticality from horse, to ground, to water. The splashing around and talk of being embraced by water creates an image of envelopment, which the continuity of reaction among her sisters in the auditorium space helps to keep afloat without breaking, supporting her buoyancy through their response, and enabling *Shirin*'s spectators to flesh out a body that derives great enjoyment from the freedom of movement through a watery expanse. The mental image of the expanse of the water and duration of her pleasure lasts until a different sound erupts, suggesting the presence of surrounding vegetation that has hitherto protected her modesty but that now also indicates a breach of privacy. The sound of the snap and crunch of twigs and branches and the faint sound of breathing breaks this momentary idyll, suggesting the proximity of someone else, someone watching her whom she suspects to be Khosrow. Although the onlooker is thereby aligned with a voyeuristic male, the continuing concentration on women spectators in the auditorium space challenges conventional gender dynamics of the gaze. A woman spectator's face registers concern, her inquisitive look and slight frown querying this interruption in a way that matches Shirin's question as to who is spying on her. The pleasure of imagining images of Shirin taking pleasure prior to the intrusion is formed in conjunction with the gaze of women who look unabashedly towards *Shirin*'s spectators, sealing an intimate female circle in this very public onscreen space. As Sara Saljoughi notes, there is a challenge to Iranian modesty laws in this film, which also conjures the very possibility of active looking on the part of women that a focus on the male gaze has long occluded.[3] From its culturally specific vantage point, this film engages critically with the history of that gaze in cinema.

In a western context, the 'to-be-looked-at-ness' that Laura Mulvey's work on classical Hollywood cinema brought to the fore when analysing women on screen posited both voyeurism and fetishism as aspects of a dominant male gaze from which women viewers were excluded and with which they needed to cross identify. Mulvey's theory of fetishistic scopophilia is informed by the Freudian account of fetishism, which has at its root that aforementioned deceptive duality of seeing and refusing to accept what is seen, and putting something else in its place. In her later work, and pertinent to the dynamics of *Shirin* exemplified particularly in this bathing scene, Mulvey counters the fetishistic gaze with one that is curious and that is aligned with an active woman's gaze. She rereads the myth of Pandora in order to articulate a feminist theory that will imagine what is in her infamous box rather than looking in and unleashing its evil contents. The eye and the mind's eye join forces here (the subtitle of the book in which she explores Pandora's myth, *Fetishism and Curiosity*, is *Cinema and the Mind's Eye*), bridging the separation of interior and exterior worlds to create a different relation to space and signification. Mulvey writes: 'I visualise (in my mind's eye) the fetishised body falling apart once it has been reconfigured, out of a spatial pattern of inside/outside, the masquerade/the abject, into an enigma or a pattern that can be decoded' (Mulvey [1996] 2013: viii). Mulvey's filmic examples that serve her theorisation of these workings of the mind's eye emerge again from classical Hollywood narrative cinema, ranging from Pandora's latter-day sisters of film noir, the *femmes fatales*, for whom she serves as archetype, through to Hitchcock's heroines who investigate the uncanny houses of his films. Mulvey writes on Kiarostami, however, in a later text. Observing that it is when he releases *Ten* (2002) that his cinema begins to turn more directly to women, she writes at length on his earlier work, commenting astutely on the blurring of imagination and reality in what she terms his cinema of uncertainty and delay (Mulvey 2006: 142). In *10 on Ten* (2004), Kiarostami talks through his filming strategies for *Ten* and other works made prior to *Shirin*, imparting a series of lessons on filmmaking. In these lessons, he underlines the importance of what goes on in the viewer's mind when watching films of the kind he makes and that he contrasts with those of Hollywood. He cites Bresson, who speaks of creating films through subtraction, in order to emphasise the role of the viewer's imagination. Kiarostami further declares: 'the combination of the filmmaker's and viewer's mind creates a film which will be more durable, original and fruitful than a film which merely aims at telling a story and impressing the viewer'. And, when speaking about the use of sound, he notes that 'if used well, sound can create an image in the viewer's mind'. Mulvey's sense of 'seeing with the mind', as outlined in *Fetishism and Curiosity*, is a critical and political way of seeing differently, prescient albeit in different terms of the more fully fleshed out and conscious kind of mental image-making that I have been arguing *Shirin* stimulates, and chiming with Kiarostami's own lessons on the importance of engaging the listener-spectator's creative imagination.

The supplement of imagining that is formative of *Shirin* has a feminist impetus that is dependent upon viewing the intrigued reactions of the women to the film-within-the-film openly in the cinema auditorium space. The prompting of imagined images by words and sound in addition to the relation to the onscreen image is always to some extent associated with this active female gaze in this film. The imagined images that take shape here, born from a context of female spectatorship in Iran, are part of a vision of change that depends upon the equal importance of both perceptual and imaginative activity. Jonathan Rosenbaum notes that to fully experience the paradox of being overpowered intimately in a public cinema as these onscreen spectators are, one needs to see *Shirin* in a theatre space with other spectators, acknowledging, however, that most will see it on DVD at home (in Saeed-Vafa and Rosenbaum [2003] 2018: 146).[4] The dual vision of *Shirin*, wherever it is experienced, is driven nonetheless by what the women watch in the auditorium space and what spectators imagine in their own space of viewing them; it bridges the visible and invisible realms and is as dependent on the mind's eye as it is on the eye.

The stimulation of the mind's eye in the supplementary activity of imagining is what I now want to extend in the direction of a contrasting series of examples, since it is not a function of Kiarostami's aesthetic in this film alone. The instances of supplementing the onscreen image that I shall go on to explore engage dual vision through a sense of tactile contact with something or someone that is not seen. We leave the representation of the auditorium space behind us from this point onwards; the filmic images that we are about to explore are lacunary and call upon tactility, in addition to what is heard, to form a visual mental image based on what is still intimated on the screen without being shown. As in *Shirin*, a literary text serves as source material for the narratives of the films that follow, and the imprint of emotion on the women's faces is exchanged for a different kind of onscreen impression.

## Imprinting, or Beginning Again with a Different Horse

In gloomy black-and-white shots, alternating with images of the sky and the earth, along with a close-up of the beady eye of a black crow, the shapes of a horse's hooves form in thick, squelchy mud, one at a time, leaving impressions that fill slowly with water. Whereas a horse was heard frequently in *Shirin*, now a horse's imprints are seen, but still without sight of the animal making them. The horseshoe imprints seem to grow from the sodden soil and be generated by it rather than imposing themselves from above. A regular clip-clopping is heard along with orchestral music in a minor key and a male voice-over that recounts in the first person a lonely horseback journey on a dull autumnal day. The rhythm of the final imprints corresponds to three horseshoe marks that overlay one another, leaving a darkened hole in the muddy ground. The invisibility of the animal making its mark and the man riding it not only instils a supernatural air, it also foregrounds the living substance of the natural world, revealing the trace it retains of animate contact that is not normally seen in the process of its making, and becoming both bearer and catalyst of a sentient filmic imagination.

Jan Švankmajer's *Zánik domu Usherů/The Fall of the House of Usher* (1980) opens thus, and is the first of two of his films of the 1980s to be discussed here that draw upon Edgar Allan Poe's writings. In Poe's short story – a frequent source of inspiration for filmmakers – a childhood friend of Usher makes a visit to his house upon receiving a letter that worries him. Usher is unwell and his troubled mental state is exacerbated by the illness of his sister Madeline, who roams around the house as an almost ghostly presence from the outset. When she dies and they bury her, the noises and strange occurrences that pervade the house, along with the persistently stormy weather, foretell the chilling revelation that they have buried her alive within the tomb. She breaks out only to die in front of them, and Usher perishes too, along with his house. Švankmajer's film follows the trajectory of the original narrative but the human protagonists are nowhere to be seen. It is the power of the missing visual, representational images of the human subjects in particular that ignites the imagination in the sense that I have been outlining in this chapter. The arrival of Usher's friend, the narrator, on horseback at the start sets the tone for the short film that ensues: the main protagonists are conspicuous in their absence, but they do in fact have a presence and weight, and leave their mark – they are just invisible to the eye. A condensed version of Poe's tale is recounted in the brisk male voice-over (provided by Petr Čepek), speaking of his experience as the visitor to Usher's house does in the literary text. The camera positioning is not always subjective, though, opening out to other perspectives, most evocative of that of Usher himself, as well as Madeline at one late point, all the while hinting too that it may be the objects and the house itself to which some of these viewpoints belong. The mental visual appearance of the absent human characters is created on the basis of descriptions from the voice-over narrative. But the formation of mental images also contends with the impression the people are said and seen to make on the material objects in the house and the natural world that surrounds it, which bear the trace of what happens to the people and convey this. The supplement of the imagined image is again, then, that without which the perceived image would not look or feel the way that it does, but Švankmajer adds to sound and vision in order to stimulate the imagination further. The narrator's spoken words imprint the emotions, feelings, and atmosphere that they bring forth into and onto the inanimate world, which is animated as a result from the very beginning. The epigraph that Poe uses in his tale from Pierre-Jean de Béranger, and that Švankmajer also cites at the beginning of the film, compares the human heart's sensitivity to a lute that resonates as soon as it is touched. Such touch is crucial to the formation of what Švankmajer himself terms 'inner Vision' (Švankmajer [1983] 2014: 81).

During an earlier period when Švankmajer was not making films because of restrictive censorship under the oppressive regime in Czechoslovakia, he was engaged in research into tactilism. The fruits of his experimentation appear in *Touching and Imagining*, five copies of which were originally published with tactile covers in 1983 as *samizdat* (self-published clandestine dissident literature) under the title *Hmat a Imaginace*. His experiments show how a tactile object arouses visual mental images and associated emotions, as he explains:

> As we touch even the most banal but invisible object, and visualize it with our inner Vision, it takes on a fantastic form which we instantly invest not only with elements common to all similar objects (if it wasn't so, we wouldn't be able to identify the object), but also a whole number of subjective associations, permanently or temporarily dependent. For instance, the same shoe will have a different effect on every perceiver that touches it and in a much larger measure than if it was pictured. (Švankmajer [1983] 2014: 81)

The emancipating imaginative effects of not seeing a picture of a shoe and touching the shoe instead are what Švankmajer carries forwards to his filmmaking in subsequent years, reintroducing sight and removing literal touch, but encouraging the same expansive activity of visualisation that emerged in the tactile experiments. The authorities' stipulated condition for allowing Švankmajer to return to filmmaking from the eighties onwards was that he worked from literary subjects rather than his own topics. His choice of Poe's and also Auguste de Villiers de L'Isle-Adam's short stories for some of his initial filmic inspiration after the censorship ban was lifted is guided by the presence of a strong tactile imagination in the writing itself, especially that of Poe, with which he feels a kinship in his own work. His early films had already grappled with the materiality of objects, animating them and showing surfaces in close-up. His later films pursue the interest in tactility and film further, deepening the relationship to the imagination. As Marina Warner notes, Švankmajer – who trained in Prague's famous puppet theatre and whose films variously combine live action with stop-frame animation, puppetry, and drawing, among other techniques – proved himself the natural heir to both Hieronymus Bosch's phantasmagoria and the darkness of Franz Kafka's fabulism (Warner 2007). His at times nightmarish and always disturbing visions are critiques of power, which are absolutely dependent on inner vision to have their effect.

One of the perspectives that I highlighted at the outset of this study as key to how filmmakers recognise the possibility of spectators imagining in images was the paradox of seeing with one's eyes closed even though they are open when watching a film. I recalled this obliquely earlier in this chapter with reference to Barthes's position in the auditorium space, but it was Švankmajer who gave such a clear instruction to this effect through the words spoken by his eponymous Alice in the opening of his first feature-length film: 'You must . . . close your eyes, otherwise . . . you won't see anything.' For inner vision to have the quality of the images of dreams or nightmares but not to be eradicated by what is seen with the eyes, the conditions for his sense of closed-eye vision need to be created on screen. In *The Fall of the House of Usher* and *Kyvadlo, jáma a naděje/The Pendulum, the Pit and Hope* (1983), which I shall discuss presently, a first-person handheld camera serves as the viewer's eyes as well as those for the most part of the person who guides them – the narrator mainly in the first film, the main character in the second – but it is what it does not show and therefore what spectators cannot see that arouses the supplementary activity of imagining. The horse of the opening of *Usher* whose prints are seen in the mud (Figure 5.3) is not described in any detail by the voice-over of the narrator, but as the narrator advances and his tale progresses, there are moments where verbal description is so detailed and the imprint of the absent figures so apparent, that they encourage the kind of vivid inner vision that Švankmajer catalogued through his earlier experiments on tactilism. The figures of Usher and Madeline serve as good, if divergent, examples in this regard.

As the narrator arrives in Roderick Usher's house, the handheld camera moves along at human eye level, roaming around the dimly lit, shadowy spaces as he walks across the threshold, travels along corridors and then goes upstairs, opening door after door, to get to the room where there is a solitary, empty wooden chair (Figure 5.4). This is where he pauses to describe what he declares to be his old friend's unforgettable countenance, which has much altered:

> A cadaverousness of complexion, an eye large and luminous, a nose of a delicate Hebrew model but with unusual breadth of nostril, lips somewhat thin and very pallid but of a beautiful curve, a finely moulded chin, speaking, in its want of prominence, of a want of moral energy, hair of a more than web-like softness and tenuity.[5]

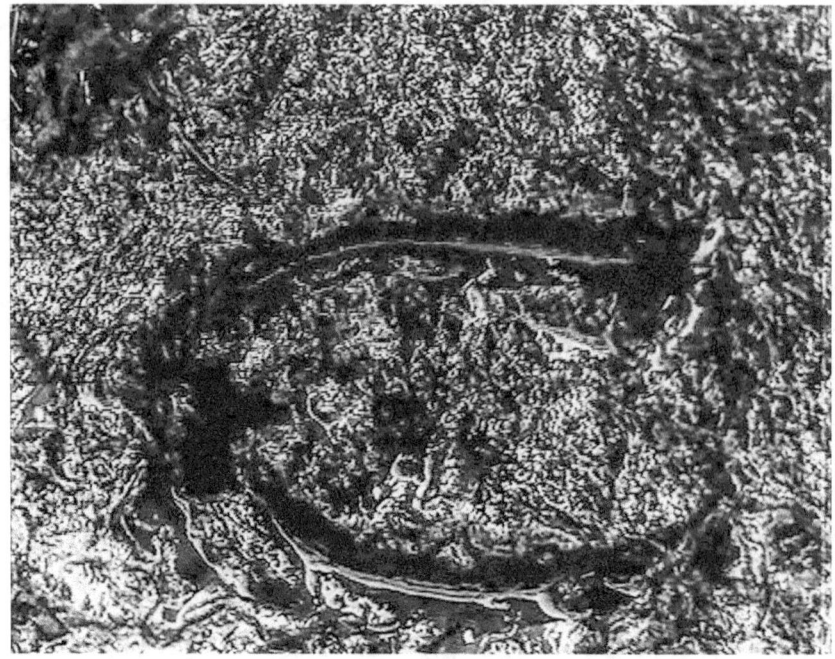

**Figure 5.3** *The Fall of the House of Usher* (Jan Švankmajer, 1980).

**Figure 5.4** *The Fall of the House of Usher* (Jan Švankmajer, 1980).

Throughout the description of Usher's at all times remarkable appearance, the camera films the nooks and crannies of the chair, showing the grain of the material, and calling tacitly for the viewer to imagine the described appearance on the basis of the contours and shine of the wood as it catches the light occasionally and that seems to still bear his weight. The pallor of a cadaverous face is illuminated by the radiant ignition, to recall Scarry, of the description of the eye that instils life and fine movement into a physiognomy that otherwise approximates that of the dead. (This light is said to go out after his sister dies.) The curve of his lips is described as the camera films the detail of the carved curves of the chair, the materiality of what is viewed in close-up here lending solidity and motion to the mental image of lips held in a very slight unconscious smile. His hair, the rarity of which – it is 'more than web-like' – contrasts with the suggested solidity of the moulded chin and the carved curves of the chair, crowns a head poised between life and death. This surface contact between rare substance and solidity, gossamer against the relative firmness of cadaverous flesh, completes the mental image.

Poe's words are crucial to the formation of the imagined image of Usher here but the film confers a setting, in addition to showing his chair, which it scrutinises as if filming the memorable face the narrator describes. The material object bears the trace of the man who is present in spite of his absence, supplemented by the imagination that creates pictures beyond what is visible on screen. Usher materialises through an inner vision formed as much by getting close enough to the wood to be able to come into contact with it as it is through words. Throughout this sequence, the camera comes close enough to touch the surface of the chair and engage haptic visuality in Laura U. Marks's sense, yet surface-to-surface contact also occurs in the mind, as well as between screen and mind, to form the imagined images of embodied vision. Marks describes her desire in her own writings to maintain what she terms 'a robust flow between sensuous closeness and symbolic distance', between words that use symbolisation – a form of representation requiring distance – and the mimesis of haptic proximity (Marks 2002: xiii). Here it is words that direct the contact between surfaces that form the imagined images in conjunction with what is on screen. Spectators do not touch the chair and nor do they see Usher, but his imagined substance emerges from what the camera films and the voice-over describes. Viewers can not only sense and feel his presence as a result, as a reading of this scene in terms of haptic visuality might substantiate, but also see him with the mind's eye.[6]

Unlike the mental image of Usher furnished through the narration and its relation to the onscreen image, Madeline is never described. At the end of this sequence, her worsening illness is referred to and she is said to pass by in a remote part of the apartment without noticing the narrator, as the onscreen image shows a door closing, the handle moving slowly upwards, signalling that someone has left the room. The absence of any description other than her passing by without noticing her surroundings leaves only the faintest mental impression of her walking around in a kind of somnambulist state. The ease of picturing rare entities that we have witnessed in earlier chapters, which is akin to the haze of mental images that form indistinctly when undirected, comes to the fore here, as Madeline glides by, unseeing and almost ghost-like, although still living. When Usher informs the narrator abruptly one day of Madeline's death, the coffin is the only thing shown as it travels of its own accord into the tomb (just as at the end of the film, the furniture leaves the house independently and piece by piece, disappearing into the tarn by the side of the house). Her ethereal presence signalled only by her impact on material objects while alive (the handle of the door that closes) is now subsumed by the wooden coffin, which, in its animated journey, parallels her earlier imagined wanderings. The coffin's journey is accompanied by banging on the soundtrack, which conjures the action that is never shown of the firm nailing down of the lid, but she is no more absent when dead than she was present while alive. The mental image of Usher's countenance may be more vivid and substantial, but in its 'cadaverousness', he is just the fleshier counterpart of his sister's more ghostly state and both are poised between life and death until they are reunited. The climax of the film in which this reunion occurs takes us back to Usher's chair and his eventual end.

In an increasingly forbidding and tense atmosphere, throughout which a storm rages and nature comes uncannily to life – trees, leaves, and mud are animated and seem to pre-empt what Usher and the narrator do not yet know for sure – Usher's chair rotates to face the door of the room they are in. He has been listening to the narrator reading the tale of *The Mad Trist* by Sir Launcelot Canning, with which there are several eerie correspondences with what is going on around them. The description of one sound of a wooden door being broken down in *The Mad Trist*, for example, corresponds with images on screen of Madeline's wooden coffin breaking open, as the narrator believes he hears the sound the story describes. Imagination and perception blur into one another at such moments for the narrator himself, recalling the Perky experiment mentioned in an earlier chapter, in aural rather than visual terms. Viewers are asked to imagine the narrator hearing a sound that he dismisses as imagined on the basis of the tale he is reading, but which turns out to be real as shown through onscreen images that reinforce the relation between perceived and imagined occurrences. This relationship will become stronger as the scene progresses to the point that the final sound described in the tale of *The Mad Trist* that the narrator is reading aloud, akin to that of a shield of brass falling heavily upon a floor of silver, is heard on the soundtrack as a panel in the house falls to the ground on screen. The story-within-the-story heightens the effect of the imagination on what the narrator and spectator perceive, and the sense of foreboding registers subsequently in Usher's declining mental and bodily state.

With the carved detail of Usher's chair viewed in close-up once again, and a sound of creaking on the soundtrack, the chair is said to begin to rock slowly from side to side as the camera mimes this action. The narrator describes vividly his partial view of Usher's features: 'his lips trembled as if he were murmuring inaudibly' and 'his head had dropped against his breast', but he knew that Usher was not asleep from the 'wide and rigid opening of the eye'. After cutting between shots of the room and layers of material peeling away erratically from different walls and surfaces, the film then draws close to the back of the chair, as the narrator describes how Usher had become rigid, 'his eyes bent fixedly before him'. The handheld camera's subjective eye approaches the house, as Usher is said to mumble with a sickly smile the realisation that they have put Madeline living in the tomb. The handheld mobile shots eventually reach the door of the room they are in, the door opens and the camera zooms in to reveal only the blank whiteness of the wall outside, with a sound signalling Madeline's anticipated return, as a dark, liquid stain then appears on a blank background. This abstract stain carries the full weight of horror of the story at this point, becoming what Švankmajer terms elsewhere 'a messenger of analogical poetic emotion' (Švankmajer [1983] 2014: 169). Madeline is said to tremble and reel from side to side on the threshold before falling heavily inwards with a low moaning cry onto the person of her brother. On screen, Usher's chair falls backwards, breaks apart, and is covered over with debris, becoming an indistinct pile. The imagined figure of Madeline acquires weight at the point of her death, not only through the tumbling description of her 'falling heavily inwards' and her cry, but also through the backwards fall of the chair seen on screen that now fails to bear her weight and that of Usher. What is absent from the screen is present in the mind but the conditions for the emergence of the mental image are part of the onscreen image. The chair's disintegration does not just accompany the imagined end of both brother and sister but bears the weight of an imagined image of their demise that spectators furnish in supplementary fashion.

When I spoke of Madeline's faint appearance when she is referred to as passing through one of the opening scenes in the film, I suggested that it was because she was not described nor her passing featured in any detail, that the mental impression of her was ghost-like. I have noted several times throughout this book, in keeping with Scarry's observations about the power of the verbal arts to prompt the creation of more vivid images, that the unguided imagination does not receive the direction necessary to form such detailed images. We have seen, however, that when verbal instruction is non-existent, sound sometimes performs a similar function through its volumising capacity to create space and conjure images within it, both in the previous chapter and earlier in this chapter with reference to *Shirin*. In the second of Švankmajer's films to be based on a short story by Poe but this time combined with one by Villiers, *The Pendulum, the Pit and Hope*, image and sound are not supported by any words, save the citations that bookend the film. The epigraph comes from Poe's story *The Pit and the Pendulum* (1842):

> The sentence – the dread sentence of death – was the last of distinct accentuation which reached my ears. After that, the sound of the inquisitorial voices seemed merged in one dreamy indeterminate hum. It conveyed to my soul the idea of revolution, perhaps from its association in fancy with the burr of a mill wheel.

The lines that appear on the screen at the end of the film come from Villiers's *Torture by Hope* (1893) (which itself features an epigraph from Poe's story) and extend the torture of Poe's text into an interminable, cyclical horror with no hope of escape: 'What! my child! on the eve, perhaps, of salvation . . . you would then leave us?' Poe's *The Pit and the Pendulum* relates to the time of the Spanish Inquisition and the same context is inferred in Švankmajer's film, but the Czech authorities clearly read it as a criticism of the regime in the present and banned it.[7] Rather than words prompting the formation of the supplement of imagination the conditions of which form part of the onscreen image, now it is the partial nature of what is shown and what the sounds alone conjure that provide the grim ingredients for immersion in this gothic nightmare that evolves between mind and screen.

The only face that appears in this film belongs to one of the hooded torturers at the start as he blows out a candle in the underground darkness of the dungeon. With sunken, barely visible eyes and high cheekbones that hollow out the face below, his pale, shadowy aspect is visible as if a death's head who is also letting spectators and the main protagonist know silently with the snuffing out of light that sight is not necessary to be able to imagine what he as one of the agents of torture can do. Nevertheless, the audio-visual capacities of film will be exploited to the full here and sight will arouse tactile imagination in both the most ordinary and extreme ways, as what Švankmajer terms inner vision again comes into play. Unlike the conditions for some of his tactile experiments that involve being blindfolded, this film's set-up, like that of *The Fall of the House of Usher*, keeps the eyes open as this inner vision is activated, such that audio-visual perception and imagination are concurrent. The imagination goes further than the audio-visual images perceived, generating horrors that are not shown, just as it permitted the picturing of Usher and other figures in the preceding film. Švankmajer speaks of tactilism as a central character in this film (Švankmajer [1983] 2014: 169–70): the protagonist's hands and feet map out the space of this dark environment. The sight of rough walls and ceilings at the start, illuminated only by the vacillating torch flame carried by one of the hooded figures ahead, along with the sound and partial sight of the protagonist shuffling along, convey visceral contact with the material surface of the space the camera moves through that is heightened the more the film progresses. The man, who appears to black out and then awakens tied to a table in one of the dungeon chambers, gradually takes stock of his surroundings, the camera's whip-pans suggesting his eye movements that dart around from one area of the torture chamber to the next, building up a fragmented onscreen picture. His torso, limbs, feet, and hands are shown from his perspective, reaching and grasping continually towards survival, and his breath is audible intermittently throughout, along with sounds of torture equipment working inexorably. The hope added to the title of the film is illusory, as in Villiers's short story, since the protagonist seems to escape the torture only to find himself trapped again by one of his captors, just moments after glimpsing possible freedom above ground.

No onscreen images are given of what happens to those struck by the pendulum, but there is a rat that is sliced open before the pendulum becomes embedded in the wooden bench from which the protagonist eventually detaches himself. The sounds and onscreen images suffice to prompt imagining of a suppositional kind of what could have happened to his body had he not broken free from his binds. The slice through the rat's body that spectators do see conjures an imagined slice through his own body that he extricates from the contraption just seconds before it is too late. The regular swing of the pendulum that is heard and seen is easily pictured slicing through the body that it narrowly misses, an imagined mimesis of the slicing of the rat and final embedding in the wood. When the man reaches the next chamber of horrors, the Bosch-like clanking wall with fire behind it, designed by Eva Švankmajerová, Surrealist artist and wife of Švankmajer, that inches towards him with knife tongues, one of which stabs him in the hand, pushes him gradually towards a pit, the bottomless darkness of which he also narrowly escapes. Moving models of bodies and body fragments creak as the machinery cranks forwards,

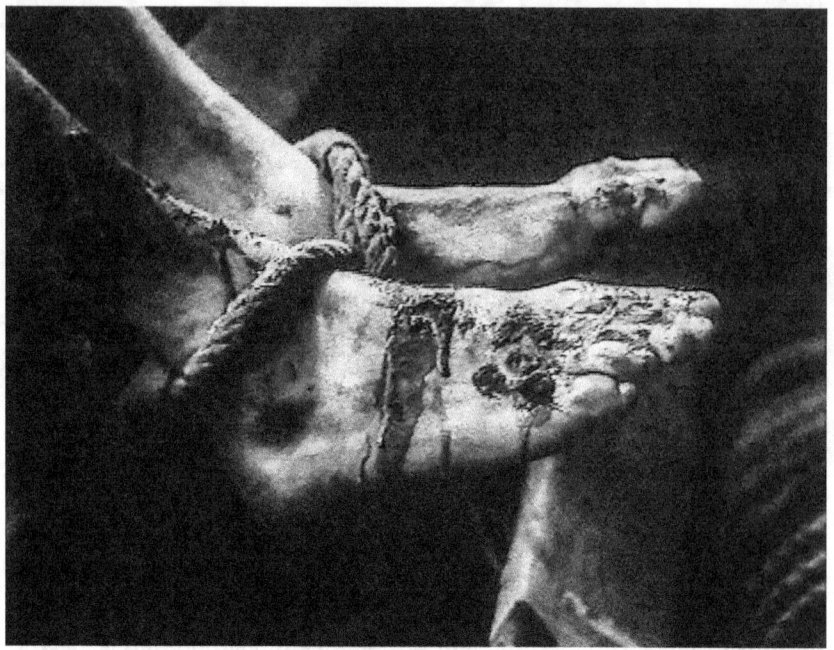

Figure 5.5 *The Pendulum, the Pit and Hope* (Jan Švankmajer, 1983).

pre-empting the painful dismemberment he could undergo if trapped by the torture wall or forced into the pit. As the man creeps down the underground corridor looking for a way out, he sees his hooded captors carry equipment into another chamber, and as he gets level with the room he sees the shackled feet of another prisoner (Figure 5.5). One of the captors reaches down to a lever near the man's feet and obscures the view in the process. Excruciating cries of pain result from the torture practice that is not shown beyond the captor bending forwards to operate the lever, but that prompts the imagination of torture to the extension of the body that is not shown on screen, while also causing the protagonist now to hurry along the corridor. As the man whose eyes viewers are seeing through and whose breathlessness they hear as if it were their own makes it out into the open air, the image of dread of the sandaled feet of one of his cloaked captors is exacerbated as the camera tilts up his body to show only darkness in the hood with no identifiable face. Over the closing credits, the same sound of machinery turning and creaking is heard as for the opening credits, giving a purely circular sense to the revolution referred to in the Poe epigraph – of never-ending torture rather than its overthrow. The sunken face visible for a moment at the start has now been removed entirely. Drawn definitively towards the increasingly unbounded horror of inner vision, torture after torture and stage after stage, the onscreen visual image now disappears and all that remains, besides the continuing sound of the torture equipment, is blackness.

The darkness that has been intermittent throughout the man's journey in this underground place is the corollary of the partial view that spectators have of the space he is in and the tortures undergone there, which are imagined rather than seen in spite of the clarity of the equipment shown on screen. From pendulum slice, through dismembering machine, to the torture of someone else, the man who guides the spectatorial gaze through these chambers of doom also witnesses sounds and images that ignite further mental images in the shadowy darkness of the imagination as he feels his way painfully through an interminable cycle. Spectators do not complete these images; rather, they layer them with what is simultaneously imagined, the conditions for which are laid bare on screen to be supplemented.

## Coda

The examples that I have discussed in this chapter involve seeing the impression that something absent from the screen makes on the onscreen image, from richly expressive faces, through imprints on the material world of objects and substances, to the slicing open of a rat and the semi-obscured torture of a man. The socio-cultural and historical conditions for the creation of the main films that I have focused on here could not be more contrasting: there is a world of difference between twenty-first-century Iran and Czechoslovakia of the early 1980s. And yet, the principles of the prompting of the imagination in supplementary fashion abide across this gulf. There is consistency to the ways in which mental imagery is prompted, the imagination stimulated, to supplement what is on screen, which does not erase the specificity of the films in question but which forges a link between them while recognising these differences. As in the previous chapter, the processes discussed here can be related to other films. In the context of the process that is the focal point of this chapter, there are more insubstantial possibilities that exist for supplementing the image than I have explored here but which invoke similar mental activities. In *Dogville* (2003), for example, Lars von Trier works with a pared down stage set, narration, and sound, as he does in the sequel *Manderlay* (2005) too, to create an imagined material setting around his characters out of thin air.

In *Dogville*, Tom (Paul Bettany) knocks on the door of the Mission House where there is no door to be seen: the sound of knocking is heard and Tom and Martha (Siobhan Fallon Hogan), who looks after the chapel, behave as if there were a door there. The possibility of spectators imagining the presence of the absent door is facilitated in part by the presence of a single wood panel adjacent to the door. While the knocking makes no contact with the wood that is there, the imagined image borrows from the materiality of the wooden slats that are visible to construct a door on the basis of the sound of knocking that is heard and believed in by the characters within the fiction. Similarly, when Ma Ginger (Lauren Bacall) rakes the earth, she holds a hoe and viewers hear the sound of earth being raked, but the hoe is raking through the air above the floor of the stage set. There is a skeletal tree sketched out on the backdrop of the scenery that will gain blossom later in the film but that here contributes to the possibility of picturing the soil from which something, even this solitary tree, might grow. The door and the earth materialise through the sounds that are heard in addition to seeing the actions the characters perform on screen, along with the presence of the wood panel and the skeletal tree, guided by the voice of the narrator (John Hurt). The impression of the imagination is not seen on screen in the same way that we have observed in the filmic examples discussed in this chapter – it does not take material, visible form (on faces, in the visibility of sodden soil, on tortured bodies) – but the air of the setting bears the weight of wood and soil through the sounds, actions, and partial materiality that can generate the image of a door and the raked earth. The actions of hands, knocking on a door and holding a tool that rakes, hark back to the 'hands-on' instruction of which Scarry speaks in relation to the verbal arts referred to in this and the previous chapter but transfers now to what is seen on screen, and it is the sounds that aid the formation of an occasional yet strong image of materiality around the characters who act as if already immersed in what is being imagined. The predefined space of the stage set thereby acquires contours in the mind in conjunction with what is seen, and the supplement of what is imagined is built invisibly into the onscreen image.

The supplementary activity of imagining across all of the examples discussed in this chapter is bound inextricably to perception. The mental visual images formed by spectators who visualise will necessarily differ, but as and when they do form, their conditions of possibility both enable and are pre-empted by the images on screen without ever appearing there. Whether imprinted materially or aurally, the presence of an absence that prompts the creation of a mental image that supplements what is on screen is an integral part of how film stimulates the imagination. The next chapter will explore how viewers are encouraged to act upon the onscreen image and imagine something different from what is seen, not just layering but actively reshaping the perceived image.

CHAPTER 6

# Reshaping

The processes involved in the formation of mental images on the part of spectators that I have been outlining across the previous chapters depend to a great extent on an ability to concentrate on what is heard and seen, even when the screen is blank. The process of reshaping that I consider in this chapter is no exception but it also relates more explicitly now, paradoxical as this may sound, to the workings of a wandering mind: in the first case it involves revisiting the meandering associated with the imagined protagonist of a film discussed in an earlier chapter, and in the second it relates to the straying mental activities of spectators before these are guided in the service of attending to and modifying what is seen. I noted in the opening chapter of this study the link that neuroscientists have made between the default mode network and mind wandering, as well as daydreaming. The kind of imagining that I have been interested in throughout, however, is a more hybrid activity, since it appears to partake of distraction – spectators are not glued exclusively to the perception of what is on screen – but is not the free-floating wandering that takes over when the mind has no external tasks to engage in, since there is guidance given on what is to be imagined in addition to a screen on which to focus. Attention comes and goes when watching any film, but there are films in which the mind drifts considerably and in some cases this is precisely the point.

Attention and distraction have been embedded in discussion of film from its moment of inception, and I mention key accounts in passing here in order to mark out the distinctiveness of my own interest in them with regard to imagining. Early film theorist Hugo Münsterberg placed the act of attention at the heart of film's means of conforming to the inner workings of the mind, setting up a synergy between mental activity and the form of film, arguing famously that the close-up played a major role in cancelling out the surrounding world to this end (Münsterberg [1916] 2006). The contrasting notion of reception in a state of distraction (*Zerstreuung*) studied by Weimar film theorist Walter Benjamin in the

1930s defines perception by experiences of fragmentation and shock (Benjamin [1936] 1992). For Siegfried Kracauer, working in the same context and valorising Soviet montage cinema as Benjamin did, the revolutionary aspect of film lay in the untapped potential in the Weimar picture palaces to aim at a kind of distraction that reveals rather than masks the subjective disintegration characteristic of modernity (Kracauer [1926] 1995). Far closer to the present, and writing on the material and psychical conditions of attentiveness at the cinema in more general terms, Steven Shaviro notes:

> The unstable screen image holds my distracted attention captive, I do not have the ability to look away. There is no way to watch a film without allowing this to happen; I can resist it only by giving up on the film altogether, by shutting my eyes or walking out. But as I watch, I have no presence of mind: sight and hearing, anticipation and memory, are no longer my own. (Shaviro [1993] 2011: 48–9)

My own discussion of attention and distraction in what follows differs from these accounts in its interweaving of both states, and involves retaining rather than losing what Shaviro terms 'presence of mind'. There is a liberating potential to the switching of attention that will be unravelled in this chapter, which values the activity associated with both a wandering gaze and mind but which does not forsake attentiveness. It is in this emancipating move through the mental activities of being both attentive and distracted that a further formative process of image-making emerges that is distinct from those considered thus far.

## Mental Landscaping

It takes a wanderer sometimes to show us what lies off beaten tracks, and we have already met one such exemplary figure in an earlier chapter. Patrick Keiller's Robinson was last visualised recounting a dream to the narrator of *London*, and I return to him first on an earlier leg of his journeying through the city in the 1990s, since his psychogeographical practice of drifting introduces the mental process of reshaping which the film's spectators are invited to partake in along the way. Early on in *London*, 'The Romantic' appears as an inter-title before Robinson's understanding of Romanticism and a Romantic life is described over an unanticipated shot of a McDonald's restaurant. The combination of inter-title, voice-over, and image displaces the historical foundations of the nineteenth-century movement to the new urban landscape around him but features this thus as part of his rather ironic latter-day *flâneurie*, as distanced from as it is deferential to the possibilities of obtaining information from his surroundings using the technique of walking and observing. On the basis of a citation from Baudelaire, the poet of modernity, read out by the narrator, Romanticism is situated in a mode of feeling; for Robinson, the essence of a Romantic life is said to be to get outside oneself and to see oneself from the outside, as if in a Romance. At this point, the image cuts to a landscape around a canal where it is reported that Robinson was searching for the location of a memory. Two shots comprise this sequence devoted to what is no longer physically there but that he remembers clearly: the first accompanies the narrator describing 'a vivid recollection of a street of small factories backing onto a canal'. He adds: 'But they no longer exist.' Wasteland showing a path to the left and a low-level bridge in the distance to the right denoting the canal furnishes the ground and substance on which to picture the absent factories (Figure 6.1). The mental image borrows from the brickwork visible in the distant constructions as it rebuilds the factories on the grass, backing onto the canal. The film then cuts to a shot from one side of the canal showing grassy banks on the opposite side and low-level buildings in front of high-rise tower blocks on the horizon, as the narrator describes Robinson using the landscape as a site for exercises in 'psychic landscaping, drifting and free association' (Figure 6.2).

Figure 6.1 *London* (Patrick Keiller, 1994).

**Figure 6.2** *London* (Patrick Keiller, 1994).

The first shot lasts for ten seconds, the subsequent shot for a few seconds longer than that, and the possibility of transforming the landscape with what has been spoken about is proffered to the spectator through these two onscreen images. The landscape does not show the visible imprint of the supplementary activity of imagining as it did in my examples in the previous chapter, ranging across faces and places, objects and rarefied air: here it has had something erased without a trace and the task of imagining is associated with that of rebuilding, thanks to Robinson's memory, described by the narrator over the landscape that viewers do see. Such mental activity on the part of spectators works in keeping with the layering described in detail the first time that we came across Robinson on his travels, outlined fully in my earlier chapter, but now it is about transforming what is perceived, rather than just superposing an image onto it, having an effect on the landscape that is present and altering it on the basis of information from Robinson's memory of how things used to be. Imagining here is a matter of time travel and reconnecting with a lost history; this changes the way in which the past relates to the present by modifying the perceived image mentally and reshaping its landscape in the process. This requires focus but is such an integral part of Robinson's meandering journey that it operates and oscillates between modes of attention and distracted looking – and wandering – away.

While the image-making capacity of imagining on the part of spectators seems ostensibly just to put something back that was lost here, this is not a simple play of nostalgia and reinvention but has serious political intent. For both Robinson and the spectator, there is no mere passive absorption within a landscape but the performance of an active, accretive mental process in relation to what is seen that adds to it and changes it in the present on the basis of past information, without regression. It is this comparative and additive gesture, moving between perception and imagination, that registers losses, that compensates for them partially, and that reflects on the meanings of the landscape of the present which adds a political awareness to looking, listening, and imagining. The role of the imagination is fundamental for Robinson in showing how landscape registers politics and in encouraging a form of rebuilding the very bridges between reality and imagination that neoliberal political decisions taken in the late twentieth and early twenty-first century have destroyed.

Imagining in images contributes to a change in the way things are seen, then, which forms the very basis of the transformations necessary in everyday life and their reshaping in more than just the mental space. In *Robinson in Ruins*, the narrator refers indeed to what he terms Fredric Jameson's anticipation of the crisis – a description which could also sum up the trajectory of Keiller's previous films, which lead up to the 2008 financial crash on the world stage and its aftermath. Over a close-up image of the slit of a red letterbox she reads: 'It seems to be easier for us today to imagine the thoroughgoing deterioration of the earth and of nature than the breakdown of late capitalism; perhaps that is due to some weakness in our imaginations' (Jameson 1994: xii). *Robinson in Ruins* registers the importance of thinking about the relationship between the fate of the earth and late capitalism, and the weakness of the imagination that Jameson laments is something that this film, like those before it, counters explicitly by valorising its potential as well as its actions. Nature, without being idealised, has cooperative systems pointed out here and there, which offer possibilities for reimagining human relationships through and around it. In Keiller's fascination with landscape, as Mark Fisher points out in his review of *Robinson in Ruins*, the filmmaker echoes concerns found in Jean-Marie Straub and Danièle Huillet's work, which returns frequently to landscapes of antagonism and martyrdom (Fisher 2010). Straub and Huillet also focus on more peaceable spaces but still with the intent of exploring change. They proffer an experience of attentive looking and distraction that contributes further facets to the kind of reshaping that Robinson has allowed us to witness on his own meandering journeys.

## Dissolving Vision: Cézanne, Straub, and Huillet

If you have ever stared at something so hard and for so long that it begins to vacillate before your eyes, you will already be receptive to one of the ways in which Straub and Huillet encourage spectators to look at the screen at times in *Cézanne* (1989). Moreover, to start to picture something other than what is on screen in this film is bound as closely to attention as it is to distraction. In order to contextualise such moments that permit us to add other examples to the initial understanding of reshaping that Robinson has just introduced, we need first to embed their approach to Cézanne and his work in a broader history of attentive looking and move gradually towards the landscape that first the painter, then the filmmakers, and then spectators engage with in transformative terms. To recall Merleau-Ponty's remarks in 'Eye and Mind', imagining 'borrows from vision and employs means we owe to it' (Merleau-Ponty [1960] 1993b: 146). Cézanne was a key point of reference from the philosopher's early investigations of perception onwards, and he writes at length on the painter in 'Cézanne's Doubt'. Merleau-Ponty observes: 'Motivating all the movements from which a picture gradually emerges there can be only one thing: the landscape in its totality and in its absolute fullness, precisely what Cézanne called a "motif"' (Merleau-Ponty [1945] 1993a: 67). Nothing appears to be missing from such vision, but the act of attending to the ostensible plenitude of the resultant landscape brings the eye into contact with more than can be seen, and it is precisely this that will lead to the modification of what is perceived.

As part of a landmark study of perception and attention that concentrates on late nineteenth-century Impressionist and Post-Impressionist painting, Jonathan Crary argues that what Édouard Manet was aware of without studiously putting into practice became an integral part of Cézanne's work: 'the creative discovery that looking at one thing intently did *not* lead to a fuller and more inclusive grasp of its presence, its rich immediacy' (Crary [1999] 2001: 288). The dissolution inherent in attentiveness that Crary describes when writing about Cézanne's late paintings crosses over into what he terms 'a more intensive re-creation of a subjective interface with the world' (ibid.: 297). Crary locates the painter's work in the interregnum between the uprooting of vision from the classical order of knowledge of the seventeenth and eighteenth centuries and the regimes of machine vision of the twentieth century (ibid.: 358). As one of the machine visions that were to develop during the twentieth century, cinema is recognised in Crary's discussion, as is the creation of two major possibilities: an 'affirmative model of automatic behavior' (which he draws from Cézanne's own vision of himself) is contrasted with 'the passive automatism' in which, in terms that concur with Deleuze, the subject becomes dispossessed of their own thought (ibid.: 358). The latter is associated more by Crary with the management of attention rather than a capacity for freedom and creation, and connects with the far wider administering of attention within the society of the spectacle to which Cézanne offers an earlier, notable contrast (ibid.: 359). The society of the spectacle refers to the development of modern society in which social life has been replaced by representation and the social relation is mediated by images; Guy Debord will later critique this society in text and film, and we will return to this in the following chapter. When Straub and Huillet make *Cézanne* and their subsequent film on the painter, *Une visite au Louvre/A Visit to the Louvre* (2003), they do so in the first instance on the basis of a commission, but as filmmakers who had long admired his painting and who frequently quoted his words.[1] They evidently recognise something in his painting that is compatible with their own lifelong challenge to spectacular culture, albeit at their later historical juncture. To look intently, for both Cézanne and Straub–Huillet, is to push vision to the point of collapse but to observe something else happening in the embodied mind in the process.

The central subject that will soon loom large in my discussion and prompt the gradual re-emergence of the mental images of reshaping that concern me in this chapter appears after two slow opening panning shots at the beginning of the film: Mont Sainte-Victoire is introduced subtly, in the distance, across an intervening townscape that marks a separation from the era when Cézanne painted it, with traffic sounds audible all the while. The film takes some time to get back to the mountain, lingering first on a photograph, a painting, and a film extract before Mont Sainte-Victoire is visible again. The shot that follows the opening panning shots, and which also marks the beginning of the voice-over, is of a small black-and-white photograph of Cézanne, pictured in profile out in the countryside, standing in front of his easel, paintbrush in hand. The photograph only partially occupies the screen image, its white border framing it upon a red surface. The photograph is filmed for almost four minutes, accompanied by passages from Joachim Gasquet's book *Cézanne* (Gasquet [1921] 1926), the second half of which is structured as a series of dialogues between the painter and Gasquet, his young admirer. These dialogues provide the basis of the voice-overs for both films, spoken by Huillet in *Cézanne* (with Straub interjecting occasionally as Gasquet), and Julie Koltaï in *A Visit to the Louvre*.[2] The photograph is the first of three that appear within the film *Cézanne* and is at one and the same time an image to be stared at and an image that disappears from view even though it remains on screen as one listens to the words that are spoken. Gazing at the photograph for almost four minutes without always fully concentrating on it may generate free-floating, unguided mental images, although in this case it is not reverie to which the words seek to give rise.

Huillet's delivery of Cézanne's words that are drawn from Gasquet's text is sometimes breathless as if ignoring punctuation altogether and at other times introduces pauses in unusual places, creating unexpected gaps that leave listener-spectators hanging momentarily before hearing the next word and being able to grasp the meaning. The painstaking attention to detail that the filmmakers pay when working on how a text will be read is evident from the detailed, multi-coloured annotations of their scripts, which highlight the importance of individual words right down to the syllable and the letter.[3] Furthermore, Straub has commented that punctuation is there to be blown up (*dynamiter*) (in Raymond 2008: 23), so it is unsurprising that the rhythms of the voice-over jar at times. Scholars have read this as part of their distancing style.[4] Yet the difficulty of listening to the uneven syncopations of the sentences can be thought of differently in this context: similar to Cézanne in his painterly environment but in more specifically filmic terms, the filmmakers focus on what it means to attend to attention itself, on how one concentrates, understands, and processes what one hears in addition to what one sees, with both the eyes and the mind's eye. The spectator's mind may wander, but this too is noteworthy.

I mentioned in an earlier chapter that faint, unbidden mental images come and go frequently when watching films, and that these are not always prompted by what spectators are supposed to be attending to on screen. Unlike the guided wandering and reshaping that Keiller's Robinson invites viewers to partake in, this kind of distraction can take them away from the film they are watching, and one particularly honest reviewer of an early film by Straub and Huillet attests to this when she talks about her viewing experience. Writing on *Chronik der Anna Magdalena Bach/ Chronicle of Anna Magdalena Bach* (1967), Penelope Gilliatt notes: 'Sometimes I watched the moments when the pretend Bach changed manuals on the harpsichord, and sometimes I fell into things that never get into reviews, like thoughts of dinner, and what to do with your life . . .' (Gilliatt cited in Roud 1971: 11–12). Here the distraction leads to concentrating on something else – her dinner, her life – with the film serving as a blank canvas or backdrop at times. Yet Gilliatt's wandering mind also points to the possibility of focusing on distraction itself, looking to those moments when the film prompts attention to distraction in the same way that it does to attention, to the binding together of both in that part of the experience of Straub and Huillet's work that involves musing on and indeed visualising other things while looking and listening, feeling and thinking. French scholar Yves Citton writes of a form of emancipatory distraction, inspired initially by Freud's notion of free-floating attention in which the analyst does not fully concentrate on what the patient is saying in order to grasp what the patient means (Citton [2014] 2017: 116–21). Straub and Huillet's films turn distraction into an emancipatory force by other means. Uninterrupted viewing of a natural landscape is rendered impossible by the very mediation of their filmic engagement with Cézanne's working processes, and yet this links the form of sustained viewing that their long takes permit to the kind of attention pushed to the point of collapse that gripped Cézanne. This occasions an encounter with their films that stands apart from the wondrous experience Lutz Koepnick describes eloquently with reference to the long take (Koepnick 2017). Durational viewing in their case is never valorised in and of itself: attention and distraction combine in the process of dissolution occasioned from word to image. In such dissolution of vision, the film's images are never blurred and nor do they disintegrate; rather, a clear point of focus is provided by the long take which is both aided and interrupted by the spoken word and also by the shots that surround it. Their approach to montage is significant in this respect and contributes to the generation of imagined images on the part of the spectator.

When speaking about the challenge of editing an extract from Jean Renoir's *Madame Bovary* (1934) for inclusion in *Cézanne*, Huillet explains that Renoir is difficult to cut because he approached montage in terms of blocks. Huillet's terminology here brings out an important connection between the earlier filmmaker and the work of Straub and Huillet, which also relates back to Cézanne (Huillet cited in Raymond 2008: 35). Straub and Huillet's own 'montage by blocks' operates by the apparent removal of the interval, creating a correspondence between that which is thereby juxtaposed and allowing no space to intervene. The forming of mental images on the part of the spectator that Eisenstein encouraged through his writings as a result of the pacier montage of his own shot combinations is absent here. Yet looking to the point of imagining more than what is seen on screen is just as important in spite of the relative infrequency of the cut, it is just stimulated differently, over the course of sequences that sometimes take the form of a single long take. In this way, Straub and

Huillet's montage builds on the layering that has been fundamental to my discussion in previous chapters. The dissolution that I have been speaking about as a function of attention also comes into play here though, as the mental image is formed by reshaping the image perceived on the screen. To refer back to Bachelard, this deformation of the perceived image is a locus of imagination, and in Straub and Huillet's case, the imagined images are created in part through the resonances of the spoken word in relation to the image blocks but also through other means.

The possibility of imagining images beyond what is seen on screen relates to the prompting of mental processes similar to those involved in reading, as we have observed with recourse to Scarry's discussion of image-making. This point of reference has helped to explain how the spoken words of film voice-overs, for example, direct the formation of mental images. But the other means of seeing beyond what is on screen to which I have just alluded are not always prompted by words or sound, even though Straub and Huillet's work is audibly verbose. When writing about their films, Deleuze cites Noël Burch to emphasise how their visual images are read at the same time as they are seen: Burch suggests that grasping images that cease to be linked together naturally 'requires a considerable effort of memory and imagination, in other words, *a reading*' (Burch cited in Deleuze [1985] 1994: 245). Continuing in his own words, Deleuze writes that 'reading is a function of the eye, a perception of perception, a perception which does not grasp perception without also grasping its reverse, imagination, memory, or knowledge' (ibid.: 245). Recognising the importance of the spoken word to their work, Deleuze points nonetheless to the many sequences in their films without words, arguing: 'A new sense of "readable" appears for the visual image, at the same time as the speech-act becomes for itself an autonomous sound image' (ibid.: 246). More attentive as I am to the mental visual images that emerge as a result of such 'reading', it is important to elaborate on what Deleuze posits as part of the reverse side of perception and to show how it is fundamental to prompting the formation of imagined images. To do this, we need to rejoin Cézanne who is now in the presence of Mont Sainte-Victoire.

As Cézanne speaks the following words through Huillet's voice-over, spectators view a long take of Mont Sainte-Victoire:

> . . . this sun. Listen. The pure chance of sunbeams [*hasard des rayons*], the progression, infiltration, incarnation of sun across the world. Who will ever paint that? Who will tell of that? That will be the physical history, the psychology of the earth.

The sun is not visible in the sky shown on screen. Its rays, though, are easily imagined while listening to the painter's words. The blue sky, wispy clouds and the combination of light-coloured rock and vegetation of the mountain furnish the material setting for the words to generate mentally 'the pure chance of sunbeams', along with the 'progression', 'infiltration', and 'incarnation' of the sun across this imposing fragment of the world. Spectators are not illuminating a blank screen, as has been the case in some of the filmic examples in previous chapters, nor are they seeing night and being asked to imagine day; rather, the film images provide a sunlit setting in which the sun is everywhere present but nowhere visible, and the mountain is its incarnation. This is the starting point for imagining fire at the heart of this rock, which will be spoken about explicitly in ensuing sentences, taking the mountain back to its origins and potentially gesturing forwards to its future explosive destruction. The imagined superimposition of geological time implied by the overlapping fire of beginnings and endings also relates to the montage of image blocks that eschews linear chronology.

The order of juxtaposition of Straub and Huillet's montage blocks upsets the direction of text-based reading, pointing to the disintegration of temporally understood grammar as might mark the progression of understanding in a sentence. Relevant to this disruption, Dominic Païni remarks on the relationship between Cézanne and the Friedrich Hölderlin philosophical poem incarnated in their earlier film *Der Tod des Empedokles/ The Death of Empedocles* (1986), an extract of which bisects the long take of Mont Sainte-Victoire just discussed, which follows the excerpt from Renoir's *Madame Bovary*.[5] The extract from *The Death of Empedocles* that features in *Cézanne*, filmed in the volcanic landscape around Mount Etna in Sicily, begins with Empedocles' reflections on light and appears after the painter's reflections on the sun that spectators have just heard. Although the Empedocles sequence follows this and begins with the mention of heavenly light, the German poet prefigures Cézanne in historical terms, as Païni suggests, 'responding to him *ahead of time*' (Païni [1999] 2006). The Straubian dialectic thus identified is that of the answer preceding the question. Hölderlin responds to the later painter's question of who will tell of the physical history, the psychology of the earth. From paint, through film, to rock, Straub and Huillet's own montage works to establish material relations across the different media, rewriting any teleological sense of historical progression or influence by placing the source after its presumed derivation or adaptation, in culture and in nature. Sense is not arrived at through progression in time but through digression, and their aforementioned explosion of punctuation is matched by their positioning of montage blocks that both hold together and dismantle the geological strata of time. While it is not possible to get back to the time when Cézanne painted (the opening shots of the film show the historical separation unequivocally), his is a way of seeing with which these filmmakers are very much identified, and as Empedocles and Hölderlin preempted Cézanne, so Cézanne has already responded to the questions the filmmakers ask of the vision they pursue.

The Empedocles episode is inserted, as I have noted, between shots of Mont Sainte-Victoire: Cézanne's reflections on the sun that lead into it emerge again on the other side of it, rising from within Mont Sainte-Victoire having passed through Hölderlin. Hölderlin's meditation on light provides an unspoken connection between Mont Sainte-Victoire and Mount Etna inscribed in the respective landscapes of the two films that links the rock invisibly to molten lava. Straub and Huillet's images thus lend themselves to being read not only through what is spoken even as the spoken word plays a crucial role in stimulating the imagination to reshape what is seen. The filmic image of Mont Sainte-Victoire that appears after the Empedocles episode is closer to the mountain than the first shot and the light is less bright; the blue sky now features wispy clouds that are faintly visible at the summit (Figure 6.3). Through the voice-over, spectators are asked to look at the mountain as the painter's words describe what he sees as he does the same many years beforehand:

Figure 6.3 *Cézanne* (Jean-Marie Straub and Danièle Huillet, 1989).

> Look at Sainte-Victoire: what momentum [*quel élan*], what imperious thirst for the sun, and what melancholy in the evening when all this heaviness drops back down. These blocks were made of fire. There is still fire in them. The shade, in the daytime seems to back off, trembling, to be afraid of them. When large clouds pass, the shadow they cast quivers on the rocks as if they were burned, drunk in suddenly by a mouth of fire.

Cézanne observes here in a statement that Straub and Huillet are fond of citing, that the blocks of Mont Sainte-Victoire were 'made of fire' and '[t]here is still fire in them'. Deleuze notes moreover: 'The visual image, in Straub, is the rock' (Deleuze [1985] 1994: 244). This rock is friable to the point of being combustible, demonstrated by the changing light that viewers imagine without seeing within this long take. The large clouds that are described as casting the shadow in the heat of the day and are said to cause the rocks to seem as though they are burning are nowhere visible. The very faint small clouds in the sky do, however, serve as a basis for building an imagined image of the larger clouds that are spoken about and of imagining the changes of light and shade across the mountain as a result of their movement relative to the sun. This shadow that 'quivers on the rocks as if they were burned' proffers the imagined reshaping of the perceived mountain as an incarnation of the invisible fire within. It is through looking intently to the point that spectators begin to imagine more than they are seeing that the surface and the solidity of the rocks are opened up to the flickering mobility of fire born of burning, dry heat and shadow. The dissolution of vision gives way to the digression of imagining that is always rooted in the real.

Cézanne declares that he could not paint Mont Sainte-Victoire at one time because, like others who look but do not see, he imagined the shadow of the mountain to be concave. But by looking at it more closely, as spectators are also invited to do throughout the duration of this long take, he declares that he realised that it was convex and that the mountain escaped from its centre. Cézanne preferred to stay with the materiality of the real rather than journeying into a purely imagined realm. Over the fifth painting filmed in *Cézanne, Rocks and Branches at Bibémus* (1900–4), for example, coupled with reflections on blocks of colour as the means of reaching the depths of things and communing with them, the painter's method is said to be that of 'the hatred of the imaginative'. Cézanne clarifies that the real is what he is interested in: the immensity of the world in a tiny portion of the earth. Yet his closed-eye explorations of his relation to nature, his notion that the artist is a recording machine (*un appareil enregistreur*) or a sensitive plate (*plaque sensible*), make reference to being a brain (*un cerveau*) – all of which references feature in Straub and Huillet's

*Cézanne*, taken from conversations with Gasquet – suggesting that the mind's eye plays a central role in his creativity even if he spurns disappearing into the imaginative dimension as such. Something passes through him that he then observes inwardly and captures. In glimpses throughout their sustained examination of his thoughts and paintings, Straub and Huillet probe the mental retina as a site of sensory impression that fleshes out what Merleau-Ponty terms the lining of sight and that provides a basis for perception and imagination, but through which the latter alters the former.

Refusing to just imagine what the shadows of Mont Sainte-Victoire look like, the painter chooses to look closely instead, but this in turn generates seeing more than is visible to the naked eye. As he notes while its sturdiness still asserts itself visually on screen: 'instead of settling, it evaporates, becomes fluid, participates in the blueness of the ambient respiration of the air'. In looking intensively at the blocks of image here of Mont Sainte-Victoire, either side of the Empedocles extract, the fire that preceded and that may once again engulf it is evident, imaginable without being viewed in the onscreen images, as is the vapour and fluidity into which the mountain is also said to vanish. The shot that has been held of Mont Sainte-Victoire is then set in motion as the camera pans slowly to the right before pausing again, and brilliant sunlight begins to seep in from above the image. Perception of solidity in the company of nature disintegrates from German poet to French painter through the renewed gaze at Mont Saint-Victoire, facilitated by the lens of the filmmaking duo and the words of Cézanne, which are filtered through Gasquet and read by Huillet. This chain reaction of reference crosses historical periods, like aftershocks of earthquakes that cause terrain to shift irrevocably and the magma that is usually encased well below the surface to emerge, as a painter speaks through writers to filmmakers, and the solid stillness of what is on screen is not the only thing that is seen.

## Re-enlivening

Mental reshaping of the onscreen image thus holds a special place in these long takes of Mont Sainte-Victoire. *Cézanne* offers a different kind of transformation of the landscape from that which Keiller's Robinson prompts spectators to visualise by rebuilding factories on a canal site and sustaining them for the length of the accompanying shots. Mont Sainte-Victoire is taken imaginatively through geological time to its magma origins and then outwards into the rarity of the air through the gaze that looks so hard that it changes what is seen using the mind's eye. It is a related kind of looking and listening that is extended into Straub and Huillet's second film on the painter, *A Visit to the Louvre*, now with reference to works of art rather than the natural landscape.

As Gilberto Perez notes, the lacunary nature of Straub and Huillet's films requires spectators to be active in response to their incompletion, with a view not to completing the films but to making the gaps their own (Perez 1998: 324). There is something in this description that is akin to the way in which the brain processes information on an everyday basis and with which Cézanne was also in tune. The brain is described in *Cézanne* on more than one occasion as independent of the artist but capable of being impregnated with the image of things: a lifelong travail of meditation prepares it for this. The field of action of the brain's plasticity and its sculptural qualities, to which philosopher Catherine Malabou refers in more contemporary times, involves neuronal information crossing voids such that something aleatory comes between the emission and receipt of information or messages (Malabou [2004] 2008: 36). For Malabou, this plasticity is the condition for resistance to the analogies that exist between neoliberal late capitalist structures and the flexibility of the brain. There is a formal reflection on plasticity, bound up with imagining, within Straub and Huillet's later film, *A Visit to the Louvre*, which connects with the broader emancipatory elements of their vision evident in *Cézanne* and that will also become apparent in the politics of resistance in one late work that I turn to in the final section of this chapter. The opening sequences of *A Visit to the Louvre* feature sections of black leader, and also focus on the statue *La Victoire de Samothrace/The Nike of Samothrace*. Sally Shafto notes that the blackness here is in fact that of black cards inserted humorously over the images of paintings that Cézanne does not like, marking out the filmmakers' complicity with the painter's views (Shafto 2009). Yet it also dissects the appreciation of the statue that the commentary provides, read this time by Julie Koltaï, introducing the aleatory and registering those all-important gaps in the process of perceiving and attending to the onscreen image.

The winged headless statue of the draped female form is viewed first from her right (Figure 6.4) and then from her left-hand side with an intervening cut to black that also precedes her first emergence. All the blood that courses through the body is said by Cézanne to have passed through the brain and into the heart: it is the movement of the entire woman, of the whole statue, of the whole of Greece that he suggests is perceptible here and he adds that when the head fell off, the marble bled. This imagined life within marble and the vivid liquidity of its substance recalls the fluidity of the rock of Mont Sainte-Victoire, and indeed its elemental

**Figure 6.4** *A Visit to the Louvre* (Jean-Marie Straub and Danièle Huillet, 2003).

fire, conjured mentally in the earlier film. With solidity and impermanence conjoined here in a different way, Cézanne offers an insight into his own mental activity: 'I do not need to see the head to imagine the gaze.' In turn, spectatorial imagining is prompted over the course of a cut to black and the static filmed images of the statue from both sides successively. This particular statue that appears in the opening of the film may not be able to perform the action Malabou says the brain can when she writes, fittingly in this regard, that '[t]he plastic art of the brain gives birth to a statue capable of self-repair' (Malabou [2004] 2008: 27–8). But the statue, like the film, is subject to its gap being focused on and filled in the mind as Cézanne says he does in his imagination. Directed but not to the point that the detail of the head or the gaze is pinned down, the formation of the mental image at this stage is a continuation of the enlivening of the sculpture as flesh, moulded to fit the body that is brought to life through description and two long takes of her enrobed form. The folds of her clothing and the angle of her body contribute to the momentum of her movement, culminating in the rebuilding of the missing gaze that leads the way forwards.

Later in this opening sequence in the glorious presence of Veronese's *The Wedding at Cana* (1563), spectators are told to close their eyes, not to think of anything, then to open them again to experience the richly coloured undulations, to bathe in the painting and become one with it harmoniously as if drinking it in. It is through looking that Cézanne suggests it is possible to feel the people in the painting breathe as they do, and such feeling passes through to what cannot be seen or, rather, what can only be seen by looking so intently that they come to life, their chests filling up, breathing 'like you and I', an act of imagining that derives from the vibrations of the painting's colour alone and that sees beyond their stasis to visualise their movement. This is the movement of materiality, encouraged by the painting itself, and prompted by the painter's instruction to the spectator to close their eyes, introducing the darkness that has manifested itself periodically on screen for the first seven minutes of the film and that now connects the body of the film to that of the spectator, from eye to brain to mental image. Imagining something different from what is on screen – the life, the breath of those seen in the painting – is not a matter of denying what is there, of disavowing or covering over what is seen, but is a subtle reshaping of vision, aided by a mental image that enlivens what is perceived.

Viewed through the lens of Straub and Huillet's critical attention to spectacular culture, but prompted by the late nineteenth-century painter's words and works, Cézanne's vision that takes attention to the point of collapse opens up vistas beyond what is shown and seen but which are nonetheless real. These may appear as mental images, off-screen and private, but they chime first with the emancipatory possibilities of distraction and then join with the powers of the imagination. Where Perez has read Straub and Huillet's *Geschichtsunterricht/History Lessons* (1972) as a representation of a coming to consciousness that asks spectators to take part in the process of that coming to consciousness (Perez 1998: 334), I understand their Cézanne films as asking spectators to take part in the play of attention and distraction that has the transformative workings of imagination at its heart. It is through this serious play, which is entrenched in the material world that is filmed so attentively, that imaginative vision has the potential to change something of the way in which people see what they see. Straub and Huillet knew this, as did Cézanne.

## Reshaping Redux, or Doubling Back and Looking Forwards

As has become apparent at intervals throughout my discussion across the successive chapters of this study, no one director is associated only with one set of processes for prompting the generation of imagined images. I want to dwell on Straub and Huillet in this final section because their work takes us back to some of the processes discussed in previous chapters – as is true in the case of Keiller too – while introducing a difference that gestures forwards to the final chapter in which I discuss the erasure of imagined images. One of the key distancing techniques with which Straub and Huillet are sometimes associated has already become apparent in *A Visit to the Louvre*: that of the insertion of entirely blank, black images which occasionally become lengthy montage blocks in their own right. This also occurs in the German version of *Cézanne*. In both the French and the German versions of the film, a second extract from *The Death of Empedocles* features later on in the film, this time with just the Sicilian landscape in view as Hölderlin's lines are delivered off-screen. In the French version of the film that I have been discussing, the images cut straight from a photograph of the painter to the *Empedocles* clip, but in the German version of the film, this second extract is preceded by forty-three seconds of black leader.[6] This intermittent presence of the blank screen harks back to the lengthier presence of blankness that was discussed with regard to volumising in the earlier chapter, and given that the words of the voice-over sometimes continue and abound across the blankness, there is an opening for the formation of layers of imagined images over the screen. The blackness introduced into the German version of *Cézanne* that marks one of the differences between the French and German films is not an isolated instance and when used in this and other films, it serves a variety of purposes. As in their usage by other directors, black inserts may point to censorship or to acknowledgement that some things either cannot or will not be represented; they may also dovetail with the prohibition against graven images. Most importantly within the context of my study, though, in Straub's more recent *Kommunisten/Communists* (2014), they accompany explicit recognition of the image-making power of the imagination and prompt this on the part of spectators too. The association between imaginative vision and the potential to change the way in which spectators see that emerged from the Cézanne films joins here most explicitly with their politics, now coupled with a strong drive towards resistance.

*Communists* is made up mainly of sections from Straub and Huillet's earlier films but has some new sequences at the start, based on André Malraux's *Le Temps du mépris/Days of Wrath* (1935). The whole film comprises existing films, extracted and edited together with this new additional material. The anthem of the former East Germany, 'Auferstanden aus Ruinen/Risen from Ruins', plays over both the credits and the black screen at the start. In the opening scene, two communists stand with their backs to the wall in a white, harshly lit room, interrogated by a man assumed to be a Nazi, heard but never seen. One man hangs his head, the other, identified by the interrogator as Kassner, answers the questions, and the focus shifts to him first. The screen then cuts suddenly to black for around four minutes as the voice-over tells of how Kassner survived his time in jail by retreating into his mind. Kassner reportedly kept a mind lucid enough to be able to defend himself while in captivity. A mental vision of torture bursts out momentarily from the words spoken against the black screen as an abrupt shift from first- to third-person narration describes how blood splatters up his face – 'a big, red line sprang up on his face, crackling and flashing'. The radiant ignition of which Scarry speaks prompts the formation of a bloody and violent mental image, there is a pause and then 'a blow to the neck' before it is announced that 'finally he fainted'. A vertiginous hunt is said to send Kassner's mind towards the images that maintained his life. He likens his use of strong mental images to revolutionary anarchist Mikhail Bakunin's practice: as a prisoner, Bakunin is said to have written every day in his imagination an entire newspaper, from the editorial to the information pages, stories, and gossip. Mental activity enables those imprisoned to fight against the passivity of incarceration, and imagining is associated with defiance of torture. This is not something that is merely theorised by the director but also put into practice in this sequence and, as with the earlier imagining of Mont Sainte-Victoire as liquid magma rather than rock while spectators view the solidity of the onscreen image, contrasting mental pictures emerge and are set in motion.

Unlike the blank image films discussed in the chapter on volumising, this segment of blackness is surrounded by representational images, situated between the interrogation scene already described and a subsequent scene of a couple on a balcony with their backs to camera, the woman seated, the man, who resembles the other man present in the interrogation of Kassner, standing. The visualisation of the torture and the strategies for coping with it form as a layer over the intervening blackness but draw from the images that have been seen on screen. A red line of blood springing up a face, a blow to the neck, and a body that faints are imagined relating to the figure named Kassner who is seen in the earlier shot, the violent movements contorting him in the imagination but with a view to setting up that mental space as one in which such violence is simultaneously countered. The imagined images that the description of the torture invites are part of a more expansive reshaping of vision that is enabled by the image-making capacity of the imagination. It is not only Kassner who puts this into practice, following Bakunin, but in the horror of his retold experience, the spectator does so too, forming mental images of torture that then give way to strategies of mental resistance.

In the work of directors who shun the society of the spectacle and who challenge the image-saturated world of the late-twentieth and twenty-first centuries, the image – and especially the mental image – still retains an important place. This is as true of Straub and Huillet as it is of the differing filmmakers whose work I discuss in the final chapter and whose contrasting relation to iconoclasm nonetheless continues to engage the power of imagining. Before this, however, it is worth pointing briefly in conclusion to another instance of reshaping that can be observed in an example from art house cinema. Rainer Werner Fassbinder's version of Theodor Fontane's nineteenth-century novel *Effi Briest* (1974) is a strong case in point. Writing of his aim in this film, Fassbinder declares:

> it's an attempt to make a film that's clearly for the mind, a film in which people don't stop thinking, but rather actually begin to think, and just as when you read, it's your imagination that turns the letters and sentences into a story, the same thing should happen with this film. (Fassbinder cited in Wetzel 1974)

The film is replete with Fontane's prose, which is voiced without always being imaged on screen and it activates the imagination knowingly as a result in ways that involve layering in particular along with distinctive, successive usage of blankness through the presence of a white, rather than black, screen. Fassbinder occasionally encourages the mental extension and completion of onscreen sequences through reshaping. A particularly good example arises when Effi (Hanna Schygulla) receives a visit from one of her admirers, Gieshübler (Hark Bohm). They sit together talking to one another, the camera focused on Gieshübler as he addresses Effi who is physically off-screen but reflected in a mirror behind and to the side of him. The scene is completed in words and the imagination alone, though, as the voice-over takes over where Gieshübler breaks off and describes how he takes his leave:

> Gieshübler would have liked to declare his love and, like El Cid, or some other hero, sought her permission to fight and die for her. Since this was not possible and his heart could bear no more, he stood up, looked for his hat, which he found at once, and after repeatedly kissing Effi's hand, quickly withdrew without a further word.

As the voice-over begins, the camera withdraws its focus on Gieshübler alone and encompasses Effi too before pulling back further (Figure 6.5), moving around a statue, and then showing both of them from a distance,

Figure 6.5 *Effi Briest* (Rainer Werner Fassbinder, 1974).

still seated in the same position. Gieshübler and Effi remain motionless as the camera makes this expansive movement and Gieshübler is imagined standing, looking for his hat, kissing her hand, and then withdrawing. The camera movement pre-empts his withdrawal and the motion contributes to the possibility of enlivening the static suitor and imagining his gestures prior to his departure.

This modifying of the onscreen image through the imagination thereby partakes of the reshaping that has been the subject of this chapter, expanding it in a different but nonetheless related sense to the process operative in the earlier examples, from Keiller's Robinson through to Straub and Huillet's films. The activity of building and rebuilding mental images has now joined with the alteration or indeed deformation of the perceived image. The next chapter will shift attention from transforming the perceived image to changing the mental image by exploring the process of erasure.

CHAPTER 7

# Erasing

Imagined images need no help to disappear. Many of those that I have described on the basis of the processes that I have identified throughout this book will last for the length of the onscreen shot or the duration of the sequence that they accompany and may sometimes recur as memory images, but they fade on their own. When we encountered the overly bright sunlight on the road to the city of Aqua Vitae in Derek Jarman's *Blue*, though, we witnessed an instance of the erasure of the mental image that required a little more activity because it was precisely an image of erasure, in this case of an experience of blinding that was to be generated by the imagination. The glare of the sun on the crystalline, mirrored labyrinth that blotted out vision with an unbearable reflection was part of the imagined activity of the sequence even though it was self-obliterating. It is not that spectators picture the glassy city of Aqua Vitae, which then diminishes to be replaced by a mental image of something else; rather, the protective walls around the city reflect light in such a way that the sun's glare makes it disappear, and it is this very disappearance that viewers are prompted to generate by means of the mind's eye.

Moving beyond this example from *Blue*, my focus in this chapter will be on mental images that spectators build and then cancel, either partially by creating a disappearance within them or fully by dismantling them as part of the activity of imagining. This iconoclastic mental activity is linked to the onscreen relation to the image in the work of the two contrasting directors that I turn to now. The reshaping processes of the previous chapter necessitated adding something to the onscreen image in order to transform it mentally: a row of small factories on wasteland; fire and liquidity to the solidity of Mont Sainte-Victoire; a gaze to the headless *Nike of Samothrace*; breath to the throng of people in *The Wedding at Cana*. The work of erasure to be explored here will involve both subtracting something from mental images formed on the basis of verbal instruction and obliterating them in their entirety: the former process is one I trace as a recurrent element of Guy Debord's first film and the latter through a series of late films by Marguerite Duras. Duras will also bring to our attention instances of re-picturing, which involve the successive forming and re-forming of mental images even as this too serves the process of dilapidation.

## Absent Images and Mental Images of Absence

Briefly but powerfully, Debord invites the formation of mental images of disappearance and absence in *Hurlements en faveur de Sade/Howls in Favour of Sade* (1952). In order to appreciate how he does this, it is necessary first to recognise the unusual form of the film in accordance with Debord's aims in making it. Even prior to the publication of *The Society of the Spectacle* in 1967 and the establishing of the Situationist International, Debord was interested in cinema being part of the societal fabric that might generate transformative situations necessitating a response connected to life rather than purely aesthetic goals. Setting himself apart from the kind of modernist experimentation with iconoclasm that still sought to remain within the aesthetic realm, and thereby distancing himself in advance from figures such as Godard and Duras, but also from his initial compatriots the *Lettristes* whose destructive goals were nonetheless geared towards a heightened aesthetic, Debord worked in the service of changing society rather than art. Debord's first film, dedicated to Gil J. Wolman, forms part of the group of *Lettriste* films. Yet, as Thomas Y. Levin points out, while the *Lettristes* devalued the image in favour of sound and the letter, this remained an aesthetic pursuit for them in a manner that differed from Debord's fundamental intentions in his own filmmaking practice (Levin 2002: 346). For the *Lettristes* indeed, *Howls* went too far in rupturing with the history of art; and this, coupled with the rift caused by Debord's part in an attack on Charlie Chaplin's politics from which Jean Isidore Isou and Maurice Lemaître distanced themselves, caused an irrevocable split among the group to which Debord initially belonged (see Coppola 2006: 39–42; Field 1999: 59). Debord, as a member of the break-away left-wing group, would form the Situationist International just a few years later in July 1957 (Merrifield 2005: 27). *Howls in Favour of Sade* was the earlier starting point of his own revolutionary filmic activity, which has its most powerful effects when screened at the cinema even though it is now more widely available on DVD. Not giving cinema-goers and film viewers what they might expect is the point of his endeavour: Debord's anti-film dismantles the architecture of the spectacular regime, inciting debate from the first to the most recent screenings, and thereby creating situations that were to be the mainstay of the Situationist enterprise. Although Debord was against the cult of creativity embraced by Isou and his followers, his mobilisation of provocative techniques to produce his own anti-film serves to create a collective experience in the cinematic auditorium space not entirely divorced from creativity on the part of spectators who gravitate between moments of attentiveness and distracted engagement. This works differently, however, from the combination of these states explored in the previous chapter.

In accordance with the conditions of blankness discussed in the chapter devoted to volumising, Debord's film features no onscreen images.[1] The screen picture, such as it is, does alternate throughout though, between black and clear leader, creating an idiosyncratic black-and-white film in blocks; the white screen has noises, sounds, and then voices over it, and the black is accompanied by silence. The black leader that is inserted at irregular intervals between the clear leader lasts for uneven amounts of time, and the final period of blackness lasts twenty-four minutes. This final number of minutes of darkness bears a relation to a key number within cinema: the usual rate of celluloid sound film projection of twenty-four frames per second. The interval of darkness that makes cinema possible is eventually the only thing that is left. Apart from the beginning of *Howls* that features Wolman performing *mégapneumie* (guttural sounds that are indecipherable), the text is a tissue of citations taken from their original contexts of the civil code, poetry, and novels, as well as random conversations and declarations, assembled together in their new environment. The origins of Debord's cinematic *détournement* lie here, which involves uprooting texts (and onscreen images in other films) from their source and placing them in an entirely different context. As a result of the juxtaposition of textual citations from so many different places in *Howls* over the alternating blank black and then white screen, there are constant jumps of sense and direction, involving leaps from one subject to the next without a connection between them necessarily to be found. It is this disparate montage that still generates occasional images, off-screen rather than onscreen, by stimulating mental activity. Whereas Eisenstein posited the production of mental images prompted by montage of onscreen images, Debord foregrounds a more haphazard process indebted largely to words. For Debord (and Wolman), and in contrast to Eisensteinian rational montage, '*détournement* is less effective the more it approaches a rational reply' (Debord cited in Field 1999: 68). It is the eclectic assemblage of words that prompts the formation of mental images that are vital to an anti-film founded on an absence of more than just onscreen images.

Specific instances of disappearance are the condition for the formation of mental images that run thematically through the opening statements of the film. Rather than the generation of a presence to make up for an absence, the mental image-making here is complicit with the self-cancelling appearances that spectators are informed about from the start. One of the statements furthers the absence writ large across the screen that is void of visual images by citing Article 115 of the civil code, which refers to someone going missing:

> Voice 3: If a person has ceased to appear at his place of residence and nothing has been heard concerning him for four years, interested parties may petition the civil court to officially recognize the absence of said person. (Debord 2003: 1)[2]

Furthermore, and in a subsequent statement, the promised presence of the director is withheld and his reported speech declares that there is no film:

> Voice 5: Just as the projection was about to begin, Guy-Ernest Debord was supposed to step onto the stage and make a few introductory remarks. Had he done so, he would simply have said: 'There is no film. Cinema is dead. No more films are possible. If you wish, we can move on to a discussion.' (Debord 2003: 2)

Guy Debord's absence can paradoxically be pictured, since what is meant to have happened prior to the start of the screening is still described. Even without a clear image in one's mind of what Debord looks like, the action of a director getting up on stage to say a few words at the beginning of a film can be imagined in spite of the fact that he did not in fact do this. As Scarry notes when describing mental processes of addition and subtraction, if an image is there and then disappears, it seems to have moved (Scarry [1999] 2001: 100). The fascination of Debord's technique lies in the appearance and disappearance combining with supposition as the imagined images recognise what he was supposed to do. Suppositional imagining can be aligned with fainter mental images, as was the case in my discussion of *Blue* in the chapter on volumising, when the cyclist nearly knocked Jarman down but did not. Here, though, it is not that the director is imagined in all his substantiality on stage with our being told that he almost did not show up; it is, rather, that he is imagined doing what he was supposed to do as well as what he did not, and his imagined absence is as powerful as his imagined presence. The mental images work in reverse of Scarry's shift from presence to absence, since he is absent from the stage, then he is there, but the situation is that of an auditorium setting that is ready to welcome him and in which he never appears. The brief glimpse of what should have happened, accompanied simultaneously by recognition of the no-show, prompts the concurrent creation and withdrawal of the mental image of the director's appearance on the imagined stage.

This self-cancelling motion is entirely in keeping with the proclamation of the death of cinema by this anti-film. The deadpan delivery of these and many of the lines from the civil code and the other disparate citations does not set out to engage its audience, even though certain exclamations may provoke a jolt. Indeed, as spectators are told, what Debord would have suggested if he had been there is to have a discussion instead, since there is no film. Anything goes, then, by way of response to *Howls*, and as the reactions at the initial and subsequent screenings attest, the effects of the opening, coupled with the indeterminate length of the black leader that interrupts the presence of voice and sound over the white screen, led to walk-outs amongst many other kinds of interventions.[3] For those who stay with it, though, and who tune in to the voices, however fragilely and intermittently, people and things arise and float by in mental pictures with neither rhyme nor reason, among the myriad abstractions, non sequiturs, and banalities. There is one particularly noticeable figure that appears on my mental retina against the blank whiteness of the screen and amidst the cacophony of voices. In keeping with the activity of erasure implicit in the simultaneous prompting and withdrawal of an imagined presence from the outset, the condition for this figure's emergence is the tragic tale of her fatal disappearance at the beginning of one of the transitions from the black to the white screen.

The death of a twelve-and-a-half-year-old radio star, Madeleine Reineri, who committed suicide by throwing herself into the river Isère in Grenoble constitutes this vivid if harrowing point of reference, drawn from a newspaper report in 1950:

> Voice 1: Lines from a 1950 newspaper: 'Popular Young Radio Actress Throws Herself Into the Isère. Grenoble. Twelve-and-a-half-year-old Madeleine Reineri, who under the stage name "Pirouette" starred in the Alpes-Grenoble radio program *Happy Thursdays*, threw herself into the Isère river Friday afternoon after having placed her schoolbag on the bank.' (Debord 2003: 4)

A poetic statement follows, read by another voice, rhyming the Isère with 'misère' (misery), before the screen cuts to black, instituting a pause and silence through which this news story continues to resonate. At the end of a subsequent segment some minutes later what is termed 'the perfection of suicide' is said to lie in ambiguity before the screen once again cuts to black. A mental image of a young girl falling into a river and that of a schoolbag on a riverbank become linked with the more abstract, colliding pronouncements of misery, perfection, and ambiguity. The production of her vanishing image is generated by her appearance on the riverbank followed by her disappearance into the water, and unlike Debord's suppositional appearance/disappearance at the start, this motion mental picture emerges from the narration of an event that is reported to have happened. The formation of her disappearing image along with that of the schoolbag that abides more statically on the riverbank is the activity of consciousness alone, and is generated from the montage of words. As a radio star, she was known primarily through her voice, and the voice that speaks of her untimely death preserves her in this aural sphere. Yet there is a loose structure of mental image creation here, in tune with a practice that is not founded in making rational connections and with the bleak irrationality of a young girl taking her own life.

Lest this be seen as just another of the many citations that follow one after the other never to be heard about again, *Howls* picks up on this story later on, and the same voice adds further details. At the beginning of the penultimate white screen segment, Voice 1 gives the young girl's name, age, and pseudonym for radio once more, repeating the earlier news of her throwing herself into the river Isère. This time Voice 2 associates her with a more specific location – she is said to come from the Quartier de l'Europe (the Europe Quarter) – and declares that her face will always have the same wonderstruck look (ibid.: 10). The addition of a specific detail, of eternal wonder, gives just enough information to prompt mental composition and to guide the formation of an expression on the young girl's face as she resurfaces in the mind. An ensuing mention of her body as 'the best of promised lands' brings in an uncomfortably sexualised gaze before a man's voice states 'je t'aime', possibly to Madeleine, the young girl, but suggestive of a change of focus and context that sets off a further chain of disconnected responses. The young girl who is evoked and described in slightly more detail than the first time still plunges into the river. Dropping into the water this one final time, the mental image of her erasure also vanishes amidst disparate citations and against the white screen almost as quickly as she was brought back to life in order for her disappearance to be recounted again.

Spectators who make it through to the end of *Howls* are already prepared for the final association between blackness and silence that has been apparent at varying intervals throughout. The twenty-four minute period of blankness that draws *Howls* to a close has the effect of interrupting any concentration the longer it goes on, rather than heightening it. As with the earlier intervals, there is a sense of anticipation but also a disconnection of the listener-spectator from the soundtrack. In the auditorium space, the darkness sheds light on the absurdity of the situation of sitting in silence in front of a screen with others when there is nothing to be heard or seen. Freed from any onscreen image and provoked not to engage through periods of silence and blackness, as well as the disconnected statements and style of delivery, this anti-film engages imagination only sporadically and in spite of itself. Yet the imagined image of the young girl who throws herself into the river, an image of a disappearance that is generated twice with a slight variation without altering the outcome, is one of the ways in which this anti-film plays intermittently in and on the mind rather than the screen. As we move forwards now to consider further examples of mental erasure in other films, onscreen images return but are still accompanied by periods of blankness.

## Bare Mental Images

Both the initial example that I recalled from Jarman's *Blue* and the brief but disturbing report of the young girl who drowns in the rather different context of Debord's *Howls* are singular instances in which spectators perform acts of erasure within images of the mind. The direction of travel for the remainder of this chapter will be towards the formation of a series of composite mental images the content of which is first altered prior to the entire scene within the image being destroyed. The instigator of these mental gymnastics is the writer-filmmaker Marguerite Duras whom we first encountered in the opening section of this book and to whose filmmaking I now return. The ensuing discussion of her work will move slowly into the more extended and comprehensive mental activity of alteration and erasure that I have just set out, which is comparable to what philosopher Maurice Blanchot speaks of with reference to her literary prose, which 'exposes itself at the same time that it is abolished' (Blanchot 1983: back matter). First, and in more specifically filmic terms, it is useful to consider what motivates the connection to the imagination in the work of a filmmaker who, as has already been observed and albeit for very different reasons from Debord (and from Jarman's *Blue*, for that matter), bears an annihilating relation to the image.

Many of Duras's films, particularly from *India Song* (1975) onwards, are renowned for their sound–image disjunctions in which the onscreen visual images differ from what is spoken about in *voix off* or voice-over. In keeping with my focus throughout this book, a corollary of this divergence – a dual focus on the level of imagery, split between visible onscreen and mental image, perception and imagination – is instigated by but not reducible to the dichotomy of what is seen and heard. It is in the context of such a disjunction that Duras initially engages the spectator's imagination in formative terms. When Duras turned to directing her own films between 1969 and 1985 – and notwithstanding successful collaborations with Alain Resnais and Paul Seban – she did so as an acclaimed writer irritated by the ways in which other filmmakers had adapted her books. In the published screenplay of her film *Le Camion/ The Lorry* (1977), she declares: 'Cinema stops the text and kills off its offspring: imagination' (Duras 1977: 75). The wager, then, for Duras, is to create a film that provides access to the very realm of imagination that a filmic adaptation of the text would block if it were only to furnish fixed interpretative images. *Le Camion* aims to stimulate imaginative activity on the part of the spectator, and what is not shown on screen but still described is as important as what appears there. This film provides a good starting point for the eventual consideration of the erasure of the mental image, since from the outset Duras relies upon pared down vocabulary to prompt the creation of the barest of mental pictures.

In *Le Camion* spectators see and hear about the contradiction of a hypothetical film that is spoken of in the conditional tense – a film as it might have been but that has not been made. The whole project is therefore suppositional, yet unlike the fainter instances of imagining things that could have happened but did not (the cyclist almost knocking Jarman down), the imagined images generated from the spoken words of *Le Camion* are more vivid, guided as they are by Duras reading out her writing. For Duras, who writes in a space she names the 'chambre noire' (her very own *camera obscura*), her darkroom becomes a 'chambre de lecture' (reading room) in this film that materialises in the form of an attic room in her house in Neauphle-le-Château (ibid.: 11). Onscreen images show Duras sitting with actor Gérard Depardieu at one of her tables, reading aloud from a batch of loose leaves of paper that constitute the screenplay of the unmade film, a copy of which he also holds in his hands. Preceding the appearance of Duras and Depardieu and then interspersed with scenes of the two of them in this indoor space are images of a thirty-two ton blue Saviem lorry and its journey through an industrial zone. Suggesting a slippage indicative of the unfixed nature of this film, Duras says that the setting could be La Beauce, near Chartres, or the Yvelines department of the Île-de-France. This gives an initial sense of how interchangeable some aspects of the film are, re-emphasising the fact that it has yet to be made but also supplanting one thing – in this case a place – with another. The lorry seen on screen sets out and then continues tirelessly, appearing and disappearing from the

**Figure 7.1** *Le Camion* (Marguerite Duras, 1977).

screen throughout the film, a visible imprint from within the walls of the 'chambre noire', but a vehicle for the imagination too. Duras's and Depardieu's voices, and especially that of Duras, transcend the indoor space and are heard as *voix off* over onscreen images of the lorry's journey, enmeshed with Beethoven's Diabelli variations on the soundtrack. It is emptiness and silence that first characterise the imagined scene shortly after the opening of the film, however, as images of the roadside are visible on screen (Figure 7.1). Duras describes a denuded scene in *voix off*: 'There is a white sky, of winter. A mist too, very light, spread right across the landscape, across the earth.' Whiteness and mist, the latter so easy to picture because of its insubstantiality, are thus instilled as qualities of the first mental images that are to emerge from Duras's darkroom in the spectator's mind, accompanying the travelling shot of the road on screen.

The story at the heart of the script that Duras reads from is simple: a lorry driver picks up an older woman hitchhiker who then travels with him on part of his route for the length of the film. Throughout the film there are no visual onscreen images of the driver, his hitchhiker passenger, or his co-driver who is said to sleep above them in the cabin for the duration of their time together: they have to be imagined. In the opening sequences, as Duras explains to Depardieu what the film would have been about, she gives a brief and unadorned initial description of the woman but still with sufficient detail for spectators to begin to flesh her out mentally. Duras's words permit the creation of an image of the woman on the

**Figure 7.2** *Le Camion* (Marguerite Duras, 1977).

basis of a mimetic relationship with Duras's onscreen image (Figure 7.2): 'on the roadside a woman is said to have been waiting. She is said to have waved. She is said to have been approached. She is a middle-aged woman. Dressed in town clothes.' She has only one possession with her: 'She is carrying a case. She gets in the lorry. The lorry sets off again. And we leave the seaside.' Duras's perceived substantiality on screen as she reads these lines lends itself to the picturing of the traveller; a scrim of Duras's gender and dress serves the formation of an image of the middle-aged imagined woman who waits in town clothes with her suitcase on the side of the road.[4] All that the lorry driver and the woman are said to share once she is in the cabin with him is the view of the road, through the screen of the windscreen, thus contributing a cinematic dimension to the space of the cabin, and bonding these invisible travellers with Duras and Depardieu (Duras 1977: 104), along with the film's spectators, as Duras explains in *voix off*: 'The only thing that they have in common is a certain violence in their gaze. Opposite this void in front of them, the naked winter, the sea.' Connecting back to the white, wintry, misty sky evoked earlier on, the mental image of a void is what both the driver and the woman are said to stare at: a stripped back winter scene by the sea. By conjuring a mental vision of emptiness and sustaining it in different ways across different descriptive passages in the opening minutes of the film, Duras creates a hollowed out imagined space for her woman hitchhiker to travel through. The seasons spoken about will change, as will the landscapes described along the way, but the constitutive and pervasive bareness of the imagined images will remain until they, like the lorry, finally vanish as an onscreen cut to black follows an abrupt declaration: 'The lorry disappeared.'

Unlike some of the examples of the spoken word that I have discussed in this book, there is nothing florid about Duras's prose. The opening of *Le Camion* shows an interest in a vital blankness that is not so far removed from the later acts of mental dilapidation that Duras will guide spectators to perform and that we will come to in due course. It suffices to note here how important *Le Camion* is in enabling Duras to open up imaginative space in some of her subsequent works, *Le Navire Night/The Ship Night*, along with the shorts *Césarée/Caesarea* and *Les Mains négatives/Negative Hands*, all made in 1979, the latter two from off-cuts of the former. The last sixteen seconds of *Le Camion* following the aforementioned cut and disappearance of the lorry from both the screen and the mind are entirely black. The black screen will appear more prominently yet intermittently in *Le Navire Night*.[5] The more frequent insistence of the black screen in her later films, which culminates in its heightened presence in *L'Homme Atlantique*, may signal the impossibility of completing the picture, onscreen or off, flagging the disintegration that the image undergoes in the era that philosopher Georges Didi-Huberman terms 'the era of torn apart imagination' (*imagination déchirée*) (Didi-Huberman 2003: back matter). Yet it is also a reminder of a longer-standing anti-spectacular and non-representational drive, a powerful iconoclasm with which Duras's work is often associated, first enacted on screen and then prompted in the mind.

*Le Navire Night* begins with a black screen that introduces viewers immediately to what Bernard Alazet terms an imaginary palimpsest, as Duras's voice declares: 'I told you it was necessary to see' (Alazet 1992: 133). Seeing in the darkness lies at the heart of this film – emphasised in the opening sequence by city images that are interspersed with a black screen. Laura McMahon speaks of Duras's wider interest in 'blindness rather than sight' (McMahon 2012: 104), and the black screen here joins with the potential violence of the cut of montage that James Williams analyses across Duras's late films more broadly (Williams 1992: 68).[6] The intermittent use of black leader here, however, although blocking out vision aggressively at times, signals an excess to the onscreen image to which the mental image also contributes, since imagining what is not there is fundamental to the content and experience of this film. For, this is a film about a relationship between a man and a woman who never meet up with one another, who are connected by a telephone line, which causes both for the most part to imagine one another only, and spectators must do this too.[7]

Whereas *Le Camion* involves an encounter between an imagined woman hitchhiker and lorry driver, *Le Navire Night* requires spectators to visualise a relationship that happens entirely within a mental space, the lovers' only contact being through their voices on the phone. Likewise, Duras (M.D.) and Benoît Jacquot (B.J.), with whom she is in dialogue in *voix off*, never appear, thereby contrasting with the visibility of Depardieu and Duras in the previous film, and invoking the liminal 'acousmatic' presence that Michel Chion finds exemplified across Duras's work (Chion [1982] 1999: 26, 120), thereby heightening the importance of what is invisible to the eye in Duras's film aesthetics. The woman of *Le Camion* is, however, said to close her eyes frequently on her journey in the lorry in order to see more than it is possible to see when looking out of the window, and the man and woman of *Le Navire Night* are said to see with their eyes closed too. Without face-to-face contact, the woman and the man look at themselves through each other's closed eyes: B.J.: 'He says that his entire body beats in the same way to the sound of her voice.' M.D.: 'She says that she knows. That she sees it. Hears it, with her eyes closed.' Listening in the dark, they both see without seeing, and listening viewers are encouraged as well to imagine on the basis of the voices heard beyond what is seen in the onscreen images.

The interior space of the house in which much of the filming takes place shows the signs of a film set: visible lighting but also blackboards on which Jacquot's and Duras's lines are written. Three actors appear occasionally in the visual images, sometimes together, sometimes separately: two women (Bulle Ogier and Dominique Sanda) and one man (Mathieu Carrière), silent for the most part, walking around the house in which they are filmed, looking, as if waiting for roles for which they are no longer required. The physical bodies of these figures may serve as the material basis for the formation of mental images of the virtual lovers that the spectators hear about – as was the case in the relation between Duras and the woman hitchhiker in *Le Camion* – but the actors differ from the descriptions given by the man and woman of themselves. Moreover, in this film that is so dependent on imagining those who are not seen, the descriptions proffered give just enough information to prompt the formation of mental images, but the relative freedom to imagine the man and woman thereafter is facilitated by a more general indistinctiveness that gives rise to figurative connections. Thus, while the set-up of this film differs from *Le Camion* in the ways already outlined, it is nonetheless just as precise yet scant in the guidance it gives for picturing the detail of the man and the woman as the earlier film was in guiding the formation of the imagined image of the woman hitchhiker. Furthermore, the pervasive wintry blank whiteness established so simply yet effectively at the beginning of the previous film gives way to a combination of colours that is also imprinted in the mental space. The bare mental image thereby assumes different hues.

The man and the woman are said to describe themselves in the following terms: B.J.: 'She describes herself as a young woman with black hair. Long.' M.D.: 'He says he is a young man too, blonde, with very blue eyes, tall, quite thin, handsome.' She gives less information to begin with than he does and emerges less distinctly as a result. Introduced as an element of precision in their respective descriptions of themselves, the colour of her hair and his eyes at once serve the image-making capacity of the imagination in literal terms and yet also form a figurative picture due to the colours lifting away from their designated relation to the couple's respective bodies, rather like the blue haze of Jarman's garden in summer. The colour palette of their combined image is recurrent in Duras's films and texts: it conveys the complexity of love and loss. It links up with the love without hierarchy that the woman of *Le Camion* advocates in the final stages of this earlier film through to a later concern on Duras's part with the plight of a fly in *Écrire*: as it lay on the floor dying, she tells of a strong connectedness without loss of difference between her and the insect, 'That queen. Black and blue' (Duras 1993: 43). These colours are also those of the title of her text on Yann Andréa, her partner during the later stages of her life (Duras 1986), and they associate too with the opening colours of *L'Homme Atlantique* in which Yann Andréa features – a black screen, followed by a deep, dark blue night sky, showing Andréa and his ghostly reflection in the window pane. The colours recall as well Aurélia Steiner of whom Duras writes: '*Yes, those eyes are blue. [. . .] Her hair is black*' (Duras [1980] 1996: 109). The precise form that the composite image of the man and the woman takes in the minds of spectators on the basis of the opening descriptions matters less than these colours, which cast the encounter between viewers' own mental pictures of the imagined couple as a painful contusion. This bruised image, black and blue, is one to which Duras returns in *Les Mains négatives* and it is in this film, as well as *Césarée*, that the pared down precision of Duras's prose gives rise to the more explicit formation of ruined mental images.

## Building Up and Bringing Down Mental Images

To break something down, it must already have been formed, and the process of creating followed by modifying and then dilapidating is what the two short films permit spectators to stage and restage in the imagination. In *Les Mains négatives* a black screen appears at the beginning and is the starting point for the formation of a mental image, which is then modified on the basis of the text Duras speaks over the presence of travelling shots through the city of Paris as the film advances from dawn into the light of day. The black screen is there while Duras explains in voice-over the definition of the 'mains négatives':

> *Mains négatives* are those handprints found on the walls of the Magdalenian caves in Western Europe. These hands were simply placed on the stone after having been coated in colour. In general they were black, or blue.

Duras's description paints a specific yet characteristically sparse image of these handprints in caves, the colours of which are definite. The image of black and blue hands is thus imprinted, through the spoken text, from the cavernous darkness of the screen, in the spectator's imagination, but only then to be altered, first in accretive terms. Unlike the reshaping of the perceived image in the imagination that we explored in the previous chapter, this is a reshaping of the mental image, based on repetition and change. The constant yet contrasting journeying of the travelling shots through Paris that accompany the voice-over throughout the film will call attention to itself as the mental images prompted by Duras's fragmented narrative also loom large, forming layers over it but also in tacit dialogue with it. What Duras achieves here on the way to the eventual collapse of the mental imagery that she stimulates is an instance of re-picturing that has been implicit in some of the examples explored throughout this book but which becomes pronounced in a more nuanced manner in this film.

The mental images that have been conjured forth in different ways in the preceding chapters do not all disappear never to be re-formed. Keiller's Robinson, Švankmajer's Usher and Madeline, or indeed Duras's woman hitchhiker may not be imagined figures who are sustained uninterrupted for the length of the films, but they are called forth several times across their respective films and this involves picturing them again and again. Debord's repeated reference to Madeleine Reineri too caused viewers to picture and re-picture her disappearance. Yet there is a specific way in which re-picturing works in Duras's *Les Mains négatives*, which relates to observations that Scarry makes about this process. For Scarry, re-picturing is associated in the first instance with the form of the circle, of doubling back, and of a mind that keeps turning back on itself. Noting how spherical shapes roll through the mind with great ease, she refers to Aristotle's declaration that the sphere is the most mobile of shapes before he concludes: 'Mind then, as well as fire, is composed of spherical atoms' (Aristotle cited in Scarry [1999] 2001: 196). Duras does not ask her spectators to picture spheres and make them move in the mind; rather, she puts the wheeling motion on screen as her camera crew films the streets of Paris from a moving vehicle. It is this repetitive motion, which spectators follow with their eyes through the city boulevards, that assists the different kind of re-picturing that the spoken text calls for, one that goes back on a previously formed mental image and changes it. The initial description of the black and blue hands in the caves over the black screen will be recalled and modified several times in the opening sequences as the movement of the onscreen vehicle that accompanies the imaginative work in the mental space goes round roundabouts, turns corners, and travels through the Parisian boulevards, gliding along as effortlessly as skaters wheeling across ice.

The spoken text that ensues after the initial black screen disappears positions listener-spectators before the ocean (*devant l'océan*), under the cliff (*sous la falaise*), directing the gaze to the wall of granite (*sur la paroi de granite*) that shows blue and black hands, palms open (*ces mains, ouvertes, bleues et noires*), the blue that of water (*du bleu de l'eau*), the black that of night (*du noir de la nuit*). A man is said to have come alone to the cave, opposite the ocean, to look at the hands, which are all of the same size, and, as Amy Flamer's screeching string music interrupts the words on the soundtrack, he is said to observe the immensity of everything (*l'immensité des choses*) against the noise of the sea before crying out: 'You who are named, who are gifted with identity, I love you.' Visually on screen while these opening words are spoken, the images show a journey through Paris in the half-light moving towards dawn (Figure 7.3). A succession of travelling shots reveals closed shops and rubbish piled high in the centre of the boulevards or strewn across the side pavements, the camera sometimes looking straight ahead, sometimes panning to the side. Aurally through the voice-over, the hands are then immediately recalled, serving as a prompt to mentally re-picture them, albeit slightly differently now: 'These hands / of the blue of water / of the black of the sky / Flat / Spread out across the grey granite / So that someone sees them'. Their colours are reiterated, causing spectators to reinstate the initial image, to recall it, but also to change it on the basis of further descriptive information provided by Duras. The hands, now described more specifically, are spread out flat across grey granite, as the mental image is articulated further – the initial description of open palms of black and blue gives way to a more precise black (of the sky) and blue (of water), but still with the relative freedom for listener-spectators to imagine what the blueness of the water and blackened sky might look like. To this description is added the specification of the size of the hands, the greyness of the stone on which they are imprinted,

Figure 7.3 *Les Mains négatives* (Marguerite Duras, 1979).

and the fact that there are a number of them, spread out across the stone just so that someone sees. Spectators are the ones seeing or rather picturing and re-picturing them, like the original man who sees them for the first time, all, of course, a product of the imagination. This, like *Le Navire Night*, is a tragic love story between people who never meet and who, in this case, are separated by millennia. Duras's voice speaks in the first person and identifies itself as that of the man of the cave who called out 'I love you' thirty thousand years ago: he who wants to love you, who loves you, and the you addressed here extends to her listener-spectators.

After an onscreen travelling shot passes a group of road sweepers who are just visible in the dawn light, the hands are recalled again with a further distinction added and with verbal intonation and grammatical omission functioning to highlight and isolate details now. They are said to remain (*resteront*) on empty land (*la terre vide*) facing the din of the ocean (*fracas de l'océan*); the subsequent term 'insoutenable' (unsustainable or unbearable) stands alone but speaks for both the durability of the hands in this environment and for pain, as Duras continues: 'Nobody will hear any longer' (*Personne n'entendra plus*) or see (*Ne verra*). The hint of a total eclipse of anything to be heard or seen is present as the reported din of the ocean combines with the image of the hands on granite, its imagined vigorous activity and noise intruding upon the isolated imprints of a witnessed presence. The mental image that is set up and modified in the opening stages of this film of the cave, the granite wall, and the imprinted hands, will eventually collapse, as we shall see, and this building and rebuilding of an image that will be made ultimately to disintegrate extends to the film *Césarée* too, which I turn to now before doubling back to *Les Mains négatives*.

The text Duras delivers in voice-over for *Césarée* evokes a place in which there is only the name that remains as a marker of the memory of a story, of history. The French name for the place, an ancient Roman city, now in Israel, has a feminine association through its double 'e' ending, and from the beginning, the place and the tragic destiny of a woman seem intermingled in that name, a move that carries distant echoes of Nevers (from the screenplay Duras wrote for *Hiroshima mon amour*) and S. Thala (from her text *Le Ravissement de Lol V. Stein/The Ravishing of Lol V. Stein*). Impossible love and its effect on the woman involved in the relation travels through the ages, and stretches back to Racine's expression of the tragic circumstance of such a liaison in *Bérénice*, and which the eponymous heroine summarises neatly at the end of the play: 'I love him, I am fleeing him; Titus loves me, he is leaving me' ('Je l'aime, je le fuis; Titus m'aime, il me quitte') (Racine [1671] 1982: 432). The pain of separation will haunt *Césarée* too. The more abundant usage of the black screen in this film does not serve the symmetrical punctuating purpose that the caesura of the classical alexandrine does in Racine's prose: its irregularity detaches from such a model drawn from writing. In keeping with her valorisation of her own darkroom or 'chambre noire' as a generative space, Duras seems to forge a broader association between the black screen and creativity, and it is light that brings with it an annihilating motion. In the mental space through which her prose travels, darkness gives way to illumination akin to Scarry's radiant ignition, but also to the setting in motion of destruction.

As spectators hear Duras pronounce the name of Caesarea several times at the opening of *Césarée*, over Amy Flamer's haunting string music that was also audible in *Les Mains négatives*, the visual images of the film begin with travelling shots that arc smoothly around and then back past one of the statues of the female form, *La Montagne* by Aristide Maillol, in the Jardin des Tuileries in Paris (Figure 7.4). The gliding, semi-circular motions are fitting, given that this film, like *Les Mains négatives*, will set up a mental scene that involves re-picturing initial imagined images and operating upon them. A brief cut to a black screen follows the opening travelling shots as Duras's voice-over prompts the formation of the first mental image, which is of whiteness: 'The ground. It is white.' As the film images cut to a fixed frame shot of a scaffold that surrounds one of the covered over white marble statues in the Paris gardens, the mental space

Figure 7.4 *Césarée* (Marguerite Duras, 1979).

in which the image of white ground is evoked is then said to be covered in marble dust and mixed with sea sand. Duras provides the foundation here on which to build subsequent mental images, but from the dustiness of this starting point, from which her prose passes through an oblique reference to the unbearable pain of separation, the ground is re-specified as a site of ruins. Onscreen travelling shots of Maillol's statues recur briefly and verbs of action also bring motion with them as the sea is said to pound heavily against the ruins (*frappe les ruines / toujours forte*) that remain of the place on the flat ground, before a black screen intervenes and spectators are then shown the upper part of a large statue under repair. The Parisian gardens are thus awash with a layering of mental images of a powerfully destructive sea. Duras then adds colour to the opening mental images in voice-over, as blue marble columns are described as having been 'thrown before the port'. This colour palette matches that of the sky and the dusty covering of the marble statue shown on screen and, through the mimetic relation to the perceived colours here, makes the mental images easy to picture, even as the onscreen images remain distinct from those that spectators are prompted to imagine on the basis of Duras's spoken words. A wrecked scene, with the sea crashing over debris, opens out the initial imagined image of white ground as listener-spectators are told twice over a close-up of the head of the statue under repair that everything has been destroyed (*Tout détruit. / Tout a été détruit*). The place name is again repeated, followed by three feminine past participles,

'Captured/Abducted/Taken into exile on the Roman vessel' (*Capturée, Enlevée, Emmenée* . . .), before the female subject, 'the queen of the Jews, the woman queen of Samaria', is introduced for the first time, along with the man responsible for her exile: 'He. The criminal.' From the opening mental image of material disintegration, and against the moving mental image of the sea hitting ruins, the female subject emerges, also in motion, being sent into exile on a Roman vessel by the criminal who destroyed the temple of Jerusalem, and she is thus momentarily reborn from the dust and rubble in the imagination.

Later, the voyage of her Roman vessel is recounted over a travelling shot that moves along water, gliding along on a straight axis now, as the queen does in the vessel conjured mentally by Duras's prose, the scrim of the perceived movement spectators experience (Figure 7.5). Later still, the exiled woman is described as very young, but in a manner that blocks the possibility of visualising her clearly: as the film cuts to black briefly, she is said to be eighteen, thirty, two thousand years old. It is not possible to picture her age, and she is timeless, cancelling the image of her that viewers may have generated when they first heard mention of the queen of Samaria. Her later arrival in the vessel from Rome, in the morning, in front of the town is a bare image of whiteness: 'Mute, white as chalk, appears.' These words are spoken over onscreen travelling shots filmed in the Tuileries, passing by a selection of statues again. From disintegrated marble and sand, to the chalky vision of the queen's floating sepulchre,

Figure 7.5 *Césarée* (Marguerite Duras, 1979).

whiteness recurs in the mental space intermittently, associated with death, loss, and ruin. After the queen of Samaria is said to re-emerge silently and white as chalk, a sudden explosion of ash is evoked in the sky (*Dans le ciel tout à coup l'éclatement de cendres*), which will fall on Pompeii and Herculaneum, burying everything. In the mental space, the explosive outburst of ash – an instance of sudden radiant ignition – lays a deadening blanket over everything, communing tacitly with the white-as-chalk muteness of the queen. In *Les Mains négatives*, to which it is now appropriate to return, this obliterating mental whiteness is disentangled from the plight of one woman and expanded.

After the opening sequence of *Les Mains négatives* in which the hands are pictured and re-pictured through the accretion or highlighting of details, the hands are described only as black now, and this is the final time in the film that the hands will be mentioned (*Ces mains-là, noires*). Although Duras's interest in these black hands is more bound up with aesthetics – the making of a mark in a cave for someone to see; the imprint of colour (black and blue) in the mental space – than a strident politics in this film, it is significant that the subsequent sequence shows in passing on screen an individual Parisian road sweeper as the voice-over gets spectators to mentally picture an obliterating white light refracted from the sea on the rock face: 'The refraction of light on the sea makes the rock face tremble.' The man who is said to speak through the millennia cries out through Duras's voice in the destructive white light: 'I am someone I am he who called out who cried out in this white light.' The radiant ignition of which Scarry speaks as a prerequisite for setting images in motion in literary texts is once again palpable here as the sturdy stone starts to shake and the movement that instigates a change in the pictured image results in dereliction while the invisible witness calls through the ages to a different Paris in which more people are emerging, dressed for office work. Duras speaks in interview of the colonial history implicit here in a hierarchy between those who work prior to dawn and those who succeed them (Duras [1984] 2001: 178). She notes the black men and Portuguese women she saw as she filmed: those who sweep the streets, clean shops and businesses, and who disappear as the day comes. There is no explicit critical commentary on this in the film itself, but the eclipse Duras speaks of here is visible between eye and mind.[8] The handprints that are singled out and re-pictured as black only at this juncture reach across to the solitary road sweeper subtly but nonetheless significantly.

As *Les Mains négatives* advances towards its conclusion, the wind is said to stir up a stormy ocean, the waves slowed by its strength, but they reach the rock face, patiently, and everything is crushed (*Tout s'écrase*).

Elemental forces fighting against each other eventually bring the initial wall of granite down in a mental image of destruction. In voice-over Duras states: 'For thirty thousand years I have been crying out in front of the sea the white spectre (*devant la mer le spectre blanc*) / I am he who cried out that he loved you.' The scene that the imagined man sees, that Duras voices, and that spectators create in their minds disappears, destroyed by the elements and by time. But he remains, through his call alone, as does the spectre of the sea – an image that is self-cancelling, but a cry that is unchanging, relentless, which is in the continuous tense (*je crie*) before slipping into the past (*je suis celui qui criait*), while still remaining in the absence of anything other than this whited out mental space as the onscreen journeying through Paris into the day continues. Within the superposition of the pulverising sea and its spectral whiteness, it is possible to discern a further, if distant, refraction of whiteness that colonises the scene and eclipses all others. Duras's onscreen Parisian images in *Les Mains négatives* constitute the making of a mark that does not resemble the mark of the hands on the granite walls that spectators are first asked to picture and then re-picture. Yet perception and imagination work in different ways here along different image-tracks, which nonetheless communicate with each other from the dawn of humanity to witness the existence of the dawn workers.

*Césarée* also returns to Paris in the voice-over in conclusion thereby joining with the onscreen Parisian images that have been visible throughout. The mental imagery generated by Duras's prose in *Césarée* is halted in the final stages of the film with what seems a definitive statement: 'There is nothing further to see' (*Il n'y a plus rien à voir*). Yet this is said the better to convey the vastness of everything there is to see: 'But everything' (*Que le tout*). In the closing moments, Duras speaks of Paris as images of the city continue to appear on screen: 'It is a bad summer in Paris. Cold. Misty.' This mundane final line belies the astonishing imaginative journey spectators have taken through imagined images, visualising the burial of a place and the demise of a woman, as the spoken word aligns ultimately with the perceived setting of the statuesque markers of the female form in the present in Paris. The mental mist generated over the final Parisian image on screen – a clear shot of a marble statue of a semi-clad woman against a pale blue sky – recalls that of one of the opening mental images of *Le Camion*, yet it is an imagined bare image of closure this time, clouding over the mental space as the film itself ends.

Duras's films reach out from the darkest of places: a man journeys into the depths of a cave to leave his handprint, to make a mark in the darkness and silence; a ship sails through the night air, with no land, light, or other vessels in sight, moving slowly in the pitch-blackness. Nothingness is all there is ahead, behind, around: the contours of the abyss are unfathomable. Lovers, like ships that pass in the night, along with other solitary figures, call out through the void of separation, desperate for someone to hear their cry. Another person, distant in place and time, is out there but invisible. To give space to what is invisible to the eye is to create a place for that other, who may not ease the suffering but who may become a fellow traveller, if only for a while. Thus, too, the writer covets her transient witness from the shadows of her cavernous darkroom, before flooding it with light. This is the light of Duras's cinema, stark and devastating.

In both of the short films discussed in this final section, light and whiteness are the sources of the creation of a ruined mental image. These concluding examples in a chapter devoted to some of the ways in which the erasure of mental pictures is enacted in the mind might be taken as a metaphor for the act that cinema performs on writing in Duras's terms, as light invades the darkness of her darkroom of writerly creativity, initiating movement within mental imagery only to form an image of annihilation. Yet something generative is still at work, akin to the clarity of vision both the woman of *Le Camion* and the protagonists of *Le Navire Night* have with their eyes closed. It is only cinema that can provide this insight, born of the dual vision in which images appear to both the eyes and the mind.

# Conclusion: Broadening Out

Whenever vivid imagined images become apparent while viewing film, something remarkable is happening, and it is precisely this striking experience of imagining in images that my book has sought to explore. When the jostling contact of the bird and the rose spoken about over a black screen in the latter half of Duras's *L'Homme Atlantique* was described in the first section of this book, it was not possible at that point to account precisely for how that mental image takes shape. Now, however, we can return to this first encounter in the light of the processes that have unfolded chapter by chapter, in order to suggest how that velour collision comes to be pictured and to place it in the wider context of this particular film throughout which all of the aforementioned processes variously succeed one another and combine.

The radiant ignition, to reiterate Scarry's term, of an imagined sunrise ('And then the sun rose') was already acknowledged in the earlier chapter as a prerequisite for creating and setting in motion the subsequent scene that is also never shown on screen: 'I heard the bird's brushing of the rose in its velvet flight. And I looked at the rose. It moved first as if animated with life and then little by little it became an ordinary rose once again.' The mental image of this encounter, wing to petal, is layered over the screen, having been positioned by Duras as a scene that is heard and seen by the speaking I. As was observed in the chapter on layering, imagined surface contact between two entities confers substantiality on both: the brushing together of the surface of a bird's wing and the petals of a flower in a way that disturbs the flower before it regains its stillness firms up the possibility of seeing the scene in the mind. It does not borrow from qualities shown on screen at this point in the film (as was the case for several examples discussed in the chapter on layering and beyond), since the screen is completely black, but it is facilitated by the fact that the words pertain to entities whose size, among other qualities that Scarry refers to, means that they can be readily imagined. As Scarry notes of flowers especially, the ease with which they can be pictured demonstrates the aspiration of imagining to bring about a mimesis of perceiving that lends the mental image vivacity (Scarry [1999] 2001: 43). The sound of the sea that is heard throughout this sequence adds spatial volume to the mental arena, contributing to the motion of the imagined scene through the rush of an ebb and flow, of a gentle yet persistent expansion and contraction, both aural and spatial, key to volumising.[1] The sea is always nearby in Duras's work, even when it is not visible or audible on screen. Although the sea does appear on screen in the earlier part of the film as well as briefly at the end of this sequence, now hushed, its continuation in aural-perceptual terms across the passages of blackness in which the garden encounter of bird and rose is described ensures its continuing presence in the space of the imagination too. The composite mental image of this scene, born of layering and volumising, fades on its own and does not partake of the explicit erasure spoken about at length in the previous chapter with regard to Duras's work. This entire film is, however, built on a succession of extinctions, which will return us ultimately to flowers and to listener-spectators being prompted consciously to imagine wilting blooms in a rose garden of the mind. For the moment, let us linger on its first half in which onscreen images are interspersed more frequently with black leader, since they show how other processes are also initiated.

The interior setting of the hotel space that is present in the first part of the film is the same as that in *Agatha et les lectures illimitées/Agatha and the Unlimited Readings*, also of 1981, in which Bulle Ogier and Yann Andréa feature. Made from the off-cuts of this film and now featuring Andréa alone, *L'Homme Atlantique* shows him early on looking out of the window, reflected in the glass at night, as well as walking and sitting in the hall of mirrors that distorts the space he is in; the mirrors expand but also disorient any exact sense of where he is positioned. He appears and disappears from the frame, sometimes into the *mise en abîme* of the hall of mirrors, sometimes just absent from the filmed images of empty chairs, sea, and sky, as well as disappearing entirely along with his setting when the black images appear: it is thus his absence that the film records as readily as his presence. Of the man who will become one with the sea, nothing will be left but this floating absence; nothing else will occur but what Duras's voice calls this 'absence drowned in regret'. When he first appears silhouetted against the deep blue sky, pale, looking obliquely out of the window and reflected faintly, ghost-like in the glass, she talks of an absolute gaze which will try to look 'to the point that [your] sight fails, to the point of blindness, and even through this [you] must try again to look'. His head turns slightly as if listening to what she is saying; the act of looking to the point of not being able to see any more and still trying to see through this speaks for the extinction of which he is a part. The focus on his face in profile, with his head cocked slightly, is not akin to the rapt, emotive attention of the spectators that we witnessed in *Shirin* whose expressions carried the imprint of the supplementary activity of imagining while watching a film. But the fact that he is directed by Duras's voice and appears to be listening to it marks the impression nonetheless of imagining on screen. The onscreen image bears the imprint of the image-making that is prompted by her words, even though they occupy separate spaces, and the propensity to imagine is inscribed in the listening ear incarnated on screen here. The supplement of imagination opens too to the reshaping of the onscreen image, albeit in a distinctive fashion that again is specific to this film but that is related to the process discussed in an earlier chapter.

Duras tells him subsequently to look at the sea, before the image cuts to black and she speaks of successive disappearances: of a dog, of the coastline, of a seagull in the Atlantic wind, all of which are conjured only to be cancelled in the mind – fleeting instances of mental erasure. As he is told to listen (in the present tense), she explains that if he does not look at what is presented to him and that will be seen on the screen, the screen will empty out. A shot of the sea accompanies the first part of this instruction, gunmetal grey against cream sand, filmed through the frame of a hotel window, before the image cuts to black when the screen is spoken about as emptying out. While the coastline becomes visible, the dog and the seagull are never shown, but they return in her voice-over, with the gull qualified and referred to subsequently as 'that tenacious gull battling against the wind' and later as 'that tragic gull struggling against the wind'. Mental images of a gull braving the wind soar against a black screen in both evocations, yet they also relate back to the coastal images that intersperse the blackness. The gull joins the memory of the coastal image shown on screen, adding to the memory of the perceived image and layering this transformed image, born of perception and imagination, over the blackness. This transformation of the sky owes something to the reshaping of the perceived image that we explored in an earlier chapter. Rather than an equivalent of, say, solid factories being rebuilt on wasteland visible on screen for the length of a shot, though, as was the case in the example of Keiller's *London*, the gull, pictured and re-pictured, tenacious and then tragic, is subject to the elemental force of the wind which, coupled with the intermittent perceived sound of the sea, is buffeted in the mind across onscreen images and blackness and, like everything else here, is just passing through.

## CONCLUSION: BROADENING OUT 159

From the beach and hotel in winter, imaged on screen at the start of *L'Homme Atlantique*, to the height of summer in a park (the seasonal trajectory of her earlier film *Le Camion* too), evoked without being shown towards the end of the film, Duras builds up images only eventually to remove them. Narrated over a black screen, the park is said to have roses in it, but they are in an area that is rarely seen. Duras writes of these roses:

> It is said that high summer is on its way, that is possible. I don't know. That the roses are already out, there, at the bottom of the park. That sometimes they are never seen by anyone while they are alive and that they hold themselves like that in their perfume, open for several days, and then they fall to pieces. Never seen by that lone woman who is trying to forget. Never seen by me, they die.

This hidden life – and death – of the roses that Duras suggests have not been seen by anyone and that is never shown on screen occasions a bringing to life of flowers that then disintegrate in the imagination. Erasure joins thus with reshaping, supplementing, volumising, and layering to form and transform the mental moving pictures generated by this film.

My argument throughout the preceding five chapters has sought to emphasise that no one process is attached solely to the examples discussed, and *L'Homme Atlantique* shows how a number of processes sometimes coalesce when viewing an individual work. The exploration of filmic examples that prompt spectators to visualise has involved attending to mental activities that owe something to processes prevalent in reading, as has been suggested by the relevance of Scarry's scholarship to the different kinds of image-making occasioned by watching and listening to film. As is the case with *L'Homme Atlantique*, several of the works that I have referred to challenge their very definition as films in their valorisation of the verbal dimension and their debt to quasi-readerly imagining, sometimes in the total absence of any onscreen image. My intention has not been to locate such examples closer to literature than to film, even though filmmakers such as Duras are also acclaimed writers and others cite directly and extensively from literary texts; filmic specificity has been foregrounded throughout rather than ignored in these and all other examples discussed. I suggested at the outset of my study that the processes of mental composition are relevant to a wider range of films beyond those that I have since focused on in detail, and I have indicated some such other examples along the way. I add to these now in conclusion in order to gesture towards ways in which the imaginative terrain of image-making might be extended still further.

Thanks to an entrancing combination of onscreen visual images and his father's poetry read in voice-over shortly after the start of *Zerkalo/ Mirror* (1975), Russian filmmaker Andrey Tarkovsky shows that he knows as well as Duras the power that Scarry refers to when writing of how birds and particularly flowers aid the creation of imagined images. The mention of flora and fauna towards the beginning of *Mirror* does not cause them to brush together as in Duras's film as part of a more brutal disturbance of suffering from love but, rather, supports and cushions the creation of a more peaceable mental image of two lovers at an earlier stage of their relationship. The poem, 'First Meetings', by his father Arseny Tarkovsky recalls the idyll of precious moments that two lovers once spent together. It is written in the first person and read out by Tarkovsky's father. The addressed lover in the poem is described as 'more daring and lighter than a bird' before the poem progresses by building a downward motion akin to vertiginous flight, 'Down the stairs, like a dizzy apparition', that contrasts with the more grounded and gentle onscreen climb of the onscreen woman, Margarita Terekhova, who plays both Maria, Alexi's young mother, and Natalia, his wife, and whom the camera follows. The poem proceeds as she pauses on screen and turns to look back: 'You came to take me on your road / Through rain-soaked lilacs / To your own possession / To the looking-glass world'. The onscreen image cuts from her turn of the head to her young son whose head turns too, continuing the circle from mother to child before he wanders along in the opposite direction outside. Lilac is resonant with spring and the first stirrings of love but is not only symbolic here: it is literal in its presence in the mental space, colouring it with a hint of floral delicacy while the onscreen hues become darker and the light begins to fade, as the scene cuts to the interior of the house showing two children eating and playing with their food at the table. The imagined lilac gives way to night in the poem as a mental image of nakedness is ignited in the darkness before the image is tilted: 'And in the darkness shining / And slowly reclining was your body naked'.[2] But the lilac then returns to colour the mental scene with a different illumination: 'My blessing was: You were fast asleep / Your closed eyelids with the universal blue / The lilac on the table so strained to sweep / Touched by the blue, your lids / Were quite serene . . .'. As the lover's sleeping eyelids are said in the poem to be touched by the universal blue that lifts off the description to float in the mind as it did in the buzzing summery image of Jarman's garden, an expansive camera movement shifts from the onscreen view of the children at the table to Maria in the darkness of the corner of the room, who looks outwards to meet the gaze of the camera in the distance. The lightness of a bird helps an imagined image to arise and the damp lilac serves to ground both lovers before the predominant colours of green and brown in the onscreen image are braided with lilac flowers in the mind, lending the entire palimpsest a hint of blue.

The visual richness of even this short scene contrasts markedly with Duras's denuded onscreen images and her pervasive recourse to blackness in *L'Homme Atlantique*. Yet as was indicated at length in an earlier chapter, blankness can be an ideal stimulus for imagining in images, as recognised in the extended discussion of works by Ruttmann and Jarman, in addition to the curatorial work of Hulse, and the brief side-glance at the presence of volumising in relation to the more momentary blankness nestling nonetheless significantly within Jonze's *Her*. This latter brief example, when positioned in the context of a sequence in which the main protagonist Theodore appears and is audible on screen, demonstrates that the spoken word and soundscape do not have to exist solely in voice-over or as *voix off* and can emerge from the diegetic space in which fictional characters are visible for the most part rather than occluded. This was also evident in the first of the processes discussed in this book in the example of the real-life figure of Jane Birkin and her dream as recounted in Varda's *Jane B. by Agnès V.* in the chapter on layering. In this and the earlier examples mentioned or recalled here, great emphasis has been placed on the sonorous and verbal means by which vivid mental pictures are prompted, yet this should not obscure the fact that these elements of film do not automatically signal that mental image-making is possible, desirable, or even necessary every time verbal elements and a soundscape predominate. We witness this wherever verbal abstraction prevails, rendering ambiguous or unclear what, if anything, is to be pictured, but it also comes to light for other reasons. In Varda's documentary short *Elsa la rose/Elsa the Rose* (1965), for example, which is devoted to Louis Aragon's passion for his wife, the writer Elsa Triolet, Aragon's love poetry that Michel Piccoli reads out in voice-over is deliberately fast-paced, and it is the incantatory, almost liturgical rhythms and timbre of the voiced words that matter rather than the individual phrases and mental pictures that might be generated were the poetry to be voiced at a slower pace. Moreover, as has been clear from the outset, even films that stimulate mental composition more deliberately do not do so uniformly for the entire length of their running time. Image-making can be sporadic and fleeting, yet it is for these very reasons that it can also be pointed to in a far wider selection of examples. The process of layering occasioned by both the spoken word and broader soundscape extended into other chapters too and was not just a function of the essay films and documentaries foregrounded in that initial discussion. Following on from its foundational place in this book and its combination with the other processes discussed in subsequent chapters, layering spans indeed a whole range of films that reverse the impulse to show rather than tell. In Ingmar Bergman's *Persona* (1966), for example, nurse Alma (Bibi Andersson) tells the story of a sexual encounter on a beach while her fiancé is away for the day to the mute actress in her care, Elisabet Vogler (Liv Ullmann). The tale brings forth a vivid scene in the mind that is intensely erotic and that works with the set-up, postures, and gazes of the women on the screen. It furnishes an instance of layering that is guided by the spoken word and that borrows from the perceived images to strengthen the imagined images.

The scene in which Alma recounts her sexual encounter lasts around seven minutes and the shots are sustained to the extent that they aid the image-making of imagination without distraction. Alma evokes a nice warm day on the beach (Scarry's radiant ignition) where she is alone at first and then joined by another girl who paddles over from a separate island. As Alma sets up the sunny scene in the imagination, Elisabet is visible in the depth of the shot, sitting upright on the bed with her back to the wall, cigarette in one hand perched on a raised knee, the other arm resting along the top of a pillow. Alma sits in an armchair to the side of the foot of the bed, her upper body visible in profile. Alma narrates how she and this other girl were lying naked in the sun wearing only cheap straw sunhats, and as she describes the hats – hers, she specifies, has a blue ribbon around it – she sketches their shape by drawing a loose circle around her head, looking to Elisabet as she does so, and also thereby aiding mental image formation. The angle of Alma's head and of her bent arm that remains raised after the description of the hats is suggestive of the brim and angle of her head and hat as she tells of how she lay peeping out from underneath it, looking at the landscape, sea, and sun. Imagining borrows thus from the perceived images and this relationship is strengthened as the film cuts to a frontal shot of Alma in the chair. Her eyes look to the side and slightly upwards – away from Elisabet who is now off-screen – as she describes how she suddenly noticed a couple of boys leaping about on the rocks above them, the angle of her gaze aiding the imagining of her upward gaze from the beach. And as she describes turning to the girl who was bathing naked alongside her to tell her about the boys, Alma looks to Elisabet and then turns her head slightly as if miming her action on the beach, which continues to assist the formation of a mental image of her turn to the girl whose name she now announces to be Katarina. Alma reports that Katarina says to let them look and rolls over on to her back. As Alma describes this, she rolls away from Elisabet in the armchair, turning her back to her and curling up, the physical roll in the present space accompanying the narration of the imagined roll of Katarina that initiates their sexual encounter with the boys. The encounter that is narrated over the ensuing minutes (what I have outlined thus far lasts just over one minute) involves the girls having sex with the boys, with Alma looking towards Elisabet to whom the film cuts when she describes how she came over and over again with one of the boys, aware of Katarina lying on her side and watching. Alma and Elisabet are at some distance from one another in the set-up of the scene (Alma will eventually close this distance when she joins Elisabet on the bed), but the cuts to each of them in isolation, with Alma narrating and Elisabet listening, brings them closer, onscreen image against onscreen image. As the recounted sex brings bodies together with flesh touching flesh inside and out, the mental images also vivify through such narrated contact. Through the avoidance of any flashback or mental memory or fantasy images on screen here, the narration and movements of Alma in relation to Elisabet help the formation and duration of the imagined scene that layers over without blocking out what is perceived, both borrowing from it and contributing to it.

The technique of focusing spectatorial attention on the onscreen image as a character narrates events that can be pictured is not of course limited to such an art house example. While the filmic examples that I have discussed throughout this book were chosen because they permitted extended exploration, there are salient instances within films beyond the art house, documentary, and more experimental contexts that have been the basis of the previous chapters. Both Vinit Masram and David Bordwell refer to the scene from *Persona* that I have just described when speaking of telling rather than showing, relating it fascinatingly to disparate examples from Bollywood to Hollywood (Masram 2016; Bordwell 2010). I refer to just two of the instances that they mention here in order to indicate how image-making is prompted in more momentary but nonetheless significant ways in the context of such narrative cinema. Indeed, here as elsewhere, wherever a voice-over is evocative as it relates to or diverges from what is seen on screen, when a soundtrack speaks louder than words, or if characters tell stories in the diegetic space without their words giving way to images that illustrate what they are narrating, there are openings for the vivid image-making of the imagination that has been my subject throughout.

In Ashutosh Gowariker's *Swades: We, the People* (2004), for example, there are occasions when the lead character Mohan (Shah Rukh Khan) speaks about events that are never shown or seen and that spectators are prompted to imagine through description. One of the pivotal scenes in this regard, which is responsible for a cumulative change in Mohan's attitude towards his Indian place of birth is when Mohan himself sits and listens to a heart-breaking tale of hardship. Mohan, a NASA engineer who immigrated to the USA years beforehand, has travelled back to India on extended leave of absence to find his beloved nanny Kaveriamma (Kishori Ballal). His journey through India is one of self-discovery in which he falls in love with a childhood friend, Gita (Gayatri Joshi), and helps the local community to which he will eventually return and settle within. When Mohan is sent by Kaveriamma to collect rent from a tenant of Gita's property, the poor man tells his sorrowful tale of how he cannot pay. He recounts how he used to be a weaver before he took up farming but the advent of machines for weaving meant that this soon ceased to be a lucrative business. He describes how he took Gita's land on lease, thinking that when crops flourished his children's life would improve, but it did not happen. He continues, outlining that the village elders did not accept his change of profession since they felt that a weaver should remain a weaver and, as a result, he became an outcast. His tale of how he cried and pleaded accompanies his tears in the present as he recounts his situation to Mohan. The imagined images of the man's experiences emerge through a mimesis of the onscreen images of him and his family as the camera gradually closes in on him and the film cuts between him and Mohan, before a succession of shots of his face, that of Mohan, and the man's wife, shows their tears.

The sustained focus on a filmed subject within a sequence that features either an onscreen or off-screen narrative, even if this does not comprise a long take, has been an important element from the very outset of my discussion of the various processes of mental composition in permitting the imagined images prompted by that sequence to abide, from Tarn's image of a young girl on a swing to Straub and Huillet's attention to Mont Sainte-Victoire. In this example from *Swades* that retains concentration on the narrated story across the cuts to different figures in the room, remaining with the telling rather than shifting to flashbacks is effective not only in revealing and lingering upon everyone's visible emotion but also in permitting spectators to imagine what led up to this point in a guided manner for the length of the sequence. In a further example, now from a film by Otto Preminger, the focus on the intensity of emotion experienced by onscreen characters is also as important as the imaginative activity that accompanies it: the framing of the classic confessional scene of *Exodus* (1960) permits guided imagining of horrors that are not shown. Dov Landau (Sal Mineo) wants to be admitted to the Irgun, a guerrilla group whose goal is to drive the British out of Palestine, and in order to join he has to explain his activities in Auschwitz during the Second World War.

## CONCLUSION: BROADENING OUT   165

Through persistent probing questions mainly from Ari Ben Canaan (Paul Newman) that eventually reveal the sickening truth of Dov's position in the Sonderkommando, he describes the camp, what happened to those sent there, and his own activities, and is asked again and again to revisit aspects of his story as his chief questioner gradually unearths his ashamed complicity in the running of the camp. The details Dov gives of what those in the camp undergo when they arrive – from the description of undressing and clipping of the hair onwards – are enough to set off the grim yet vivid process of mental composition that leads to the gas chambers and mass disposal of bodies. Ari moves around the room towards the start of his questioning, arcing around the table and back again, while Dov remains seated, the stillness of his position corresponding to abiding contact with the imagined images that arise from his stories. Ari's movements dovetail with his requests to Dov to recreate his experience again for him and pre-empt his subsequent circling back to Dov's earlier responses when he too is seated, prompting the mental activity of re-picturing as Dov revisits, adds to, and updates his story. In an intense shot/reverse-shot exchange, Ari discredits and accordingly erases Dov's account of blowing up Nazis with dynamite in the Warsaw ghetto and then initiates the adjustment of imagining Dov as the camp cleaner and kitchen worker he positions himself as before Ari's questioning begins. In Ari's corrective of Dov's earlier accounts of how it was at Auschwitz, Dov becomes an agent of the very activities he first described without implicating himself, pictured mentally now as a demolition squad worker who blew holes in the ground to bury the bodies. The deception of Dov's recounted memory and its subsequent correction initiates alterations in what and how he is imagined in the camp that work in tune with the movements, stillness, emotions, and gravity of the scene on screen, borrowing from it and layering over it to form a superposition of imagining and perceiving.

These examples from *Swades* and *Exodus*, drawn respectively from Masram's and Bordwell's mention of the films following their comments on *Persona*, serve here to demonstrate how strategies of telling rather than showing ignite imagining in ways that might extend the parameters of this study into other filmic territory. A more expansive critical reading of both films would situate such mental image-making in the wider context of each, attending to their respective ideologies, and while this lies beyond the scope of this conclusion, it leads me usefully to the question of how vivid mental image-making emerges as more than just an end in itself. One of the main aims of this study has been to outline the processes at work in making mental motion pictures, and to recognise this as an important part of the film experience. I isolated the processes that give rise to imagining in images in Part II of this book in order to give them their due. But just as I stressed a connection to other aspects of mental activity when outlining dual vision in Part I, the detailed filmic analyses that enabled the various processes to be explored at length in Part II also situated image-making in relation to the wider context of each film. As the varied examples discussed throughout my study have suggested, guided imagining does not always and only accompany purely aesthetic concerns. The dovetailing of such imagining with ethically and especially politically motivated concerns has been evident in diverse examples, from the works of Jarman through Kiarostami to Švankmajer, Keiller, Straub–Huillet and Debord. Yet even films that seek for political and ethical reasons to imagine things on screen also occasionally encourage spectatorial imagining in ways relevant to the processes discussed in the preceding chapters. A pertinent example in this regard is Rithy Panh's *L'Image manquante/The Missing Picture* (2013), in which the missing picture referred to in the title of the film relates to the true conditions of those like Panh and his family who were expelled from Phnom Penh in 1975 by the Khmer Rouge and deported to camps. Rather than be complicit with the censorship practices of the propaganda machine of the so-called revolution, Panh's film reimagines the conditions on screen using figurines in conjunction with available archival footage. However, the words of the voice-over sometimes prompt the imagining of horrors that are missing from the regime's official footage, which Panh does not seek to reconstitute. Just over two-thirds of the way through the film is a sequence in which he films in colour the making of one of the figurines that help to recreate what it was like to live under the Khmer Rouge. The voice-over continues to speak of what life was like for the people in the camps, asking: 'Who filmed the sick people? Who filmed the pagodas turned into hospices? The worm-eaten knee of my bunk neighbour? Or this young woman who can't deliver, who screams all night, alone, hitting her belly, to death?' The film cuts briefly after this without comment to black-and-white footage of a woman lying on the floor looking uncomfortably towards the camera, yet what cannot be shown has already been created in the imagination – a brutal image of the desperate erasure of life. The words give just enough information for mental composition to add a chilling layer to that which elsewhere is recreated and shown on screen, and the film thus builds and also encourages the further construction of counter narratives and counter images to the official line. This is part of a political and ethical project devoted to the people who died as a result of brutality and starvation, and the images that are imagined here contribute to the ongoing need to bear witness to their experience and to keep their memory alive.

# CONCLUSION: BROADENING OUT

The image-making of the imagination that has been explored throughout this book can serve an urgent ethics and politics as readily as it dovetails with varying aesthetics, then, diverging from or aligning with what is on screen as the imagined images guided by words and sounds form, transform, deform, re-form, and disappear. Yet it can also float free. Such mental composition as has been described in this book conjures qualities of vivacity and substantiality worthy of the perceived world from which it borrows. Although transient, these images of the mind eschew transparency, commanding attention within the broader film experience. In the garden, on the terrace, illuminated by the rising sun, the rose that is jostled by the wing of a passing bird and felt as the contact between feather and petal is also the contact of mental images coming into being in the light of the mind. This light is one that the author of this initial image also shuns readily, playing as other directors have done too with the dynamics of presence and absence, the internal and external, the onscreen and off-screen world in films that invite spectators to visualise more than there is to see on screen. These imagined images that accompany perception testify to the duality of seeing pictures when watching film and to the enduring strength of that experience.

# Postscript

In *Chroma*, Derek Jarman addresses his readership in a manner that pre-empts my own sentiment as I draw this book to a close with a few final words. Jarman writes: 'If I have overlooked something you hold precious – write it in the margin. [. . .] I know that my colours are not yours. Two colours are never the same, even if they're from the same tube' (Jarman [1994] 1995: 42). My imagined images will never be yours, but my hope is that the processes that I have outlined in the preceding pages help to explain some of the ways in which image-making takes place if and when you experience it when you view films. Moreover, the broadening out of the previous chapter is a potentially infinite activity that calls to be continued. Therefore, as I hand this book over, I invite my readers to extend its reach, to broaden the picture still further, and to take guided imagining into as yet unexplored terrain.

# Notes

## Chapter 1

1. There is also an appeal to the imagination in their online advertisement for 3D cinema: 'open your eyes, open your ears and open your imagination' ('Real D 3D', available at <https://www.odeon.co.uk/3d/>, last accessed 25 February 2019).
2. Imagination is key to many cognitive film theories. See especially Currie 1995 for a general theory of imagining and Smith 1995 for a study of the spectator as imaginative agent. For a broader theory of the arts in which imagination is pivotal, see Walton 1990. See also Smith 2017: 178–85 for an exploration of empathy as a kind of imagining.
3. Currie is referring to Mary Warnock's understanding of imagination (Warnock 1976). Engaging in critical dialogue in response to Currie's foundational work more recently, Rafe McGregor concurs that 'there seems little, if any, visualization required in watching a film' (McGregor 2012).
4. See Collins 1991a, 1991b; Esrock 1994; Schwenger 1999; Scarry [1999] 2001.
5. The most comprehensive article on this subject to date is Hanich 2018. See also Hanich 2010: ch. 4. See Barker 2006 for discussion of visualisation and adaptation studies.
6. Scarry's book is in part a defence of reading in an increasingly image-saturated culture, and to draw inspiration from her work in a film-centred text might be understood to go against the grain of this. I am not however advocating that anyone watch films in place of reading and believe that the two activities can and do complement each other.
7. See, for example, Grinnell 2016 and Klein 2017 for research into 'aphantasia' or the absence of mental pictures.
8. The scholarship on mental imagery within the imagery debate is voluminous. For a helpful overview, see Thomas 2014.
9. For a restatement and an update of his initial theory, see also Pylyshyn 2002.
10. Between the publication of his 1983 text and this text, Kosslyn updates the depictive theory with an account of how imagery can be neurologically embodied. See Kosslyn 1994.
11. Gregory Currie speaks of one kind of imagining as a form of simulation, which involves running our mental states off-line (Currie 1995: 144–61). For a critique of this analogy, see Grødal 2009: 182–6.

12. The telephone exchange and computer are the two principal metaphors she discusses. She revises her position on the computer in a later text in the light of developments in Artificial Intelligence. See Malabou 2017. I thank Michael Grace for bringing this text to my attention.
13. Their subsequent book, *Sight Unseen*, reflects on their research in the light of rapid advances in visual neuroscience in the intervening decade and the development of fMRI (Milner and Goodale 2005). In the second edition of *The Visual Brain in Action* they suggest more of a relation between the two streams (Milner and Goodale 2006).
14. See his interview with Rob Hopkins (Hopkins 2018). See also Schlegel et al. 2013. It may be more accurate to align the kind of guided imagining that will concern me in this book with what scientists have labelled the task positive network: as will become increasingly apparent, I am interested in mental images that emerge under attentive instruction rather than those of daydreams or a wandering mind. Scholars of neuroscience have however noted that the concept of two large anti-correlated networks (the default mode or task negative network and the task positive network) mediating attention switching in the brain may be overly simplistic. See Blumenfeld 2016: 19. As he reports, this field of research is still very much in evolution.
15. See, for example, Jacobson 2014 and Haigh et al. 2013 for studies of activity in the visual cortex of blind people as a result of sensory substitution devices that enable them to navigate the world on the basis of the soundscapes the devices create.
16. Like many theorists of imagination, McGinn distinguishes between sensory imagining (forming a mental image) and cognitive imagining (conceptually entertaining a possibility), but he also considers transitions between the two. Although my own interest is in the former domain, I too am not denying a relation between image-making and other aspects of cognitive activity or indeed image-making and other aspects of imagining.
17. For the catalogue of Alexander James's works, see <http://www.DistilEnnui.com> (last accessed 25 February 2019).
18. For a broad discussion of imagining in the wake of the death of imagination as a fixed faculty, see Casey [1976] 2000.
19. There has been more recent philosophical debate on the question of whether or not dream contents are experienced as believed or imagined. For a succinct overview of the positions, see Gendler 2011.
20. For a further philosophical reading of the relationship between film image and dream, see McGinn 2005.
21. The (male) spectator theorised by apparatus theory is duped by what is seen and cinema provides only an imaginary pleasure, a dream world that does not form critical subject-positions attuned to the functioning of ideology. In later Lacanian theory, Todd McGowan shifts focus from the imaginary dimension and towards the Lacanian Real, arguing for a closer relationship between film and dream, which in turn is more attentive to the functioning of ideology. See McGowan 2007.

22. Other scholars have considered daydreams and dreams, along with fantasy, in order to explore how film mobilises imagination variously in the service of illusion and reality. See, for example, Allen 1997; Scruton 1983.
23. Originally published with this title in July 1936 in *The Stage*, the article was republished on 27 November 1936 in the *Portsmouth Evening News* as 'I Make Suspense My Business'. I cite from the latter.
24. Brakhage also describes 'closed-eye vision', which is discernible in dreams as well as behind closed eyes in the daylight and involves seeing moving shapes and forms through the redness of the eyelid (Brakhage 1963b: 22).
25. Most notably in this book, the testimony of Hugues de Montalembert in Chapter 3 on Layering and Derek Jarman in Chapter 4 on Volumising, both of whom retain a strong capacity to visualise as their sight diminishes or disappears completely. For a contrasting example, see John M. Hull's *Touching the Rock* (Hull [1990] 2013), and the documentary it inspired, *Notes on Blindness* (Peter Middleton and James Spinney, 2014). Hull testifies to the fading of mental images the deeper he moves towards acceptance of blindness. Neurologist Oliver Sacks, who writes the preface to Hull's book, notes how he received indignant responses from some other blind people after this was published because they did not share this diminishing of the visual aspect of their inner life (Sacks 2010).
26. Barthes 1970 and Bonnefoy 1988 have also commented on the significance of lifting their head from the book they are reading.
27. Home entertainment systems now permit viewers to slow, rewind, and pause film images, making it possible to do what Barthes deemed impossible. See Mulvey 2006 for an elegant discussion of this.
28. *Wishful Thinking* is episode three of Wharry's *General Picture* series. It is a black-and-white 16mm sound film that lasts for four minutes and fifteen seconds.
29. I am grateful to Martin Brady for bringing Kluge's writings to my attention.
30. More specifically, Wittgenstein's remark is aimed at revealing differences in people's language games regarding perceiving and imagining. See also Wollheim 1973: 56.

# Chapter 2

1. All translations from Duras's films throughout my study are my own because there are no official English translations in existence; for this reason, I also use their French titles when discussing them. Most of the other foreign-language films that I discuss in this book have also been released with English titles and subtitles, and I use these instead.
2. Scarry outlines five principal means by which writers get readers to move mental images: radiant ignition; rarity; addition and subtraction; stretching, folding, and tilting; and floral supposition.
3. For example, Luce Irigaray writes that Merleau-Ponty 'accords an *exorbitant* privilege to vision' (Irigaray [1984] 1993: 174); and Jacques Derrida argues that he 'confers on vision a heavy primacy' (Derrida [2000] 2005: 206).

4. Sobchack 1992 is a founding text in this field.
5. For more on Merleau-Ponty, imagination, and film, see Cooper 2018a.
6. Although there is a difference between closing one's eyes and looking at a blank black screen in the darkness, I align the activities here on the basis of the removal of anything to be seen. For a discussion of the neural distinctiveness of blink-related and blank-related activities with regard to the default mode network, see Nakano et al. 2013.
7. Merleau-Ponty is speaking about ideas when he writes about Proust and notes: '[w]e do not see, do not hear the ideas, and not even with the mind's eye or with the third ear: and yet they are there' (Merleau-Ponty [1964] 1968: 151). My own observations on imagination couple the felt presence of the invisible with what it *is* possible to imagine in images through audio-vision.
8. For more on Deren's imagistic imagination, see Cooper 2018b.
9. For a compelling study of memory and imagination in film, see Lombardo 2014.
10. Tangential to this, work on silent cinema has demonstrated how sound can be visualised through the power of onscreen images. See, for example, Szaloky 2002.

## Chapter 3

1. Julian Hanich remarks upon this phenomenon in the context of horror and thriller films (Hanich 2010: 125).
2. Inter-titles on screen at the start announce that *Robinson in Ruins* was constructed from 'a box containing 19 film cans and a notebook' discovered in a derelict caravan. In 2012, it gave rise to *The Robinson Institute*, an installation at Tate Britain. Keiller's book *The Possibility of Life's Survival on the Planet* derives from these projects (Keiller 2012).

## Chapter 4

1. I thank Mike Witt for referring me to Hulse's work.
2. Third Coast International Audio Festival, 'The Audible Picture Show', Chicago Conference, 2004, available at <https://www.thirdcoastfestival.org/explore/feature/audible-picture-show> (last accessed 25 February 2019).
3. Beyond my own focus here on the aural shaping of images in the mind, there is a fascinating field of scholarship on the aural imagination of film, much of which engages in dialogue with Michel Chion's *Audio-Vision* (Chion [1990] 1994). See, for example, Sobchack 2005; Stadler 2018; Fox 2018.
4. Michael Cowan notes however that this latter film experiment has been lost. See Cowan 2014: 86.
5. It premiered with a performance in Berlin on 15 May 1930 and the first broadcast was on 13 June 1930. It was also screened at the second International Congress of Avant-Garde Film in Brussels (27 November–1 December 1930)

and was presented multiple times thereafter as a film, with the first cinema screening taking place in Berlin on 29 March 1931 at the Rote Mühle. See Goergen 1994: 2. See also Daniels 2017.
6. For a study of the intermediality of *Weekend*, see Birtwistle 2016.
7. As Scarry emphasises, 'handmade' pertains to things that have been made by human hands with or without the help of machines or factories – artefactual rather than natural objects (Scarry [1999] 2001: 146). The broader machinery of the opening of *Weekend* falls into this category, but the fact that this is less easily pictured as a hand-operated tool – that is, one that can be gripped and manipulated – is part of what weakens its mental visual presence here, in contrast to the hammer and saw.
8. See, for example, Townsend 2008; Remes 2015; Sobchack 2011; Crook 1999; Dillon 2004.
9. In addition to premieres at cinema venues, subsequent release on the home entertainment market (video and DVD), and its more recent appearance on the Internet, the film was broadcast on Channel 4 on 19 September 1993, with a simulcast on Radio 3. Radio listeners could send off for a large blue postcard to look at during transmission. More recently, *Blue* featured as an installation in a darkened room within the broader gallery space of Tate Britain, London (autumn 2017).
10. I join here with Maggie Nelson, whose beautiful *Bluets* testifies to a similar passion: 'Suppose I were to begin by saying that I had fallen in love with a color?' (Nelson 2009: 1). I thank Emma Wilson for the gift of this book.
11. A handmade, large-scale promotional book in the Tate Britain archive includes information about the film, then titled *Bliss*: 'The film's central image will be a tender portrait of an aged couple – two men of sixty three years old – the age that Klein would have reached had he not died prematurely. Images will recur, punctuating the film, such as a diver plunging into deep blue waters; images of the eternal cosmos, the infinite void; images created by the camera racing through the blue sky, brushing against the clouds . . .' (Derek Jarman Archive, Tate Britain, TGA 20157/1/3).
12. I borrow this sense of supposition from Scarry [1999] 2001: 158–92.
13. In the drafts of scripts for the film, the location is 'Soho Café' and the sound effects are 'Streets of Sarajevo, Café Atmosphere', suggesting the interleaving of the two places. See Derek Jarman Archive, Tate Britain, TGA 20157/1/4/29.
14. Jarman's 'Notes on "Alchemical Blue"' features the following line: 'The "Pothos", a blue Larkspur or delphinium placed on graves' (Tate Britain, Derek Jarman Archive, TGA 20157/2/3/3). James Hillman refers to this *pothos* in his own work on 'Alchemical Blue' (Hillman [1989] 1992: 38).

## Chapter 5

1. The women who took part in this film were also reacting to an imagined situation, although this is not revealed in the film itself. Kiarostami reports that

he did not know what the fiction would be when he filmed the women and there was therefore no film on a screen in front of them. See the documentary on the making of *Shirin*, *Taste of Shirin* (Hamideh Razavi, 2008).
2. This was the narrative premise, but Kiarostami reveals that he filmed each actress in his living room, as part of the same material he used in *Shirin*. See Saeed-Vafa and Rosenbaum [2003] 2018: 134.
3. The Islamic Codes of Modesty enforced on Iranian cinema in 1982 are post-revolutionary restrictions on the representation of women. Sara Saljoughi notes how Kiarostami observes the modesty law on a basic level by filming the women in their veils, but that the meditation on the female face constitutes 'a bold challenge to the law's emphasis on *not* looking at women' (Saljoughi 2012: 533). Furthermore, Najmeh Moradiyan Rizi argues that the representation of the love story of *Khosrow and Shirin* on the soundtrack hints at the restricted representation of heterosexual love in post-revolutionary Iran, suggesting that the elimination of the image serves to emphasise that the referential point is the representation of women, as both spectators and actresses (Rizi 2016: 48).
4. Kiarostami reported that the film did not get a commercial run in Iran because it was too challenging and unorthodox for a general audience (Saeed-Vafa and Rosenbaum [2003] 2018: 135).
5. As with the other films I discuss in this book, I cite the English subtitles from the DVD edition of the films I discuss wherever these are available and these are from the BFI DVD collection 'Jan Švankmajer: The Complete Short Films'. Although subtly different from the Poe original in terms of order of description and omission of some terms, they retain the essential detail. It is not the accuracy of the Czech translation of Poe retranscribed back into English subtitles that is under scrutiny here, which could lead to getting caught up in arguments about the precision of individual words, but the overall effect of the broader description combined with the images on screen in prompting the spectator's imagination.
6. For studies of imagination in relation to Švankmajer's films that do not however broach the formation of mental images, see Noheden 2013; Dryje 1995.
7. For a reading of both of the Švankmajer films discussed in this chapter that shows how redolent they are of the history of Czechoslovakia, see White and Winn 2006.

# Chapter 6

1. *Cézanne* was commissioned by Virginie Herbin, Director of the Audio-visual Department at the Musée d'Orsay, to accompany a 1988 exhibition devoted to the painter's early years, but the precise brief was dropped and the film was eventually rejected.
2. A citation from Gasquet's book also furnishes the epigraph to Merleau-Ponty's 'Eye and Mind'.

3. Examples of their intricate annotations are included in Straub and Huillet 2016.
4. With particular regard to distancing, Straub and Huillet's work has been discussed with reference to Brecht. See Walsh 1981; Byg 1995; Brady 2006, 2016.
5. Sally Shafto notes that Hölderlin wrote two versions of this poem in 1798 and 1800, and a final version in 1820, all of which remain unfinished (Shafto cited in Païni [1999] 2006). *The Death of Empedocles* (1986) is based on Hölderlin's first version; *Schwarze Sünde/Black Sin* (1989) is based on the third version.
6. For a discussion of the German version of the film, see Böser 2004: 159–204.

# Chapter 7

1. An early screenplay for the film was published in the sole number of the *Lettriste* journal *Ion* (April 1952). In the final released version of *Hurlements* that I discuss here, representational images that were part of an initial plan have entirely vanished. See Field 1999 for further discussion.
2. I refer to the published translation of the film script when talking about *Howls* because it identifies and distinguishes helpfully between the voices.
3. The initial screening of *Hurlements* in Paris on 30 June 1952 was shut down reportedly after twenty minutes because people reacted badly to the experience Debord prompted. See Jappe [1993] 1999: 49. More positively, at a more recent screening at the Lincoln Center in New York on 1 March 2009, there was chatter, song, security guard interventions, and general restlessness within the auditorium space, with an audience primed and ready to engage with, rather than refuse, the provocation. See Winestine 2009. See also Cabañas 2014: 98.
4. Duras declares later in the film that she recognises herself in the figure of the woman traveller and identifies with her banality. My point about drawing upon the onscreen image of Duras to firm up a mental image of the woman traveller is not however intended to collapse the differences between the two figures. For more on the importance of maintaining a distinction between the identity of Duras and the woman, see Cooper 2019.
5. Duras speaks of the place of blackness (the black screen) in her films in relation to the removal of visual representation, linking it to a state of suspended thought that she connects to orgasm. See Duras [1980] 1996: 93.
6. Williams suggests that the ideal image for Duras lies in the cut, observing that Duras's 'erotic crimes of montage' have a castrating power, exercised over Depardieu in the earlier film *Le Camion* (Williams 1992: 68).
7. Duras explains the genesis of this film in Duras 1979: 7–8. The short text that gave rise to the film also gave rise to a play. See McWilliams 1986 for a discussion of the relationship between the three versions of the tale.

8. For James Williams aesthetics prevails over racial politics in Duras's filming of the dawn workers. He extends the logic of fetishism that he analyses with reference to sexual difference in *Le Camion* to racial difference and its disavowal here. See Williams 1998: 84.

## Conclusion

1. Chion comments on the sound of waves being indistinguishable from minute bits of background noise on the soundtrack (Chion [1982] 1999: 120). Whether the sound of the sea is heard or imagined, it is still contact with a perceived sound that generates a mental image here.
2. The published translation of this line refers to shared nakedness of lovers, as opposed to one naked body referred to in the subtitles of the Curzon Artificial Eye DVD: 'And in the dark our nakedness was radiant / As slowly it inclined' (Tarkovsky 1986: 101). The principle of radiant ignition holds here regardless, whether 'shining' or 'radiant', and mention of 'recline' or 'incline' still tilts the mental image.

# Filmography

*10 on Ten*, Abbas Kiarostami, 2004.
*Agatha et les lectures illimitées/Agatha and the Unlimited Readings*, Marguerite Duras, 1981.
*Alice*, Jan Švankmajer, 1988.
*A Sense of Place*, Tony Hill, 2003.
*Au Hasard Balthazar*, Robert Bresson, 1966.
*Battleship Potemkin*, Sergei Eisenstein, 1925.
*Berlin: Die Sinfonie der Grosstadt/Berlin: The Symphony of a Great City*, Walter Ruttmann, 1927.
*Black Sun*, Gary Tarn, 2005.
*Blue*, Derek Jarman, 1993.
*Césarée/Caesarea*, Marguerite Duras, 1979.
*Cézanne*, Jean-Marie Straub and Danièle Huillet, 1989.
*Chacun son cinéma/To Each His Own Cinema*, Gilles Jacob, various directors, 2007.
*Chronik der Anna Magdalena Bach/Chronicle of Anna Magdalena Bach*, Jean-Marie Straub and Danièle Huillet, 1967.
*Der Tod des Empedokles/The Death of Empedocles*, Jean-Marie Straub and Danièle Huillet, 1986.
*Des Haares und der Liebe Wellen/Waves of Hair and Love*, Walter Ruttmann, 1929.
*Dogville*, Lars von Trier, 2003.
*Effi Briest*, Rainer Werner Fassbinder, 1974.
*Elsa la rose/Elsa the Rose*, Agnès Varda, 1965.
*Exodus*, Otto Preminger, 1960.
*Geschichtsunterricht/History Lessons*, Jean-Marie Straub and Danièle Huillet, 1972.
*Heart of a Dog*, Laurie Anderson, 2015.
*Her*, Spike Jonze, 2013.
*Hiroshima mon amour*, Alain Resnais, 1959.
*Hurlements en faveur de Sade/Howls in Favour of Sade*, Guy Debord, 1952.
*India Song*, Marguerite Duras, 1975.
*Jane B. par Agnès V./Jane B. by Agnès V.*, Agnès Varda, 1988.
*JLG/JLG: autoportrait de décembre/JLG/JLG: Self-Portrait of December*, Jean-Luc Godard, 1995.
*Klassenverhältnisse/Class Relations*, Jean-Marie Straub and Danièle Huillet, 1984.
*Kommunisten/Communists*, Jean-Marie Straub, 2014.

*Kyvadlo, jáma a naděje/The Pendulum, the Pit and Hope*, Jan Švankmajer, 1983.
*La Fin du monde/The End of the World*, Abel Gance, 1931.
*Le Camion/The Lorry*, Marguerite Duras, 1977.
*Le Mépris/Contempt*, Jean-Luc Godard, 1963.
*Le Navire Night/The Ship Night*, Marguerite Duras, 1979.
*Les Dites Cariatides/The So-Called Caryatids*, Agnès Varda, 1984.
*Les Mains négatives/Negative Hands*, Marguerite Duras, 1979.
*Lettre de Sibérie/Letter from Siberia*, Chris Marker, 1957.
*L'Homme Atlantique/The Atlantic Man*, Marguerite Duras, 1981.
*L'Image manquante/The Missing Picture*, Rithy Panh, 2013.
*London*, Patrick Keiller, 1994.
*Madame Bovary*, Jean Renoir, 1934.
*Manderlay*, Lars von Trier, 2005.
*Melodie der Welt/Melody of the World*, Walter Ruttmann, 1929.
*Meshes of the Afternoon*, Maya Deren and Alexander Hammid, 1943.
*Notes on Blindness*, Peter Middleton and James Spinney, 2016.
*Opus I–IV*, Walter Ruttmann, 1921–5.
*Persona*, Ingmar Bergman, 1966.
*Robinson in Ruins*, Patrick Keiller, 2010.
*Robinson in Space*, Patrick Keiller, 1997.
*Romeo and Juliet*, Franco Zeffirelli, 1968.
*Sans Soleil/Sunless*, Chris Marker, 1982.
*Schwarze Sünde/Black Sin*, Jean-Marie Straub and Danièle Huillet, 1989.
*Shirin*, Abbas Kiarostami, 2008.
*Swades: We, the People*, Ashutosh Gowariker, 2004.
*Taste of Shirin*, Hamideh Razavi, 2008.
*Ten*, Abbas Kiarostami, 2002.
*The Hateful Eight*, Quentin Tarantino, 2015.
*Thirty Two Short Films about Glenn Gould*, François Girard, 1993.
*Un Chien Andalou/An Andalusian Dog*, Salvador Dalí and Luis Buñuel, 1929.
*Une visite au Louvre/A Visit to the Louvre*, Jean-Marie Straub and Danièle Huillet, 2003.
*Wishful Thinking*, David Wharry, 1978.
*Wochenende/Weekend*, Walter Ruttmann, 1930.
*Zánik domu Usherů/The Fall of the House of Usher*, Jan Švankmajer, 1980.
*Zerkalo/Mirror*, Andrey Tarkovsky, 1975.

# Bibliography

Adorno, Theodor W. [1967] (1981), 'Transparencies on Film', trans. Thomas Y. Levin, *New German Critique*, 24/25, pp. 199–205.
Alazet, Bernard (1992), *Le Navire Night de Marguerite Duras: écrire l'effacement*, Lille: Presses Universitaires de Lille.
Allen, Richard (1997), *Projecting Illusion: Film Spectatorship and the Impression of Reality*, Cambridge: Cambridge University Press.
Anderson, Laurie (2016), 'Q&A with Director Laurie Anderson', *Heart of a Dog*, Dogwoof DVD edn.
Aristotle (1986), *De Anima*, trans. Hugh Lawson-Tancred, London: Penguin.
Arnheim, Rudolf [1936] (1971), *Radio: An Art of Sound*, trans. Margaret Ludwig and Herbert Read, London: Faber and Faber.
Arnheim, Rudolf [1962] (2000), 'To Maya Deren', in P. Adams Sitney (ed.), *Film Culture Reader*, New York: Cooper Square Press, pp. 84–6.
Bachelard, Gaston [1943] (1988), *Air and Dreams: An Essay on the Imagination of Movement*, trans. Edith R. Farrell and C. Frederick Farrell, Dallas: Dallas Institute Publications.
Bachelard, Gaston [1957] (1994), *The Poetics of Space*, trans. Maria Jolas, Boston: Beacon Press.
Barker, Martin (2006), 'Envisaging "Visualisation": Some Challenges from the International *Lord of the Rings* Audience Project', *Film-Philosophy*, October, 10:3, pp. 1–25.
Barthes, Roland (1970), 'Écrire la lecture', *Le Figaro littéraire*, 9 March.
Barthes, Roland (1975), 'En sortant du cinéma', *Communications*, 23, pp. 104–7.
Barthes, Roland [1980] (2000), *Camera Lucida: Reflections on Photography*, trans. Richard Howard, London: Vintage.
Baudry, Jean-Louis [1975] (1986), 'The Apparatus: Metapsychological Approaches to the Impression of Reality in Cinema', in Philip Rosen (ed.), *Narrative, Apparatus, Ideology*, New York: Columbia University Press, pp. 299–318.
Benjamin, Walter [1936] (1992), 'The Work of Art in the Age of Mechanical Reproduction', in *Illuminations*, trans. Harry Zohn, London: Fontana, pp. 211–44.
Birtwistle, Andy (2016), 'Photographic Sound Art and the Silent Modernity of Walter Ruttmann's *Weekend* (1930)', *The New Soundtrack*, August, 6:2, pp. 109–27.

Blanchot, Maurice (1983), *La Communauté inavouable*, Paris: Minuit.
Blumenfeld, Hal (2016), 'Neuroanatomical Basis of Consciousness', in Steven Laureys, Olivia Gosseries and Giulio Tononi (eds), *The Neurology of Consciousness: Cognitive Neuroscience and Neuropathology*, 2nd edn, London: Elsevier Academic Press, pp. 3–31.
Bonnefoy, Yves (1988), 'Lever les yeux de son livre', *Nouvelle Revue de psychanalyse*, Spring, 37, pp. 9–20.
Bordwell, David (2010), 'Observations on Film Art', 'Tell, Don't Show' <http://www.davidbordwell.net/blog/2010/01/06/tell-dont-show/> (last accessed 25 February 2019).
Böser, Ursula (2004), *The Art of Seeing, the Art of Listening: The Politics of Representation in the Work of Jean-Marie Straub and Danièle Huillet*, Bern: Peter Lang.
Bouissounouse, Janine [1931] (1994), 'WEEKEND von Walter Ruttmann', trans. Helma Schleif and Jeanpaul Goergen, in Jeanpaul Goergen, *Walter Ruttmanns Tonmontagen als Ars Acustica*, MuK 89, Siegen: Massenmedien und Kommunikation, pp. 46–7, <https://www.jeanpaulgoergen.de/home/Bucher_files/MuK%2089%20Ruttmanns%20Tonmontagen.pdf> (last accessed 25 February 2019).
Bowen, Peter (2007), 'Seeing in the Dark', <http://filmmakermagazine.com/archives/issues/winter2007/features/seeing_dark.php#.V8VENiMrL-Y> (last accessed 25 February 2019).
Brady, Martin (2006), 'Brecht and Film', in Peter Thomson and Glendyr Sacks (eds), *The Cambridge Companion to Brecht*, Cambridge: Cambridge University Press, pp. 297–317.
Brady, Martin (2016), '"The Attitude of Smoking and Observing": Slow Film and Politics in the Cinema of Jean-Marie Straub and Danièle Huillet', in Tiago de Luca and Nuno Barradas Jorge (eds), *Slow Cinema*, Edinburgh: Edinburgh University Press, pp. 71–84.
Brakhage, Stan (1963a), *Metaphors on Vision*, ed. with an introduction by P. Adams Sitney, originally published in *Film Culture*, 30, Fall 1963, <https://monoskop.org/images/d/de/Brakhage_Stan_Metaphors_on_Vision.pdf> (last accessed 25 February 2019).
Brakhage, Stan (1963b), 'Interview with P. Adams Sitney in Denver 1963', in *Metaphors on Vision*, ed. with an introduction by P. Adams Sitney, originally published in *Film Culture*, 30, Fall 1963, <https://monoskop.org/images/d/de/Brakhage_Stan_Metaphors_on_Vision.pdf> (last accessed 25 February 2019).
Brann, Eva T. H. (1991), *The World of the Imagination: Sum and Substance*, Lanham, MD: Rowman & Littlefield.
Breton, André [1924] (1985), *Manifestes du surréalisme*, Paris: Gallimard Folio.
Brown, William (2018), 'In Order to See, You Must Look Away: Thinking About the Eye', in Tessa Dwyer, Claire Perkins, Sean Redmond and Jodi Sita (eds), *Seeing into Screens: Eye Tracking and the Moving Image*, New York: Bloomsbury, pp. 15–27.

Byg, Barton (1995), *Landscapes of Resistance: The German Films of Danièle Huillet and Jean-Marie Straub*, Berkeley: University of California Press.
Cabañas, Kaira M. (2014), *Off-Screen Cinema: Isidore Isou and the Lettrist Avant-Garde*, Chicago: University of Chicago Press.
Casey, Edward S. (1976), 'Comparative Phenomenology of Mental Activity: Memory, Hallucination, and Fantasy Contrasted with Imagination', *Research in Phenomenology*, 6:1, pp. 1–25.
Casey, Edward S. [1976] (2000), *Imagining: A Phenomenological Study*, 2nd edn, Bloomington: Indiana University Press.
Chion, Michel [1990] (1994), *Audio-Vision: Sound on Screen*, ed. and trans. Claudia Gorbman, New York: Columbia University Press.
Chion, Michel [1982] (1999), *The Voice in Cinema*, ed. and trans. Claudia Gorbman, New York: Columbia University Press.
Citton, Yves [2014] (2017), *The Ecology of Attention*, trans. Barnaby Norman, Cambridge: Polity Press.
Cixous, Hélène (1993), *Three Steps on the Ladder of Writing*, trans. Sarah Cornell and Susan Sellers, New York: Columbia University Press.
Coleridge, Samuel Taylor (1895), 'A Day-Dream', in *The Golden Book of Coleridge*, London: J. M. Dent, pp. 193–4.
Collins, Christopher (1991a), *Reading the Written Image: Verbal Play, Interpretation, and the Roots of Iconophobia*, Philadelphia: Pennsylvania State University Press.
Collins, Christopher (1991b), *The Poetics of the Mind's Eye: Literature and the Psychology of Imagination*, Philadelphia: Pennsylvania State University Press.
Cooper, Sarah (2018a), 'Merleau-Ponty and Film: Documenting the Imagination', in Ariane Mildenberg (ed.), *Understanding Merleau-Ponty, Understanding Modernism*, New York: Bloomsbury, pp. 157–69.
Cooper, Sarah (2018b), 'Meshes of Muteness: Maya Deren's Languages', *Screen*, Dossier on 'Cinema and Language', ed. Tijana Mamula, Winter, 59:4, pp. 523–30.
Cooper, Sarah (2019), 'Imagining on the Outskirts of the City: Duras's *Le Camion* and the *marcheuse*', in Siobhán McIlvanney and Gillian Ni Cheallaigh (eds), *Women and the City in French Literature and Culture: Reconfiguring the Feminine in the Urban Environment*, Cardiff: University of Wales Press, pp. 97–114.
Coppola, Antoine (2006), *Introduction au cinéma de Guy Debord et de l'avant-garde situationniste*, Paris: Éditions Sulliver.
Cowan, Michael (2014), *Walter Ruttmann and the Cinema of Multiplicity: Avant-garde – Advertising – Modernity*, Amsterdam: Amsterdam University Press.
Crary, Jonathan [1999] (2001), *Suspensions of Perception: Attention, Spectacle, and Modern Culture*, Cambridge, MA: MIT Press.
Crook, Tim (1999), *Radio Drama: Theory and Practice*, London: Routledge.
Currie, Gregory (1991), 'Visual Fictions', *The Philosophical Quarterly*, April, 41:163, pp. 129–43.

Currie, Gregory (1995), *Image and Mind: Film, Philosophy, and Cognitive Science*, Cambridge: Cambridge University Press.
Daniels, Dieter (2004), 'Sound and Vision in Avant-Garde & Mainstream', trans. Michael Robinson, <http://www.medienkunstnetz.de/themes/image-sound_relations/sound_vision/10/> (last accessed 25 February 2019).
Daniels, Dieter (2017), 'Absolute Sounding Images: Abstract Film and Radio Drama of the 1920s as Complementary Forms of a Media-Specific Art', trans. Annie Buenker, in Holly Rogers and Jeremy Barham (eds), *The Music and Sound of Experimental Film*, Oxford: Oxford University Press, pp. 23–43.
Davey, Christopher G., Jesus Pujol and Ben J. Harrison (2016), 'Mapping the Self in the Brain's Default Mode Network', *NeuroImage*, 15 May, 132, pp. 390–7.
Debord, Guy (2003), *Complete Cinematic Works: Scripts, Stills, Documents*, trans. and ed. Ken Knabb, Oakland, CA: AK Press.
Debord, Guy [1967] (2004), *The Society of the Spectacle*, trans. Ken Knabb, London: Rebel Press.
Deleuze, Gilles [1985] (1994), *Cinema 2: The Time-Image*, trans. Hugh Tomlinson and Robert Galeta, London: Athlone Press.
Deleuze, Gilles [1983] (2005), *Cinema 1: The Movement-Image*, trans. Hugh Tomlinson and Barbara Habberjam, London: Continuum.
Dennett, Daniel C. (1981), 'The Nature of Images and the Introspective Trap', in Ned Block (ed.), *Imagery*, Cambridge, MA: MIT Press, pp. 51–61.
Dennett, Daniel C. (1991), *Consciousness Explained*, New York: Back Bay Books.
Deren, Maya [1960] (2005), 'Cinematography: The Creative Use of Reality', in Bruce R. McPherson (ed.), *Essential Deren: Collected Writings on Film by Maya Deren*, New York: McPherson, pp. 110–28.
Derrida, Jacques [1967] (1997), *Of Grammatology*, trans. Gayatri Chakravorty Spivak, Baltimore: Johns Hopkins University Press.
Derrida, Jacques [2000] (2005), *On Touching – Jean-Luc Nancy*, trans. Christine Irizarry, Stanford: Stanford University Press.
Didi-Huberman, Georges (2003), *Images malgré tout*, Paris: Minuit.
Dillon, Steve (2004), *Derek Jarman and the Lyric Film: The Mirror and the Sea*, Austin: University of Texas Press.
Domhoff, G. William and Kieran C. R. Fox (2015), 'Dreaming and the Default Network: A Review, Synthesis, and Counterintuitive Research Proposal', *Consciousness and Cognition*, 33, pp. 342–53.
Donoghue, Denis (1976), *The Sovereign Ghost: Studies in Imagination*, New York: Ecco Press.
Dryje, František (1995), 'The Force of Imagination', in Peter Hames (ed.), *The Dark Alchemy: The Films of Jan Švankmajer*, Westport, CT: Praeger, pp. 119–68.
Duras, Marguerite (1977), *Le Camion: suivi de entretien avec Michelle Porte*, Paris: Minuit.

Duras, Marguerite (1979), *Le Navire Night – Césarée – Les Mains négatives – Aurélia Steiner – Aurélia Steiner – Aurélia Steiner*, Paris: Mercure de France.
Duras, Marguerite (1986), *Les Yeux bleus cheveux noirs*, Paris: Minuit.
Duras, Marguerite (1993), *Écrire*, Paris: Gallimard.
Duras, Marguerite [1980] (1996), *Les Yeux verts*, Paris: Éditions de l'Étoile/ Cahiers du cinéma.
Duras, Marguerite [1984] (2001), *La Couleur des mots: entretiens avec Dominique Noguez*, Paris: Benoît Jacob.
During, Elie (2016), 'Materiality of the Image', Lecture to the European Graduate School, 27 March, *YouTube*, <https://www.youtube.com/watch?v=Vf5J-l4DMcI> (last accessed 25 February 2019).
Eberwein, Robert T. (1984), *Film and the Dream Screen: A Sleep and a Forgetting*, Princeton: Princeton University Press.
Eisenstein, Sergei [1939] (1970), 'Word and Image', in *The Film Sense*, trans. Jay Leyda, Orlando: Harcourt Brace, pp. 3–65.
Eisenstein, Sergei M., V. I. Pudovkin and G. V. Alexandrov [1928] (1985), 'A Statement', in Elisabeth Weis and John Belton (eds), *Film Sound: Theory and Practice*, New York: Columbia University Press, pp. 83–5.
Eisner, Lotte H. [1930] (1994), 'Reichsrundfunk sendet akustische Filme', in Jeanpaul Goergen, *Walter Ruttmanns Tonmontagen als Ars Acustica*, MuK 89, Siegen: Massenmedien und Kommunikation, pp. 32–4, <https://www.jeanpaulgoergen.de/home/Bucher_files/MuK%2089%20Ruttmanns%20Tonmontagen.pdf> (last accessed 25 February 2019).
Esrock, Ellen J. (1994), *The Reader's Eye: Visual Imaging as Reader Response*, Baltimore and London: Johns Hopkins University Press.
Evans, Georgina (2008), 'Imagination and the Senses: Krzysztof Kieslowski's *Trois Couleurs: Blanc*', *Paragraph*, Special Issue: 'Cinema and the Senses', ed. Emma Wilson, 31:2, pp. 223–35.
Field, Allyson (1999), '*Hurlements en faveur de Sade*: The Negation and Surpassing of "Discrepant Cinema"', *SubStance*, Special Issue: 'Guy Debord', 90, 28:3, pp. 55–70.
Fisher, Mark (2010), 'Robinson in Ruins: A Radical English Pastoral', *BFI Film Forever*, November, updated 24 January 2017, <http://www.bfi.org.uk/news-opinion/sight-sound-magazine/features/robinson-ruins-patrick-keiller-radical-english-pastoral> (last accessed 25 February 2019).
Fox, Albertine (2018), *Godard and Sound: Acoustic Innovation in the Late Films of Jean-Luc Godard*, London: I. B. Tauris.
Frampton, Daniel (2006), *Filmosophy*, London: Wallflower.
Freud, Sigmund [1900] (1991), *The Interpretation of Dreams*, vol. 4, The Penguin Freud Library, trans. James Strachey, London: Penguin.
Gasquet, Joachim [1921] (1926), *Cézanne*, Paris: Éditions Bernheim-Jeune.
Gendler, Tamar (2011), 'Imagination', Section 2.5, in Edward N. Zalta (ed.), *Stanford Encyclopedia of Philosophy*, Spring 2011 edn, <https://plato.stanford.edu/archives/spr2011/entries/imagination/> (last accessed 25 February 2019).

Goergen, Jeanpaul (1994), *Walter Ruttmanns Tonmontagen als Ars Acustica*, MuK 89, Siegen: Massenmedien und Kommunikation, <https://www.jeanpaulgoergen.de/home/Bucher_files/MuK%2089%20Ruttmanns%20Tonmontagen.pdf> (last accessed 25 February 2019).

Goudal, Jean [1925] (1988), 'Surrealism and Cinema', in Richard Abel (ed.), *French Film Theory and Criticism: Volume 1, 1907–1929*, Princeton: Princeton University Press, pp. 353–62.

Griffith, F. L. and Herbert Thompson (eds) [1904] (2007), *The Leyden Papyrus: An Egyptian Magical Book*, <https://archive.org/stream/TheLeydenPapyrus/GriffithThompson-TheLeydenPapyrus_djvu.txt> (last accessed 25 February 2019).

Grinnell, Dustin (2016), 'My Mind's Eye Is Blind: So What's Going on in My Brain?', *New Scientist*, 20 April, <https://www.newscientist.com/article/2083706-my-minds-eye-is-blind-so-whats-going-on-in-my-brain/> (last accessed 25 February 2019).

Grødal, Torben (2009), *Embodied Visions: Evolution, Emotion, Culture, and Film*, Oxford: Oxford University Press.

Haigh, Alastair, David J. Brown, Peter Meijer and Michael J. Proulx (2013), 'How Well Do You See What You Hear? The Acuity of Visual-to-Auditory Sensory Substitution', *Frontiers in Psychology*, 18 June, <http://journal.frontiersin.org/article/10.3389/fpsyg.2013.00330/full> (last accessed 25 February 2019).

Hake, Sabine (2008), *Topographies of Class: Modern Architecture and Mass Society in Weimar Berlin*, Ann Arbor: University of Michigan Press.

Hanich, Julian (2010), *Cinematic Emotion in Horror Films and Thrillers: The Aesthetic Paradox of Pleasurable Fear*, London: Routledge.

Hanich, Julian (2018), 'Omission, Suggestion, Completion: Film and the Imagination of the Spectator', *Screening the Past*, 'Dossier: Materializing Absence in Film and Media', ed. Saige Walton and Nadine Boljkovac, April, 43, <http://www.screeningthepast.com/2018/02/omission-suggestion-completion-film-and-the-imagination-of-the-spectator/> (last accessed 25 February 2019).

Higginson, Kate (2008), 'Derek Jarman's "Ghostly Eye": Prophetic Bliss and Sacrificial Blindness in *Blue*', *Mosaic*, March, 41:1, pp. 77–94.

Hillman, James [1989] (1992), 'Pathologizing: The Wound and the Eye', in Renos K. Papadopoulos (ed.), *Carl Gustav Jung: Critical Assessments. Vol. 3: Psychopathology and Psychotherapy*, London: Routledge, pp. 28–46.

Hitchcock, Alfred (1936), 'I Make Suspense My Business', *Portsmouth Evening News*, 27 November, p. 12.

Hobbes, Thomas [1651] (2008), *Leviathan*, Oxford: Oxford University Press.

Hopkins, Rob (2018), 'Interview with Alex Schlegel: Alex Schlegel on Imagination, the Brain, and the "Mental Workspace"', 4 January, <https://www.robhopkins.net/2018/01/04/alex-schlegel-on-imagination-the-brain-and-the-mental-workspace/> (last accessed 25 February 2019).

Hull, John M. [1990] (2013), *Touching the Rock: An Experience of Blindness*, London: Society for Promoting Christian Knowledge.

Hulse, Matt (2004), 'The Audible Picture Show', Third Coast International Audio Festival, Chicago Conference, <https://www.thirdcoastfestival.org/explore/feature/audible-picture-show> (last accessed 25 February 2019).

Hulse, Matt (2011), 'A Reverberation from Matt Hulse', January, included in *BIGMAG.#4: Tessera*, Rotterdam: DePlayer.

Huxley, Aldous (1954), *The Doors of Perception*, London: Vintage Books.

Irigaray, Luce [1984] (1993), *Ethics of Sexual Difference*, trans. Carolyn Burke and Gillian C. Gill, Ithaca, NY: Cornell University Press.

Jacobson, Roni (2014), 'App Helps the Blind "See" with Their Ears', *National Geographic*, 5 April, <http://news.nationalgeographic.com/news/2014/04/140403-eyemusic-ssd-visual-impairment-software-science/> (last accessed 25 February 2019).

Jameson, Fredric (1994), *The Seeds of Time*, New York: Columbia University Press.

Jappe, Anselm [1993] (1999), *Guy Debord*, trans. Donald Nicholson-Smith, Berkeley: University of California Press.

Jarman, Derek (1991), *Modern Nature: The Journals of Derek Jarman*, London: Century.

Jarman, Derek [1994] (1995), *Chroma: A Book of Colour – June '93*, London: Vintage.

Jarman, Derek [2000] (2001), *Smiling in Slow Motion*, London: Vintage.

Kearney, Richard (1988), *The Wake of Imagination*, London: Routledge.

Keiller, Patrick (2012), *The Possibility of Life's Survival on the Planet*, London: Tate Publishing.

Keiller, Patrick (2013), *The View from the Train: Cities and Other Landscapes*, London: Verso.

Khodaei, Khatereh (2009), '*Shirin* as Described by Kiarostami', *Offscreen.com*, January, 13:1, <https://offscreen.com/view/shirin_kiarostami> (last accessed 25 February 2019).

Klein, Alice (2017), 'People with No Mind's Eye May Help Us Boost Our Creativity', *New Scientist*, 13 March, <https://www.newscientist.com/article/2124346-people-with-no-minds-eye-may-help-us-boost-our-creativity/> (last accessed 25 February 2019).

Kluge, Alexander (1981), 'On Film and the Public Sphere', trans. Thomas Levin and Miriam Hansen, *New German Critique*, 24/25, pp. 206–20.

Koepnick, Lutz (2017), *The Long Take: Art Cinema and the Wondrous*, Minneapolis: University of Minnesota Press.

Kosslyn, Stephen Michael (1983), *Ghosts in the Mind's Machine: Creating and Using Images in the Brain*, New York: W. W. Norton.

Kosslyn, Stephen M. (1994), *Image and Brain: The Resolution of the Imagery Debate*, Cambridge, MA: MIT Press.

Kosslyn, Stephen M., William L. Thompson and Giorgio Ganis (2006), *The Case for Mental Imagery*, Oxford: Oxford University Press.

Kracauer, Siegfried [1926] (1995), 'Cult of Distraction: On Berlin's Picture Palaces', in *The Mass Ornament*, trans. Thomas Y. Levin, Cambridge, MA: Harvard University Press, pp. 323–8.

Lefebvre, Martin (1999), 'On Memory and Imagination in the Cinema', *New Literary History: Cultural Inquiries*, Spring, 30:2, pp. 479–98.
Levin, Thomas Y. (2002), 'Dismantling the Spectacle: The Cinema of Guy Debord', in Tom McDonough (ed.), *Guy Debord and the Situationist International: Texts and Documents*, Cambridge, MA: MIT Press, pp. 321–453.
Lewin, Bertram D. (1946), 'Sleep, the Mouth, and the Dream Screen', *The Psychoanalytic Quarterly*, 15:4, pp. 419–34.
Lombardo, Patrizia (2014), *Memory and Imagination in Film: Scorsese, Lynch, Jarmusch, Van Sant*, Basingstoke: Palgrave Macmillan.
McGinn, Colin (2004), *Mindsight: Image, Dream, Meaning*, Cambridge, MA: Harvard University Press.
McGinn, Colin (2005), *The Power of Movies: How Screen and Mind Interact*, New York: Vintage.
McGowan, Todd (2007), *The Real Gaze: Film Theory After Lacan*, New York: State University of New York Press.
McGregor, Rafe (2012), 'The Problem of Cinematic Imagination', *Contemporary Aesthetics*, January, <https://contempaesthetics.org/newvolume/pages/article.php?articleID=629> (last accessed 25 February 2019).
McMahon, Laura (2012), *Cinema and Contact: The Withdrawal of Touch in Nancy, Bresson, Duras and Denis*, London: Legenda.
McWilliams, Dean (1986), 'Aesthetic Tripling: Marguerite Duras's *Le Navire "Night"*', *Literature/Film Quarterly*, 14:1, pp. 17–21.
Malabou, Catherine [2004] (2008), *What Should We Do With Our Brain?*, trans. Sebastian Rand, New York: Fordham University Press.
Malabou, Catherine (2017), *Métamorphoses de l'intelligence: que faire de leur cerveau bleu?*, Paris: Presses Universitaires de France.
Marks, Laura U. (2002), *Touch: Sensuous Theory and Multi-sensory Media*, Minneapolis: University of Minnesota Press.
Masram, Vinit (2016), 'Tell, Don't Show', *YouTube*, <https://www.youtube.com/watch?v=NaTOpzYtV2I> (last accessed 25 February 2019).
Mayer, Robert (2004), 'Not Adaptation but "Drifting": Patrick Keiller, Daniel Defoe, and the Relationship between Film and Literature', *Eighteenth-Century Fiction*, July, 16:4, pp. 803–27.
Merleau-Ponty, Maurice [1964] (1968), *The Visible and the Invisible*, trans. Alphonso Lingis, Evanston, IL: Northwestern University Press.
Merleau-Ponty, Maurice [1945] (1993a), 'Cézanne's Doubt', in Galen A. Johnson (ed.), *The Merleau-Ponty Aesthetics Reader: Philosophy and Painting*, Evanston, IL: Northwestern University Press, pp. 59–75.
Merleau-Ponty, Maurice [1960] (1993b), 'Eye and Mind', in Galen A. Johnson (ed.), *The Merleau-Ponty Aesthetics Reader: Philosophy and Painting*, Evanston, IL: Northwestern University Press, pp. 121–49.
Merleau-Ponty, Maurice [1945] (2002), *Phenomenology of Perception*, trans. Colin Smith, London: Routledge.
Merrifield, Andy (2005), *Guy Debord*, London: Reaktion.

Metz, Christian [1977] (1982), *The Imaginary Signifier: Psychoanalysis and Cinema*, trans. Celia Britton, Annwyl Williams, Ben Brewster and Alfred Guzzetti, Bloomington: Indiana University Press.
Milner, David and Melvyn Goodale (1995), *The Visual Brain in Action*, Oxford: Oxford University Press.
Milner, David and Melvyn Goodale (2005), *Sight Unseen: An Exploration of Conscious and Unconscious Vision*, Oxford: Oxford University Press.
Milner, David and Melvyn Goodale (2006), *The Visual Brain in Action*, 2nd edn, Oxford: Oxford University Press.
Mulvey, Laura (2006), *Death 24x a Second: Stillness and the Moving Image*, London: Reaktion.
Mulvey, Laura [1996] (2013), *Fetishism and Curiosity: Cinema and the Mind's Eye*, 2nd edn, London: BFI.
Münsterberg, Hugo [1916] (2006), *The Photoplay: A Psychological Study*, New York: Hardpress.
Nakano, Tamami, Makoto Kato, Yusuke Morito, Seishi Itoi and Shigeru Kitazawa (2013), 'Blink-Related Momentary Activation of the Default Mode Network While Viewing Videos', *Proceedings of the National Academy of Sciences of the United States of America*, 110:2, pp. 702–6.
Nelson, Maggie (2009), *Bluets*, London: Jonathan Cape.
Noheden, Kristoffer (2013), 'The Imagination of Touch: Surrealist Tactility in the Films of Jan Švankmajer', *Journal of Aesthetics & Culture*, 5:1, <https://www.tandfonline.com/doi/full/10.3402/jac.v5i0.21111> (last accessed 25 February 2019).
Païni, Dominic [1999] (2006), 'Straub, Hölderlin, Cézanne', trans. Sally Shafto, *Senses of Cinema*, May, 39, <http://sensesofcinema.com/2006/cinema-and-the-pictorial/straub_holderlin_cezanne/> (last accessed 25 February 2019).
Perez, Gilberto (1998), *The Material Ghost: Films and Their Medium*, Baltimore: Johns Hopkins University Press.
Perky, Mary Cheves West (1910), 'An Experimental Study of Imagination', *The American Journal of Psychology*, July, 21:3, pp. 422–52.
Pylyshyn, Zenon W. (1973), 'What the Mind's Eye Tells the Mind's Brain: A Critique of Mental Imagery', *Psychological Bulletin*, 80:1, pp. 1–24.
Pylyshyn, Zenon W. (2002), 'Mental Imagery: In Search of a Theory', *Behavioral and Brain Sciences*, 25:2, pp. 157–82.
Racine, Jean [1671] (1982), *Théâtre complet I*, Paris: Gallimard.
Ramain, Paul [1925] (1988), 'The Influence of Dream on the Cinema', in Richard Abel (ed.), *French Film Theory and Criticism: Volume 1, 1907–1929*, Princeton: Princeton University Press, pp. 362–4.
Raymond, Jean-Louis (ed.) (2008), *Rencontres avec Jean-Marie Straub et Danièle Huillet*, Paris: Beaux-Arts de Paris.
Reitz, Edgar, Alexander Kluge and Wilfried Reinke [1965] (1988), 'Word and Film', trans. Miriam Hansen, *October*, 'Alexander Kluge: Theoretical Writings, Stories and an Interview', Autumn, 46, pp. 83–95.

Remes, Justin (2015), *Motion(less) Pictures: The Cinema of Stasis*, New York: Columbia University Press.
Rizi, Najmeh Moradiyan (2016), 'The Acoustic Screen: The Dynamics of the Female Look and Voice in Abbas Kiarostami's *Shirin*', *Synoptique*, Summer/Fall, 5:1, pp. 44–56.
Roud, Richard (1971), *Jean-Marie Straub*, London: Secker Warburg.
Ruttmann, Walter (1930), *Weekend*, <http://www.medienkunstnetz.de/source-text/96/> (last accessed 25 February 2019), originally published in *Film-Kurier*, 15 February 1930, 41, Berlin.
Ruttmann, Walter [1928] (2016), 'Principles of Sound Film', trans. Alex H. Bush, in Anton Kaes, Nicholas Baer and Michael Cowan (eds), *The Promise of Cinema: German Film Theory 1907–1933*, Oakland, CA: University of California Press, pp. 555–6.
Sacks, Oliver (2010), 'The Mind's Eye', in *The Mind's Eye*, London: Picador, pp. 202–40.
Saeed-Vafa, Mehrnaz and Jonathan Rosenbaum [2003] (2018), *Abbas Kiarostami*, expanded 2nd edn, Urbana: University of Illinois Press.
Saljoughi, Sara (2012), 'Seeing, Iranian Style: Women and Collective Vision in Abbas Kiarostami's *Shirin*', *Iranian Studies*, 45:4, pp. 519–35.
Sartre, Jean-Paul [1940] (2010), *The Imaginary: A Phenomenological Psychology of the Imagination*, trans. Jonathan Webber, London: Routledge.
Sartre, Jean-Paul [1936] (2012), *The Imagination*, trans. Kenneth Williford and David Rudrauf, London: Routledge.
Scarry, Elaine [1999] (2001), *Dreaming by the Book*, Princeton: Princeton University Press.
Schiavi, Lea [1932] (1994), 'Ein Interview mit Walter Ruttmann, dem Regisseur des Films ACCIAIO', trans. Wolfgang Boerner, in Jeanpaul Goergen, *Walter Ruttmanns Tonmontagen als Ars Acustica*, MuK 89, Siegen: Massenmedien und Kommunikation, pp. 49–52, <https://www.jeanpaulgoergen.de/home/Bucher_files/MuK%2089%20Ruttmanns%20Tonmontagen.pdf> (last accessed 25 February 2019).
Schlegel, Alexander, Peter J. Kohler, Sergey V. Fogelson, Prescott Alexander, Dedeepya Konuthula and Peter Ulric Tse (2013), 'Network Structure and Dynamics of the Mental Workspace', *PNAS*, 1 October, 110:40, pp. 16277–82, <https://www.pnas.org/content/110/40/16277> (last accessed 25 February 2019).
Schwenger, Peter (1996), 'Derek Jarman and the Colour of the Mind's Eye', *University of Toronto Quarterly: A Canadian Journal of the Humanities*, Special Issue: 'Cultural Studies: Disciplinarity and Divergence', ed. Faye Pickrem and Linda Hutcheon, Spring, 65:2, pp. 419–26.
Schwenger, Peter (1999), *Fantasm and Fiction: On Textual Envisioning*, Stanford: Stanford University Press.
Scruton, Roger (1983), 'Fantasy, Imagination and the Screen', in *The Aesthetic Understanding*, London: Methuen, pp. 149–59.
Shafto, Sally (2009), 'On Straub-Huillet's *Une visite au Louvre*', *Senses of Cinema*, December, 53, <http://sensesofcinema.com/2009/feature-articles/on-straub-huillets-une-visite-au-louvre-1/> (last accessed 25 February 2019).

Shaviro, Steven [1993] (2011), *The Cinematic Body*, Minneapolis: University of Minnesota Press.

Simondon, Gilbert [1965–6] (2014), *Imagination et invention, 1965–1966*, Paris: Presses Universitaires de France.

Smith, Murray (1995), *Engaging Characters: Fiction, Emotion, and the Cinema*, Oxford: Oxford University Press.

Smith, Murray (2015), 'Is *Weekend* a Film?', Abstract, *Film-Philosophy Conference 2015: The Evaluation of Form*, <http://www.film-philosophy.com/conference/index.php/conf/FP2015/paper/view/1179> (last accessed 25 February 2019).

Smith, Murray (2017), *Film, Art, and the Third Culture: A Naturalized Aesthetics of Film*, Oxford: Oxford University Press.

Sobchack, Vivian (1992), *The Address of the Eye: A Phenomenology of the Film Experience*, Princeton: Princeton University Press.

Sobchack, Vivian (2005), 'When the Ear Dreams: Dolby Digital and the Imagination of Sound', *Film Quarterly*, Summer, 58:4, pp. 2–15.

Sobchack, Vivian (2011), 'Fleshing Out the Image: Phenomenology, Pedagogy, and Derek Jarman's *Blue*', in Havi Carel and Gregory Tuck (eds), *New Takes in Film-Philosophy*, Basingstoke: Palgrave Macmillan, pp. 191–206.

Stadler, Jane (2018), 'Cinesonic Imagination: The Somatic, the Sonorous, and the Synaesthetic', *Cinephile*, Special Issue: 'Philosophy and New Media', Spring, 12:1, pp. 8–15.

Straub, Jean-Marie and Danièle Huillet (2016), *Writings*, ed. and trans. Sally Shafto with Katherine Pickard, New York: Sequence Press.

Švankmajer, Jan [1983] (2014), *Touching and Imagining: An Introduction to Tactile Art*, trans. Stanley Dalby, London: I. B. Tauris.

Szaloky, Melinda (2002), 'Sounding Images in Silent Film: Visual Acoustics in Murnau's *Sunrise*', *Cinema Journal*, Winter, 41:2, pp. 109–31.

Tarkovsky, Andrey (1986), *Sculpting in Time: Reflections on the Cinema*, trans. Kitty Hunter-Blair, Austin: University of Texas Press.

Thomas, Nigel J. T. (2014), 'Mental Imagery', in Edward N. Zalta (ed.), *Stanford Encyclopedia of Philosophy*, <http://plato.stanford.edu/archives/fall2014/entries/mental-imagery/> (last accessed 25 February 2019).

Townsend, Chris (2008), *Art & Death*, London: I. B. Tauris.

Walsh, Martin (1981), *The Brechtian Aspect of Radical Cinema*, ed. Keith M. Griffiths, London: BFI.

Walton, Kendall L. (1990), *Mimesis as Make-Believe: On the Foundations of the Representational Arts*, Cambridge, MA: Harvard University Press.

Warner, Marina (2000), 'The Structure of the Imagination: Darkness Visible in the Mind's Eye', in Wendy Pullan and Harshad Bhadeshia (eds), *Structure: In Science and Art*, Cambridge: Cambridge University Press, pp. 163–91.

Warner, Marina (2007), 'Dream Works', *The Guardian*, 16 June, <https://www.theguardian.com/film/2007/jun/16/film> (last accessed 25 February 2019).

Warnock, Mary (1976), *Imagination*, Berkeley: University of California Press.

Weill, Kurt [1925] (2016), 'Possibilities for Absolute Radio Art', trans. Michael Cowan, in Anton Kaes, Nicholas Baer and Michael Cowan (eds), *The Promise of Cinema: German Film Theory 1907–1933*, Oakland, CA: University of California Press, pp. 586–9.

Wetzel, Kraft (1974), 'Interview with Rainer Werner Fassbinder', *Kino*, 18/19, BFI programme notes R. W. Fassbinder, *Effi Briest*, April 2017.

White, Timothy R. and J. Emmett Winn (2006), 'Tomorrow Could Bring Salvation: Jan Švankmajer's Adaptations of Edgar Allan Poe', *Kinema: A Journal for Film and Audiovisual Media*, Fall, <http://www.academia.edu/10684773/Tomorrow_Could_Bring_Salvation_Jan_%C5%A0vankmajer_s_Adaptations_of_Edgar_Allen_Poe> (last accessed 25 February 2019).

Williams, James (1992), '*Le système D. – le malheur merveilleux*: Marguerite Duras and the Erotic Crimes of Montage in *Le Camion* and *Aurélia Steiner*', *Paragraph*, 15:1, pp. 38–72.

Williams, James (1998), 'The Point of No Return: Chiastic Adventures Between Self and Other in *Les Mains négatives* and *Au-delà des pages*', in Catherine Rodgers and Raynalle Udris (eds), *Marguerite Duras: lectures plurielles*, Amsterdam: Rodopi, pp. 77–94.

Williams, Linda (1981), *Figures of Desire: A Theory and Analysis of Surrealist Film*, Berkeley: University of California Press.

Winestine, Zack (2009), 'Howls for Guy Debord', *Film Quarterly*, 62:4, pp. 14–15.

Wittgenstein, Ludwig (1967), *Zettel*, ed. G. E. M. Anscombe and G. H. von Wright, trans. G. E. M. Anscombe, Oxford: Basil Blackwell.

Wollheim, Richard (1973), 'Imagination and Identification', in *On Art and the Mind: Essays and Lectures*, London: Allen Lane, pp. 54–83.

Yates, Frances A. (1966), *The Art of Memory*, London: Routledge.

Zacks, Jeffrey M. (2015), *Flicker: Your Brain on Movies*, Oxford: Oxford University Press.

Zellner, Margaret R. (2013), 'Dreaming and the Default Mode Network: Some Psychoanalytic Notes', *Contemporary Psychoanalysis*, 49:2, pp. 226–32.

# Index

*Note: Films are indexed under directors, who can be identified from the Filmography.*

absence
  of image, 19, 67, 136, 159; *see also* blank screen
  and presence, 27, 88, 90, 101, 105, 112, 135–7, 167
Adorno, Theodor, 44
Alazet, Bernard, 144
Alexandrov, G. V., 75
Anderson, Laurie, 54, 59, 64, 65, 89
  *Heart of a Dog*, 46–52, 48 Fig. 3.2, 51 Fig. 3.3, 57
Andersson, Bibi, 162
Andréa, Yann, 146, 157
Aragon, Louis, 161
Aristotle, 24, 147
Arnheim, Rudolf, 30, 71, 72
attention; *see* distraction and attention

Bacall, Lauren, 112
Bachelard, Gaston, 18, 20, 26, 54, 64, 82, 89, 122
Bakunin, Mikhail, 131
Ballal, Kishori, 164
Bardot, Brigitte, 92
Barthes, Roland, 18, 97, 103
Baudelaire, Charles, 53, 61, 115
Baudry, Jean-Louis, 14
Benjamin, Walter, 53, 113–14

Béranger, Pierre-Jean de, 102
Bergman, Ingmar, *Persona*, 162–3, 165
Bergson, Henri, 30
Bettany, Paul, 111
Birkin, Jane, 60–4, 79, 84, 89, 161
Blake, William, 5
Blanchot, Maurice, 140
Blank, Manfred, 55
blank screen
  general, 20, 27, 52, 67–8, 85, 89, 161, 172n; and Debord, 136, 139–40; and Fassbinder, 132; and Wharry, 19
  all black, and Duras, 22, 23, 28, 144, 146–7, 148, 150, 151, 156, 158, 159, 172n, 175n; and Jonze, 87, 88, 161; and Ruttmann, 70, 71, 72, 74; and Straub and Huillet, 127, 130–1
  all blue *see* Jarman, *Blue*
  all white, 19, 132, 136, 138, 139; *see also* whiteness
blindness, 17, 21, 27, 39, 42, 45, 46, 67, 70, 92, 144, 157, 170n, 171n
  and Jarman, 76–7, 80, 81, 83, 84

Bohm, Hark, 132
Bordwell, David, 163, 165
Bosch, Hieronymus, 103
Bouissounouse, Janine, 71, 73
Brakhage, Stan, 15, 17, 45, 171n
Brann, Eva, 6, 29, 30, 43, 45
Bresson, Robert, 99
  *Au Hasard Balthazar*, 93
Breton, André, 12, 13, 14, 35
Brown, William, 8, 18
Buñuel, Luis and Dalí, Salvador, *Un Chien Andalou/An Andalusian Dog*, 11
Burch, Noël, 122

Carrière, Mathieu, 145
Casey, Edward, 31, 35, 66
Čepek, Petr, 101
Cézanne, Paul, 118–29
  *Rocks and Branches at Bibémus* [painting], 125
Chaplin, Charlie, 135
Chion, Michel, 49, 145, 172n, 176n
Citton, Yves, 121
Cixous, Hélène, 10, 12
Cocteau, Jean, 42, 84
Coleridge, Samuel Taylor, 17
Cowan, Michael, 75, 172n
Crary, Jonathan, 118–19
Currie, Gregory, 4, 169n

Dalí, Salvador and Buñuel, Luis, *Un Chien Andalou/An Andalusian Dog*, 11
Daniels, Dieter, 69
Dardenne brothers, 93, 97
  *Dans l'obscurité/Darkness* [short in Gilles Jacob, *Chacun son cinéma*], 92

daydreaming, 8, 9, 12, 15, 24, 29, 40, 44, 47, 56, 113, 170n, 171n
De Montalembert, Hugues, 34, 39, 41–2, 45–6, 52, 59, 77, 79, 89, 171n
Debord, Guy, 53, 119, 147, 166
  *Hurlements en faveur de Sade/ Howls in Favour of Sade*, 135–40, 175nn
default mode network, 8, 9, 113, 172n
Defoe, Daniel, 55
Delaunay, Robert, 74
Deleuze, Gilles, 32–3, 119, 122, 125
Dennett, Daniel, 6, 34, 82
Depardieu, Gérard, 141, 142, 143, 145
Dequenne, Émilie, 93
Deren, Maya, 29, 30, 31, 32, 35
Deren, Maya and Hammid, Alexander, *Meshes of the Afternoon*, 29–30
Derrida, Jacques, 89, 171n
Didi-Huberman, Georges, 144
Dillon, Steve, 84
distancing, 120, 130, 175n
distraction, 113–14
  and attention, 9, 18, 35, 113, 114, 116–22, 125–9
  emancipatory distraction, 121
Donoghue, Denis, 4
double exposure, 29–30, 35
dreaming, 9–16, 25, 26, 27, 28, 33, 34, 44, 45, 46, 47, 57, 77, 82, 89, 95, 103, 170–1nn
  and Keiller, 58–60, 114
  and Varda, 60–5, 84, 161;
  *see also* daydreaming; mind wandering

dual vision of imagination and perception, 9, 15–16, 20–1, 22–3, 28, 29–35, 43, 46, 92, 97, 100, 155, 166
Duras, Marguerite, 22–3, 26, 27, 28, 32, 35, 40, 42, 43, 62, 68, 88, 135, 140–55, 160, 161
  *Agatha et les lectures illimitées/ Agatha and the Unlimited Readings*, 157
  *Césarée/Caesarea*, 144, 146, 150–3, 151 Fig. 7.4, 152 Fig. 7.5, 154
  *Écrire* [book], 146
  *Hiroshima mon amour* [screenplay], 150
  *India Song*, 140
  *Le Camion/The Lorry*, 141–4, 142 Fig. 7.1, 143 Fig. 7.2, 144, 145–6, 154, 155, 159, 175nn
  *Le Navire Night/The Ship Night*, 144–6, 149, 155, 175n
  *Le Ravissement de Lol V. Stein / The Ravishing of Lol V. Stein* [book], 150
  *Les Mains négatives/Negative Hands*, 144, 146–50, 149 Fig. 7.3, 153–4
  *L'Homme Atlantique/The Atlantic Man*, 22–3, 26, 27, 28, 144, 146, 156–9, 160, 161, 167
During, Elie, 67

Eberwein, Robert, 14
Eisenstein, Sergei, 29, 30–1, 32, 75, 121, 136
  *Battleship Potemkin*, 31
Eisner, Lotte H., 72

erasing, erasure, 85, 87, 130, 133, 134–55, 157, 158, 159, 165, 166; *see also* absence; blank screen; re-picturing
ethics, 166–7
Evans, Georgina, 21

Fassbinder, Rainer Werner, *Effi Briest*, 132–3, 133 Fig. 6.5
feeling
  of mental image formation, 22–35, 88, 129, 167
  of mental space, 66, 82
  and the senses, 51, 102, 105
fetishism, 97, 98–9, 176n
Fisher, Mark, 117
Flesch, Hans, 69
Fliess, Wilhelm, 11
Fontane, Theodor, 132
Frampton, Daniel, 21
Freud, Sigmund, 11–12, 13, 14, 15, 82, 98–9, 121

Gance, Abel, *La Fin du monde/ The End of the World*, 69
Ganjavi, Hakim Nezami, 91
Gasquet, Joachim, 119, 120, 126, 174n
Gesner, Conrad, 82
Gilliatt, Penelope, 120–1
Girard, François, *Thirty Two Short Films about Glenn Gould*, 49
Godard, Jean-Luc, 17–18, 19, 21, 27, 135
  *JLG/JLG: autoportrait de décembre/JLG/JLG: Self-Portrait of December*, 17–18
  *Le Mépris/Contempt*, 92
Goergen, Jeanpaul, 68, 69, 70
Golbou, Farideh, 91

Goodale, Melvyn, 8, 170n
Goode, Sally, 67, 75, 82
Goudal, Jean, 12–13, 14, 15, 24, 29
Gould, Glenn, *The Idea of North* [radio play], 49
Gowariker, Ashutosh, *Swades: We, the People* 163–4, 165

Hake, Sabine, 68, 69
Hammid, Alexander and Deren, Maya, *Meshes of the Afternoon*, 29–30
Hanich, Julian, 169n, 172n
HB (Jarman's companion and lover), 76, 80
Heidegger, Martin, 56
Higginson, Kate, 86
Hill, Tony, *A Sense of Place*, 67, 75, 82
Hitchcock, Alfred, 16–17, 21, 27, 32–3, 99
Hobbes, Thomas, 24
Hogan, Siobhan Fallon, 111
Hölderlin, Friedrich, 123, 124, 175n
Huillet, Danièle *see* Straub, Jean-Marie and Huillet, Danièle
Hull, John M., 171n
Hulme, T. E., 30
Hulse, Matt, 66–7, 87, 161
  'The Audible Picture Show', 66–7, 75, 76, 85
Hurt, John, 112
Huxley, Aldous, 5

illumination *see* radiant ignition
image, mental *see* daydreaming; dreaming; memory; mental image debate; visualisation
imagining, 169nn, 170nn, 171nn
  aural, 172n
  felt experience of, 4–5, 27, 34; *see also* feeling
  guided, 9, 20, 23, 32, 47, 54, 66, 95, 112, 113, 120, 141, 162, 164, 166, 167, 168, 170n
  as not perceiving, 24, 25, 26
  as perceptual mimesis, 28, 43, 45, 51, 60, 63, 68, 75, 92, 96, 105, 109, 143, 151, 157, 164; *see also* dual vision of imagination and perception
  suppositional, 79, 87, 109, 137, 139, 141, 171n, 173n; *see also* Scarry
  unguided, 9, 52, 108, 120; *see also* mind wandering
Iñárritu, Alejandro González, *Anna* [short in Gilles Jacob, *Chacun son cinéma*], 92, 93, 97
Isou, Jean Isidore, 135, 136

Jacob, Gilles, various directors, *Chacun son cinéma/To Each His Own Cinema*, 92
Jacquot, Benoît, 145, 146
James, Alexander, 10–11
Jameson, Fredric, 117
Jarman, Derek, 68, 75, 90, 140, 141, 146, 160, 161, 166, 168, 171n
  *Blue*, 68, 75–81, 83–7, 134, 137, 140, 173nn
  *Chroma: A Book of Colour – June '93* [book], 76, 86, 168
Johansson, Scarlett, 87
Jonze, Spike, *Her*, 87–8, 161
Joshi, Gayatri, 164

Kafka, Franz, 55, 103
Kearney, Richard, 12
Keiller, Patrick, 52, 64, 120, 126, 130, 133, 147, 166
  *London*, 53, 54–5, 57–9, 58 Fig. 3.4, 114–17, 115 Fig. 6.1, 116 Fig. 6.2, 158
  *Robinson in Ruins*, 52, 55, 56–7, 59, 117–18, 172n
  *Robinson in Space*, 53, 54, 55
Khan, Shah Rukh, 163
Kiarostami, Abbas, 166
  *10 on Ten*, 99
  *Shirin*, 91–2, 93–100, 94 Fig. 5.1, 96 Fig. 5.2, 108, 158, 173–4nn
  *Ten*, 99
  *Where is My Romeo?* [short in Gilles Jacob, *Chacun son cinéma*], 93, 174n
Klein, Yves, 75, 77, 173n
Kluge, Alexander, 20, 28, 32
Koepnick, Lutz, 121
Koltaï, Julie, 120, 127
Kosslyn, Stephen Michael, 6–7, 16, 19, 83, 169n
Kracauer, Siegfried, 114

*La Victoire de Samothrace/The Nike of Samothrace* [statue], 127–8, 128 Fig. 6.4, 134
Lacan, Jacques, 14, 170n
layering, 28, 29, 35, 39–65, 66, 74, 89, 112, 122, 161–2
  and Anderson, 49
  and Bergman, 163
  and Duras, 151, 156–9
  and Fassbinder, 132
  and Gowariker, 163–5
  and Jarman, 79, 81, 85
  and Jonze, 87
  and Keiller, 52, 56, 59, 116
  and Preminger, 164–5
  and Tarn, 45, 46
  and Varda, 63, 161
Lefebvre, Martin, 31
Lemaître, Maurice, 135
Levin, Thomas Y., 135
Lewin, Bertram, 14
Lewis, Mark, 67

McClure, Michael, 17
McGinn, Colin, 9, 170n
McMahon, Laura, 144
Maillol, Aristide, *La Montagne* [statue], 150, 151 Fig. 7.4
Malabou, Catherine, 7, 127, 128, 170n
Malraux, André, *Le Temps du mépris/Days of Wrath* [book], 130
Manet, Édouard, 118
Marker, Chris
  *Lettre de Sibérie/Letter from Siberia*, 53
  *Sans Soleil/Sunless*, 42, 53
Marks, Laura U., 51, 105
Masram, Vinit, 163, 165
Matta-Clark, Gordon, 46
Mayer, Robert, 55
memory
  memory image, 11, 13, 20, 23, 29, 31, 39, 41, 56, 82, 93, 134, 158
  relation to imagination, 29–32, 82, 172n
mental image debate
  in pictorial or depictive theory, 5, 6–7, 34, 169n
  in propositional or descriptive theory, 5, 169n

Merleau-Ponty, Maurice, 25–7, 28, 30, 43, 45, 60, 74, 118, 126, 171n, 172n
Metz, Christian, 15, 18, 20
Middleton, Peter, and Spinney, James, *Notes on Blindness*, 171n
Milner, David, 8, 170n
mind wandering, 8, 9, 113, 114, 120, 121, 170n
Mineo, Sal, 164
Mont Sainte-Victoire in Straub and Huillet, *Cézanne*, 119, 122–6, 124 Fig. 6.3, 127, 131, 134, 164
Moses (phone line repairer in Anderson, *Heart of a Dog*), 47–9, 52, 56
Mulvey, Laura, 98–9, 171n
Münsterberg, Hugo, 113

Nakano, Tamami, 8, 172n
Nelson, Maggie, 173n
Newman, Paul, 165

Ogier, Bulle, 145, 157

Païni, Dominic, 123
Panh, Rithy, *L'Image manquante/The Missing Picture*, 166
Peirce, Charles Sanders, 33
Perez, Gilberto, 127, 129
Perky, Mary Cheves West, 39–40, 41, 106
Phoenix, Joaquin, 87
Piccoli, Michel, 92, 161
Poe, Edgar Allan, 53, 101, 102, 105, 110
  *The Pit and the Pendulum*, 108

political issues, 40–1, 46, 53, 76–7, 85–6, 97–100, 102, 108, 117, 127, 130–2, 135–6, 166–7, 174n, 176n
Polo, Marco, 84
Preminger, Otto, *Exodus*, 164–5
presence and absence, 27, 88, 90, 101, 105, 112, 137, 138, 167
Proust, Marcel, 27, 43, 172n
Pudovkin, V. I., 75
Pylyshyn, Zenon, 5, 169n

Quentin, John, 76

Racine, Jean, *Bérénice*, 150
radiant ignition, 22, 68, 77, 84–5, 105, 131, 150, 153, 156, 162, 171n, 176n; *see also* Scarry
Rahmanian, M., 91
Ramain, Paul, 12
Razavi, Hamideh, *Taste of Shirin*, 174n
re-picturing, 135, 147–9, 150, 153, 154, 158, 165; *see also* Scarry
Redgrave, Vanessa, 53, 57
Reed, Lou, 46
Reineri, Madeleine, 138–40, 147
Reinke, Wilfried, 20
Reitz, Edgar, 20
Renoir, Jean, *Madame Bovary*, 121, 123
reshaping, 60, 112, 113–33, 134, 147, 158, 159
  and Fassbinder, 132–3
  and Robinson, 114–18, 120, 126

and Straub and Huillet,
118–32
Resnais, Alain, 141
*Hiroshima mon amour*, 150
Rosenbaum, Jonathan, 100
Ruttmann, Walter, 68, 76, 82, 87,
90, 161
*Berlin: Die Sinfonie der
Grosstadt/Berlin: The
Symphony of a Great
City*, 68
*Des Haares und der Liebe
Wellen/Waves of Hair and
Love*, 69, 172n
*Melodie der Welt/Melody of the
World*, 69
*Opus I–IV*, 69
*Wochenende/Weekend*, 68–75,
78, 80, 172–3nn

Sacks, Oliver, 171n
Saljoughi, Sara, 98, 174n
Sanda, Dominique, 145
Sander, August, 55, 56
Sartre, Jean-Paul, 24–5, 26, 34,
54, 64, 89
Scarry, Elaine, 4, 5, 9, 18, 22,
23, 24, 28, 43–4, 51, 61–2,
68, 70, 77, 80, 84, 93,
105, 108, 112, 122, 131, 137,
147, 150, 153, 156–7, 159,
160, 162, 169nn,
171n, 173nn
Schaeffer, Pierre, 69
Schiavi, Lea, 71
Schlegel, Alexander, 8, 170n
Schygulla, Hanna, 132
Scofield, Paul, 53, 55
Seban, Paul, 141
Ségard, Jérémie, 93

seeing
with eyes (dual visual systems
model), 8, 35; *see also*
blindness
with mind *see* dreaming;
visualisation
Shafto, Sally, 127, 175n
Shaviro, Steven, 114
Simondon, Gilbert, 34
simulation, 7, 169n
Smith, Murray, 69, 169n
Soupault, Philippe, 13
Spinney, James and Middleton,
Peter, *Notes on Blindness*,
171n
Straub, Jean-Marie,
*Kommunisten/Communists*,
130–2
Straub, Jean-Marie and Huillet,
Danièle, 117–18, 126, 129,
130, 132, 133, 164, 166,
175nn
*Cézanne*, 118–26, 127, 130,
174n
*Chronik der Anna Magdalena
Bach/Chronicle of
Anna Magdalena Bach*,
120–1
*Der Tod des Empedokles/The
Death of Empedocles*, 123–4,
130, 175n
*Geschichtsunterricht/History
Lessons*, 129
*Klassenverhältnisse/Class
Relations*, 55
*Schwarze Sünde/Black Sin*,
175n
*Une visite au Louvre/A Visit to
the Louvre*, 119, 120, 127–9,
128 Fig. 6.4, 130

supplementing, 88, 89–112, 116, 158, 159; *see also* absence and presence
Švankmajer, Jan, 10, 102–3, 107, 109, 147, 166, 174nn
   *Alice*, 10, 11, 14, 15, 19, 27, 103
   *Kyvadlo, jáma a naděje/ The Pendulum, the Pit and Hope*, 103, 108–11, 110 Fig. 5.5
   *Touching and Imagining* [*samizdat* book], 102
   *Zánik domu Usherů/The Fall of the House of Usher*, 101–2, 103–8, 104 Fig. 5.3 and 5.4, 109
Švankmajerová, Eva, 109
Swinton, Tilda, 76, 83

Tarantino, Quentin, *The Hateful Eight*, 3–4, 5, 7, 35
Tarkovsky, Andrey, 42
   *Zerkalo/Mirror*, 160–1
Tarkovsky, Arseny, 160
Tarn, Gary, 39, 54, 59, 64, 65
   *Black Sun*, 39–46, 40 Fig. 3.1, 48, 49, 52, 164
task negative network *see* default mode network
task positive network, 170n
Terekhova, Margarita, 160
Terry, Nigel, 76

*The Lone Ranger* soundtrack, 59
Triolet, Elsa, 161
Turner, Simon Fisher, 76

Ullmann, Liv, 162

Vaneigem, Raoul, 53
Varda, Agnès
   *Elsa la rose/Elsa the Rose*, 161
   *Jane B. par Agnès V./Jane B. by Agnès V.*, 60–4, 63 Fig. 3.5, 161
   *Les Dites Cariatides/ The So-Called Caryatids*, 61
Veronese, *The Wedding at Cana* [painting], 129, 134
Villiers de L'Isle-Adam, Auguste de, 102
   *Torture by Hope* [book], 108, 109
visualisation, 4–5, 6–7, 11, 16–18, 19, 23, 24, 28, 59, 62, 67, 69, 71, 73, 75, 77, 80, 82, 83, 90, 99, 102, 112, 121, 126, 129, 131, 145, 154, 159, 167, 169n, 171n, 172n
volumising, 66–88, 89, 90, 92, 94, 108, 137, 157, 159
   and blankness, 130, 131, 136, 161
von Trier, Lars
   *Dogville*, 111–12
   *Manderlay*, 111

Wallace, David Foster, 47
Warner, Marina, 82, 102–3
Warnock, Mary, 169n
Weill, Kurt, 71, 72
Wells, H. G., 58
Wharry, David, 21, 27, 42
   *Wishful Thinking*, 19, 20, 171n

whiteness, 107, 138, 142, 146, 150, 152, 153, 155
  and racial politics, 153–4, 176n
Williams, James, 144, 175n, 176n
Williams, Linda, 14
Williams, Luisa, 92

Wittgenstein, Ludwig, 20, 25, 171n
Wolman, Gil J., 135, 136

Zacks, Jeffrey M., 7
Zeffirelli, Franco, *Romeo and Juliet*, 93

EU representative:
Easy Access System Europe
Mustamäe tee 50, 10621 Tallinn, Estonia
Gpsr.requests@easproject.com

www.ingramcontent.com/pod-product-compliance
Lightning Source LLC
Chambersburg PA
CBHW071844230426
43671CB00012B/2060